NO ONE
WINS ALONE

NO ONE WINS ALONE

Leading Others, Building Teams, Inspiring Greatness

MARK MESSIER

WITH JIMMY ROBERTS

GALLERY BOOKS

New York London Toronto Sydney New Delhi

G

Gallery Books
An Imprint of Simon & Schuster, Inc.
1230 Avenue of the Americas
New York, NY 10020

Some dialogue has been re-created.

First Gallery Books trade paperback edition October 2022

For information about special discounts for bulk purchases,
please contact Simon & Schuster Special Sales at 1-866-506-1949
or business@simonandschuster.com.

The Simon & Schuster Speakers Bureau can bring authors
to your live event. For more information or to book an event,
contact the Simon & Schuster Speakers Bureau at 1-866-248-3049
or visit our website at www.simonspeakers.com.

Interior design by Lexy Alemao

Photo on p. 341 © David E. Klutho/*Sports Illustrated*/Getty Images.
Insert photos courtesy of the author unless otherwise indicated.

Manufactured in the United States of America

10 9 8 7 6 5 4 3 2 1

Library of Congress Control Number: 2021942823

ISBN 978-1-9821-5856-9
ISBN 978-1-9821-5857-6 (pbk)
ISBN 978-1-9821-5858-3 (ebook)

To my parents, Doug and Mary-Jean

CONTENTS

NO ONE
WINS ALONE

PROLOGUE

R ain had fallen early that final day of March in 2004, but it was now a clear spring afternoon as I ducked into the back of the black Lincoln on Eighty-Fifth Street, headed for Madison Square Garden. The distinctive smell of the season's arrival always made me feel like I should be getting ready for the playoffs. This year, though, I wouldn't have the honor of competing for the game's ultimate prize, and it colored everything just a little bit gray.

When I first moved to New York thirteen years earlier, Brian Leetch and I were the only Rangers players who lived in Manhattan. Our apartments were just a few blocks away from each other's, so we would travel together to games and practices. We soon became like brothers. At the beginning we would take the subway, or hail a yellow cab. I laugh now thinking about the time our cab got stuck in traffic during a rainstorm. We jumped out and ran the last twenty blocks. When we got to the Garden, our suits and ties were soaking wet. What a sight. Anywhere else, that might have looked odd, but what New Yorker hasn't gotten caught running through the streets in a downpour? Perhaps it was a rite of passage, or a welcome note to keep in mind: This place was not for the faint of heart.

But after we won the Stanley Cup in 1994—the first time the Rangers had won in fifty-four years—stepping onto a subway train headed to the Garden or standing on a Manhattan street corner looking for a ride became a much more "social" experience. Because when you achieve something big in New York—whether it's in sports, arts, or politics—people are not afraid to share their appreciation.

I couldn't even begin to count the number of people over the years who have wanted to congratulate and thank me for that electrifying run to the '94 Cup. Every one of those encounters meant something to me.

Not long ago, I was in a cab, and when I went to pay the driver, he fell silent for a moment as he looked at me through the clouded Plexiglas security divider.

One of the great things about New York City is that everybody seems to have come here from somewhere else. I did. As he was sizing me up in the rearview mirror, I thought there might be some kind of problem. Then through a heavily accented voice, he said:

"Mess-yay! Your money's no good with me. Mess-yay no pay!"

A moment like this was a reminder that our success on the ice wasn't really about sport, but community. It was a piece of New York pride that two strangers could share.

Brian had been such an enormous part of that success, but as I made the fifty-block ride through Manhattan now, he wasn't with me. To this day, it's one of the most disappointing moments that I had as a Ranger. A month earlier, in a sad and surprising trade deadline deal, one of the franchise's greatest players ever—who thought he was going to retire a

Ranger—was dealt to Toronto, on his thirty-sixth birthday. So, as the carnival of New York City at rush hour unfolded outside the car window, I was alone with my thoughts. It was a crowded car.

That night was to be my 1,755th game. At the time, only the great Gordie Howe had suited up for more. I'd skated thousands of minutes. Had hundreds of teammates. I was forty-three. In a hockey sense, it was indisputable: I was old.

But I'd flourished over four decades in the NHL by remembering to live by the advice of the best coach I'd ever had—my father. He said: Trust your instincts and never waver in the belief in yourself. If you can live up to the expectations of the person who holds you to the highest standard—yourself—and if you can be honest with that person, then all you need to do is tune out the noise.

My honest assessment was that I had become an aging player. I could never carry a team alone—even in my prime—but I felt there was no way at this point I could play the kind of game you would need from your top-tier players. The problem wasn't that my skills had eroded. I could still hit the corners with a shot, find a teammate with an effortless saucer pass over an opponent's stick, or take someone into the boards. It wasn't even that games took more out of me at that age.

It was something more insidious and cruel. The older I got, the more I was forced to live with a reality I never saw coming. I could still lift the weight and do the reps. The hard part was recovering. It was a vicious circle: I couldn't go all out when I trained, and had to reserve my energy for games, which in turn meant I couldn't get the maximum benefit from training.

No matter what you do for a living, a long night makes for a harder morning at forty-three than it does at twenty-three.

Every day during the season, when I wasn't on the ice, I was lying down, with the ice on *me*.

The black car continued south. It was the Rangers' last home date, and second-to-last game of the season. We were up against the Buffalo Sabres, who were hanging on to their play-off hopes by a slender thread. For us, the thread had already snapped.

But there was something more going on as well. The players' collective bargaining agreement with the league was set to expire at season's end. With a potential lockout looming, the prospect for any season at all the following year was up in the air.

Seven months earlier, my wife, Kim, and I had our first baby, Douglas. So if the NHL season was going to be wiped out, heading over to play for a professional team in Europe—which was really the only viable alternative—wasn't very appealing. My contract with the Rangers was up as well. If I wasn't going to Europe, and there wasn't going to be any hockey in North America, how realistic was it to think that I would sit out a year—at this age—and then resume my career?

With all these what-ifs hanging over a season waiting to be put out of its misery, I had become the story. Everyone seemed to be asking: Would this be my last game in New York? Would this be my last game anywhere?

I was uncomfortable that people would make this night about me and not the team, but I also understood that my career had been unusual.

Very unusual.

I'd scored 693 goals, the eighth most of all time, and as- sisted on 1,193 others, which was third best. I'd played on fifteen all-star teams, and was the league MVP twice. As proud as I was of the awards and honors, I was more satisfied by the unrelenting hard work that had produced it all over a quarter century. But there was something else that made my career even more atypical.

Since its founding in 1917, thousands of players had skated in pursuit of the NHL's ultimate prize: winning the league championship and having their names inscribed on Lord Stanley's Cup. I'd been a part of teams that had accomplished this incredible feat six times. And in almost a century, only nine names were engraved more times on the game's holy chalice than mine. That, to me, was what it was all about.

We're in this business to win, and I had always felt like the most important job I had was to make whatever organization I was part of successful; being part of the formula and, if I was in a position to influence others, making sure I did so effectively. I lived by a very simple ethic: Winning isn't an accident, it's a strategy, and you get out of it what you put in. I had learned that at a very early age.

Playing hockey started for me the way I'm guessing it does for most Canadian kids. Before I'd completely figured out walking, my dad strapped a pair of blades on my feet. At first it was nothing but fun, gliding over the ice and trying to stay upright.

As I got older, and took more interest in the game, I discovered my first hockey hero: Bobby Orr. In my neighborhood, my friends and I were riveted by the way the charismatic Bruins defenseman played the game. He was like no one else. We wanted to be like him.

When we played street hockey out in front of our houses, we even imitated the way he took a breather. Most players would rest by leaning on their stick as it lay across their thighs. But Orr did this thing where he grabbed the butt end of his stick with his right hand, turned the blade down toward the ice with his left hand, and then leaned on his kneepads. It was a signature move. We even tried to bow our legs like number 4 did.

But more than anything, I learned very early that playing was more fun if you're doing it successfully, and sharing the effort with other people. Success ultimately meant getting behind my teammates, or out in front of them; finding a way to unlock their potential. Nudge them, push them, support them—lead them.

To me, helping people be their best was the game within the game. It was fascinating and frustrating, challenging, and most of all, rewarding. At the end of my career, I was the only person to have ever captained two different NHL teams to a championship.

As my car turned onto Thirty-Third Street, that last Stanley Cup—the magical one in 1994 that had electrified New York—was now a decade-distant image in the rearview mirror. It still lived vividly for me, but there was no denying time had passed. Everything was different now. Everything.

Before 9/11, we were able to drive right up the ramp into the Garden, but those security protocols had long since changed. So I got out of the car outside the building and walked to the elevator, taking a last few minutes of solitude and a chance to gather my thoughts before the familiar routine of a home game at this remarkable place.

Playing in New York is a rush that's near impossible to describe: the manic energy and the limitless possibilities; the worship of excellence and intolerance of failure. The feeling that something fabulous was always happening in some corner of this outrageous town. And Madison Square Garden was the stage at its center—a place worthy of the biggest names.

Growing up, I'd been a big fan of the Rolling Stones and Muhammad Ali. They'd both done some pretty good work in this building.

Ali had been my sports hero. His posters were all over my bedroom walls. I'd followed his story, how he didn't believe in the war, and they took away his title because he wouldn't go fight. "I ain't got no quarrel with them Viet Cong," he said.

He stood for something and he never wavered. He showed that champions need to be committed, and that commitment comes with a price.

I remember listening to the famous fight he had against Joe Frazier in this building. I was ten years old, underneath the covers of my bed and listening on a transistor radio. I cried when he lost the decision.

And the Stones. Bands go through a similar process to sports teams. At the start, individuals have to interview to make the band. They have to find out if they're talented enough, responsible enough, committed enough. Then they find out if they're compatible with everybody else.

Eventually you make the team or the band and you have to fight through all the obstacles, the things that can tear groups apart: success, indiscretions, ego.

Through the years, how many times had the Rolling Stones thought about calling it quits? But they came out the other side and remained committed to one another because they had more music to make, more magic to create.

At this point, they'd been together for forty-two years. Was there a better "team" than the Rolling Stones?

The NHL has played in some unique and extraordinary places: Chicago Stadium, the Montreal Forum, Maple Leaf Gardens in Toronto. For me personally, Northlands Coliseum in my hometown of Edmonton will always be special. But there is no place like what the people of New York proudly call "The World's Most Famous Arena."

To me, it isn't so much a building as a living, breathing organism, its DNA made of the people inside of it, like the obsessive outer-borough fans in Nick Fotiu and Eddie Giacomin jerseys, who poured off the trains under the Garden at Penn Station, and then up into the raucous section near the rafters, which would always be known as "the blue seats" even though they had been renovated and were no longer blue. And the scores of security and facilities people, who always made the place feel like I was walking into my own home, were just as much a part of it.

This night, though, as I made my way to the elevator, somewhere in the back of my mind I was trying to push aside a disquieting idea. This could be the last time I'd be doing something I'd never taken for granted and always loved so much: just coming to work.

I traded a smile with Mario Obando, who worked the players' elevator. He'd come to the Garden in 1990, a year before I had. Game day for me always started with Mario sending me off with the encouraging shout, "We're gonna win tonight!"

I got off at the fifth floor. I remembered when I was a rookie on the Edmonton Oilers in 1979 and played my first game against the Rangers, I was so amazed that the ice was on the *fifth* floor. How was that even possible? Someone had told me that when the circus came to town, they used the ramp and brought elephants up here. There was a bowling alley and a theater underneath the ice! I'd never seen anything like that before. Only in New York.

As I walked into the dressing room, I thought about all the

people who had suited up in this room over the years, guys like Rod Gilbert, Brad Park, Vic Hadfield, and Harry Howell. The great Guy Lafleur played for the Rangers late in his Hall of Fame career as well.

Lafleur was supremely skilled. He played most of his career with the Canadiens, the game's most famous franchise, and when he hung up his skates, he was their leading all-time scorer. But "The Flower" wasn't only about the numbers. He leveraged his skills to win, and he was indomitable. In a period of seven years, he won five Cups with the Canadiens.

I idolized Orr, but after the Bruins played the Canadiens in the 1977 Stanley Cup final, it was Lafleur who captured my attention. I was sixteen years old, a hockey sponge, trying to absorb how the truly great players excelled in high-pressure situations. Montreal had won the first two games in the final series, and before game three at the Boston Garden, the Bruins provocateur John Wensink said that Lafleur—who'd had three points in the first two games—"wouldn't get out of the Garden alive."

These days, something like that might be dismissed as trash talk, but back then, when the league had a much different perspective on physical play, those words had an unambiguous interpretation, particularly in Boston: Lafleur had a bounty on his head.

Hockey arenas today are like football fields—they're all the same—but back then, they were like baseball fields, all different. Boston Garden's rink was smaller and had squared-off corners from which there was no easy exit. It was a perfect venue for the Bruins' aggressive style of play, which sometimes bordered on mayhem. There were more than a few visiting players who, on the morning of games in Boston, came down with a mysterious case of "the flu."

The story goes that Lafleur was so full of nervous energy, he got to the Boston Garden and got dressed four hours earlier than normal, then sat there in his dressing room stall, waiting for the game to start. This night had his attention. He scored two goals, and assisted on the Canadiens' other two in a 4–2 win.

What made his performance that much more impressive was that he hadn't allowed himself to become distracted. Attempting to bully skilled players is a tactic as old as the game itself. Lafleur took his hits, but he remained focused, with a steely resolve.

Montreal ended up sweeping the series and Lafleur won the Conn Smythe Trophy as the playoffs' MVP. It was an early lesson for me, and one that I later tried to share as a leader: You play hockey with your mind, your body, and your spirit, and if you're a real champion, you focus on your task, despite whatever obstacles others might throw in your path.

The Rangers' locker room at Madison Square Garden was a cramped, unremarkable little chamber, which was joined to the New York Knicks' dressing area by a shared bathroom and medical training space.

As we got ready to play the Sabres, I looked around the dressing room and it occurred to me that there were five guys on our team who hadn't even been born when I made that first trip here in 1979.

I have a ritual that sets my pregame preparation in motion: sitting down to tape my sticks. It's something every player does before each game, and every player does it differently. The process is as individualistic as a fingerprint, as idiosyncratic as the way you brush your teeth. For me, the entire blade had to be covered from heel to toe, the better to cushion the puck and grip it. I'd done it so many times, I could have taped my sticks blindfolded and completed each one in thirty seconds.

But taping had never been solely a physical task; it was a meditation, a time to get focused and flush out the toxin that could sabotage even the most successful teams: distraction.

It was something we'd faced in 1994, when we had been up 3–1 in our series against Vancouver and on the brink of winning the Stanley Cup. But as we came back to New York to play game five, the distractions were overwhelming.

We had an off day and everybody started reading the papers, which of course were just giddy, all but saying we'd already won the Cup. Guys were making arrangements to fly their families into town for the big celebration, and getting them tickets. The route for the parade had already been mapped out.

The difference between concentrating and being immersed in total concentration is subtle but critical. It can be hard to recognize. It can also be the difference between winning and losing, especially against a great team like the Canucks.

We lost game five, and then we lost game six. I'd like to say we were just making things dramatic. The truth is, the distractions got the better of us in game five, and then momentum swung against us in game six.

Ten years later, the Stanley Cup wasn't on the line for us against Buffalo, but as I finished taping my sticks it was still hard to keep my thoughts where they needed to be. As much as I wanted this to be like any other game night, it clearly wasn't.

I'd been honest with anyone who'd asked. I really hadn't made up my mind about what I was going to do at the end of the season. But it seemed my friends and family had a better sense than I did, because they'd descended on the Garden en masse—my parents, Doug and Mary-Jean; my sisters,

Mary-Kay and Jennifer; my brother, Paul; my older son, Lyon; my nieces and nephews; my close friend and former teammate Mike Richter and his wife, Veronica. Even Brian Leetch's parents came. It was the first time they'd been back in the Garden since Brian had been unceremoniously sent away.

Normally I taped three sticks. On that night, I taped twelve. Deep down I suppose it was my grudging way of saying it without uttering a word: If this *was* to be my last home game, there should be something physical for me and my loved ones to hold, touch, and remember it by.

Mike Richter stopped by the locker room to share a few minutes with me before the game. He had been the greatest goaltender in Rangers history, but after a pair of concussions, he'd been forced to retire a year earlier. I remember how sad he was and what he later told me: "When you're playing, it's the greatest thing on earth and you'll miss it. You'd do anything to get it back. Giving the game up is as close to death as you're gonna get when you're an athlete. These things have a fuse. And when you're young and healthy and strong and winning championships, you never think there's an end to it, but there is, and it's tough to swallow."

But all of that was left unsaid in the few, quiet pregame moments we shared. He didn't want to intrude, and he was mindful of another painful recent lesson he'd learned. One minute you're one of us. The next minute, you're a guy in a suit who doesn't play. You might have played once, but this isn't what you do anymore. There's a bigger wall there than you'd expect.

We went out for the pregame skate. The fans were wild, like it was the playoffs. There were fan-made signs in the Garden for me everywhere.

We came off the ice and our trainer Jim Ramsay walked

over to me. There were twelve minutes before the puck dropped and he was holding out his phone.

"It's Wayne," he said.

There are plenty of sports where talk-radio callers argue endlessly about who might be the greatest player ever.

LeBron or Jordan?

Jack or Tiger?

Federer, Nadal, or Djokovic?

But that debate doesn't exist in hockey.

By the time Wayne Gretzky finished his career, he'd accumulated more points (goals plus assists) than anyone in NHL history. But if you took away every single one of his 894 goals, his 1,963 assists alone would *still* be enough to make him the league's all-time points leader. He was a nine-time league MVP. Nobody else had ever won the award more than six times. He was known far and wide as The Great One.

I knew him as that, but also as one of my best friends. We were born eight days apart. We started together as eighteen-year-old rookies—kids, really. Outside of my family, there weren't many people who knew me as well as Wayne did, and really, in a way, we *were* family.

Wayne was calling from Phoenix, where he'd been spending time as a part owner of the Coyotes franchise. He understood what this night might mean. He told me I should be proud of my career. He said he knew how difficult it was going to be for me to move on, but when he'd retired five years earlier, it had changed his life in a positive way that he didn't really see coming.

"You play on birthdays and New Year's," he said. "You play at Christmastime. There are all those things that you miss out on, but hockey is your priority, so you forgo them. Now you won't have to anymore. You're gonna get closer to your family than you could ever imagine."

As usual, The Great One with the perfect setup. We exchanged a few thoughts the way brothers do, and then I gave the phone back to Jim and headed out to the ice.

After the anthem, I skated out to center ice to take the draw. The Buffalo center Chris Drury was waiting there.

Drury had grown up in Connecticut as a rabid Rangers fan. As a kid, he'd played on the team that won the Little League World Series, but he'd eventually given up baseball for hockey. When we won the Cup in '94, he had just graduated from high school and was living with his brother in Boston. They watched every playoff game that spring. Drury later went on to win a Stanley Cup with the Colorado Avalanche, and then, after retiring from playing, started working for the Rangers. In May 2021, he became the Rangers' president and general manager.

Before the referee Kerry Fraser moved into the circle to drop the puck, Drury skated up to the dot and looked at me. He was a mostly quiet guy and would later say he never talked to opponents on the ice. It just wasn't his style. He didn't say much, but what he did say meant a lot to me.

"Thanks a lot," he said. "For everything."

Then Kerry skated in and dropped the puck.

Thinking back on it now, the game is a bit of a blur. I remember feeling a little sluggish. I hadn't skated very much in the previous week or so. I was nursing a swollen elbow and had it drained the day before. I scored the first goal, though.

"Of course Messier scored the first goal," our PR guy John Rosasco joked later to a reporter. "Of course he did."

Still, we lost 4–3. People cried: Kim, Veronica Richter, my

mom, even my tough-guy dad. I think this kind of thing is especially difficult on moms and dads. As a player, you've already made your peace in a certain way, even if you haven't made up your mind. But parents have watched you from the time you were five or six years old. My parents had been coming to my games for close to forty years at this point. It was something they loved.

Afterward, Rosasco, who'd come to work for the team as an eighteen-year-old intern who idolized the Rangers captain Barry Beck, came over to my locker. He put his foot up on the bench and started to say something, asking how I wanted to handle the large number of reporters who were gathering to talk to me. But he'd barely started before he was overcome with emotion.

I ended up going out and talking to the media, but truth be told, I barely remember any of that, either.

I know I was hurting, but I also know my desire had been no different than it was in the first game I played for the Oilers as a teenager. I had always lived a life in this sport fueled by an intense desire to perform, and an understanding that what we do is mostly influenced by how we look at things and the choices we make. As a kid, I'd been strongly influenced by Indigenous cultures and spiritual concepts. I'd once heard a story about choices that made a lasting impression on me.

One evening, an old Cherokee told his grandson about a battle that goes on inside people.

"The battle is between two wolves who live inside us all," the grandfather said. "One wolf is evil. It is anger, envy, jealousy, sorrow, regret, greed, arrogance, self-pity, guilt, resentment, inferiority, lies, pride, superiority, and ego. The other is good.

It is joy, peace, love, hope, serenity, humility, kindness, benevolence, empathy, generosity, truth, compassion, and faith."

The grandson thought about it for a minute and then asked his grandfather: "Which one wins?"

The old Cherokee told his grandson the answer was simple: "The one you feed."

On paper, that story seems simple. In life, the choices aren't always so obvious or easy—but they define us, and set the stage for what we can and can't accomplish.

How did I get here? How did I become who I am? My head was swimming with thoughts.

As it turned out, this was indeed the end. And so it was hard not to think about the beginning.

CHAPTER ONE

MY ORIGINAL TEAM

To understand me, you have to know that hockey is *not* the most important thing in my life—family is.

I know how that must sound—like a bunch of cookie-cutter autobiographical rhetoric. Obviously, I love the game. It's been central to so much of what and how I've lived. But almost every experience I've had in hockey connects back to my family or its influence, right from the very beginning.

In some ways, for me, hockey is simply an extension of family. I mean that literally.

I'm like a lot of people. I grew up wanting to be like my dad, and although he earned a living most of my childhood as a teacher, my earliest memory of him is as a professional hockey player.

When I first put on skates, at the age of three, our family was living in Portland, Oregon, and Dad was playing for the Portland Buckaroos, one of six teams in the Western Hockey League. Some of the WHL teams were affiliated with NHL teams; others, like the Buckaroos, were unaffiliated. Until 1967, there were only six NHL teams and the farthest west was in Chicago, so professional hockey in vast swaths of North America was about elite, professional leagues like the WHL.

I was in grade school when my dad retired from playing hockey and became a full-time teacher, but over the years I've come to learn everything there is to know about his career. He was a hockey lifer. He would go anywhere to play and he often did. He was chasing a dream. He was a hard-nosed defenseman who had 265 points in eleven seasons. He was the tough guy on every one of his teams. In an era of physical hockey, he was not the type of player you turned your back on. As my brother, Paul, likes to say: He played for keeps.

He was exactly what you might expect, and also exactly what you wouldn't. At home, he was an attentive father and a patient teacher, and to say he was a supportive husband is an understatement. On the other side of things, one year with the Buckaroos, he led the league in penalty minutes. A reporter came to our house to do a feature on him and the guy seemed genuinely baffled to find a soft-spoken man with his wife and a bunch of mannerly kids. This was the home life of the Buckaroos' tough guy? As much as Doug lived for hockey, he always put family first, and he had interests in life that went beyond the sport. After he retired from hockey, he got a master's degree in education and taught kids with special needs.

DAD GREW UP IN THE prairie towns of eastern Alberta, where his father, Edmond, was a driller on oil rigs. It was a big family (Dad had four brothers and a sister) and they moved around a lot, to wherever the fields were plentiful. By the time he was fifteen, the family had moved four times, eventually ending up in Edmonton. The oil company my grandpa worked for,

Regent Drilling, was operated by Paul Bowlen, whose son Pat would go on to own the NFL's Denver Broncos.

One summer, Doug worked as a roughneck on the rigs, too, muscling 500-pound pipes as they swung by chains into fittings. He was only seventeen years old. It was dangerous, dirty, and grueling work; eight-hour shifts, seven days a week, with a day off only every third week.

He and his dad bunked together that summer in a farmhouse, sleeping in a little top-floor bedroom where the storm windows had been left on from the winter. Sometimes they worked the overnight shift and had to sleep during the days, which was challenging and somewhat less than restful as the searing prairie heat turned the sealed little dorm into an oven.

In every new home, one thing was consistent: Doug was among the best hockey players in his youth programs. When he was between fifteen and seventeen years old, playing at what was called the Midget level at that time, he competed with and against players including Johnny Bucyk and Norm Ullman, both future Hall of Famers.

Doug loved hockey but the family's move to Edmonton brought him to the true love of his life, my mother, Mary-Jean Dea. Mom grew up in Edmonton. She had a pretty good life there but was no stranger to hardship—she lost her father when she was eight, and an uncle had died in World War II. Her dad, John Lorne Dea, was actually a goalie for the Edmonton Eskimos, an elite local hockey team. She lived with her mother, Alice, and grandmother Jen Styles in the family home, but also spent time on a farm in Innisfail, to the south, owned by some relatives. Dad's younger brother Larry knew Mary-Jean and set them up on a date. Once they met, he courted her quickly. It didn't hurt that, at sixteen years old, Mom was

Miss Teen Edmonton. When they married, she was seventeen, and Dad twenty-one.

Newly married, Dad was hoping for a chance to go to the NHL Red Wings training camp, but that opportunity didn't materialize. Instead, he signed for fifty dollars a week and lodging to play for the Nottingham Panthers of the British National League.

One big reason for the move: Mom was pregnant with my older brother, Paul, and the timing was a little controversial. It was clear Paul was conceived before the wedding, so to obscure that fact, Mom and Dad quickly got married in Edmonton, got on a boat to England, and had Paul there. Maybe that doesn't seem like such an issue today, but at the time, 1957, they felt this was best.

These days, hockey in Great Britain might seem to be a strange idea, but there was a time when the sport was a big deal there. Great Britain was a founding member of the International Ice Hockey Federation. Though it hasn't had a team qualify for the Olympics since 1948, Britain won the gold medal at the 1936 games, dramatically beating Canada 2–1 in the semifinal.

In the postwar period, the British National League was a six-team operation that attracted thousands of fans to its games. Two of the players on each roster had to be from Britain, but the rest could come from anywhere, so a lot of North American players went over. In the late summer of 1957, Dad, along with a number of other "imports," did just that, taking the *Queen Mary* from New York to London. He always liked to remind the four of us—my brother, Paul, and my sisters, Mary-Kay and Jennifer—that we might want to think twice about ever giving our mother a hard time. She had made that transatlantic passage on a ship without stabilizers, one that was skirting a hurricane, while she was pregnant! She was tough. She refused to take any medication on that heaving weeklong journey to ease the morning sickness, which ended up being a good thing since what she would have been prescribed was Thalidomide, later shown to cause horrific birth defects.

It wasn't easy playing in Britain. The rosters in the BNL contained only ten players plus a goalie. NHL rosters are much bigger, and even in the games I played where it felt like I was constantly on the ice, I would end up logging around twenty-five minutes. In the BNL, Doug would have been on the ice for more than thirty, maybe even forty minutes a game, especially as a defenseman. That's a big difference. As hard as it must have been, all that extra ice time helped his overall game improve.

Dad played for one year with the Nottingham Panthers. He and my mom spent most of that time in Britain. With the pregnancy and then a newborn, they didn't get a lot of chances to travel. But the Panthers team did make some trips: once for ten days to Germany, and a memorable trip to Czechoslovakia.

The players had heard that in those days of the Iron Curtain, the Czechs had a healthy appetite for any consumer goods from the West. Apparently, nylon stockings were a particularly hot commodity, so Doug and his teammates stocked up on them at fifty cents a pair before they left Britain.

When the team got to Czechoslovakia, they saw what appeared to be nylons featured in several store windows, but were in fact knockoffs called "sylons," definitely not as good as the real thing. The players set up one of their hotel rooms as a kind of trading post for locals. They had to be careful who they trusted, but Doug managed to trade his haul of nylons for a crystal decanter, a movie camera, and a set of glasses that he still has.

He also took a new heavy winter coat to sell, which one man wanted to acquire, but the buyer was nervous about the transaction. He told Doug to take the coat out with him to a park, where the man would be. If Doug saw the fellow flick his cigarette, then he should put the coat in the open back window of his car—which he did.

It turned out all the cloak-and-dagger caution was for naught. The buyer was the Czech security official who'd been assigned as their minder. He was just waiting for an opportunity to carefully make his own acquisition from the visiting team.

The time in Britain went by quickly. Paul was born in January, in London, with the help of a midwife. Then they came back to North America to continue the hockey odyssey.

They started in Grand Forks, where Dad played for the University of North Dakota and took college courses. He also worked three jobs to make ends meet: cleaning a shop where the university's newspaper was printed, pumping gas, and driving a semitruck loaded with ice cream on an eight-hour round-trip run between Grand Forks and Minot.

Mom and Dad wanted to get home, though, so after a year in North Dakota, they moved to Edmonton, and my sister Jenny was born. Dad enrolled at the University of Alberta and played two seasons of hockey for both the school and the Lacombe Rockets, a senior team in the Central Alberta Hockey League. He also signed a deal to teach in the Lacombe school system in his "spare time." Doug never really lectured me about hard work, and he didn't have to. Growing up and listening to his stories of those times, I understood viscerally about the cost of getting to where you wanted to go and never complaining about what it took to get there. It was hard to make excuses about not having enough time to get things done to a man whose days seemed to be twenty-five hours long.

During his second year playing with the Rockets, Dad pivoted again, this time to take advantage of what looked like his big break. One night, the Rockets played an exhibition game against the Detroit Red Wings' top farm club, the Edmonton Flyers, and although Lacombe lost 3–2, Doug had a pretty good game. The Flyers' coaching staff noticed and invited him to their September 1961 training camp in Detroit.

This was too good an opportunity to pass up. As important as finishing his education and getting the training for a teaching career was, he was still determined to pursue hockey as far as he could—something my mother fully supported, even though it was tough on her. It wasn't just about chasing a dream, though: Hockey provided income for the growing family, and that was always the top priority.

Before heading off to the Wings' training camp, he went up to my uncle Mike Dea's cabin on Wabamun Lake for a few days of relaxation. My uncle Mike was an amazing guy. A schoolteacher with a kind soul, he'd spend hours a day showing kids how to water-ski. Doug was a pretty good water-skier, but my uncle introduced him to something new: letting the boat pull him along on a three-foot disk rather than skis. He figured it out, but in doing so, badly pulled a groin muscle.

Back then, training camps were long and designed to get players in shape for the season. Most players worked different jobs over the off-season and didn't have the luxury of training and conditioning year-round. It was a time for players to get stronger, so it was unfortunate when a couple days into training camp the injury got worse. It didn't help that, back then, teams worked out twice a day. The pain he endured just to play was excruciating. Still, in spite of it, he was performing well, and in the inter-squad matchups scored a few game-winning goals. The Red Wings had missed the playoffs the year before, and Gordie Howe noticed Doug's play.

"Keep going, kid," Howe told him. "We need some new players here."

Eventually, he could barely skate due to his worsening injury and was forced to sit out three weeks. He endured a number of painful injections in some pretty indelicate spots. But he managed to get back on the ice, and he made the Flyers. He was officially a member of the Red Wings' top minor league club.

He took a year off from his studies, and in his first season with the Flyers, played 63 games and had 34 points and the highest penalty minutes on his team by far. He then scored 7 goals in the playoffs to help Edmonton win the 1962 championship.

It was nearly the same story during his second season, except that he struck an unusual deal in which the team agreed he would play only home games, plus those in Calgary—which was just three hours away—so he could get back to finishing his degree at the University of Alberta. However, the aroma of competition proved irresistible, luring him to play more than he had planned, so he ended up playing 56 games and scoring 37 points, while still notching by far the most penalty minutes on the team.

Though it took him longer than he wanted, he got his degree. It's amazing he did it at all. I had been born during his first season with the Flyers, meaning he now had three kids. On top of helping my mom out with us, playing hockey, and finishing school, he was working multiple jobs to support the family. My sister Mary-Kay was born in fall 1963, bringing the count to four.

The 1963–64 season was a challenging one for Doug, and the family. Dad was away a lot. Within Detroit's system, he was moved from the Flyers to the Indianapolis Capitals. The team then became the Cincinnati Wings midway through the season, so he moved again. Finally, he was transferred to the Pittsburgh Hornets. All of this happened in quick succession. In the fall of 1963, Mom flew the family two thousand miles from Edmonton to meet him in Pittsburgh, but arrived just as Doug was heading out on a road trip and spent the next few days alone in a hotel room, with four kids—all of whom had the measles. There's no question the sacrifices they both made were massive. It came down to their commitment to make it work, and the love and respect they had for each other.

Later that year, in early 1964, he was lent to the Portland Buckaroos of the Western Hockey League, and we moved with him. That's where the hockey life started for me.

I REMEMBER GOING TO PRACTICE with Doug, sometimes at the Buckaroos' home stadium, the Portland Memorial Coliseum, and sometimes at a rink in a shopping mall called Silver Skate, where the team practiced when they couldn't get time in the arena.

Portland loved the Buckaroos. Long before the NBA's Trail Blazers arrived and hours from the big college sports towns of Corvallis and Eugene, the Buckaroos were literally the only game in town. It wasn't unusual for ten thousand people to fill the Coliseum to watch a game. Although the Portland fans were passionate, at the time there wasn't much participatory youth hockey culture, so Doug started a summer program for kids at Silver Skate, which I joined at the age of three.

The program was open to almost anyone, and everybody who came was a beginner, but they weren't all as little as me. Dad tells stories about the college football players at Portland State who came out wearing their big football shoulder pads.

Two years later, when I was five, I was playing on my first organized team, which was sponsored by a local roofing company. Mom used to drive me to the games because Dad was often on the road with the Buckaroos. But I remember a game we played when Dad came to watch, which was a treat, as was the discussion we had after—the first real discussion I ever had with Doug about hockey. We were in the car on the way home and he said: "Mark, you know, you're a pretty good skater. When the puck goes down into the other team's zone and into the corner, if you're the first guy down there, you should go get it."

"Uh-uh," I told him, disagreeing. "The coach says I should go in front of the net." I was respecting authority, in this case my coach's, as Doug had taught me.

At that age, it was totally lost on me that I might be best served listening to my father—a professional hockey player— rather than my volunteer youth league coach, C. J. Lindsay, who was a very nice man, but whose primary hockey credential was that he sang the national anthem before Buckaroos games. Of course, there's no point going to the net if your team doesn't have the puck, and Dad must have been laughing inside. Doug's hockey class began for me that day, and never stopped.

THOSE PORTLAND YEARS WERE WHERE the bond was formed with my original team: my siblings. The four of us—my brother, Paul; my older sister, Jenny; me; and my younger sister, Mary-Kay—are separated by a little more than five years.

We did everything together, and we were always outside. Our house was in the southwest part of town, out toward Beaverton, on four acres. We had horses, which were a passion of my dad's dating back to his childhood. There was a barn out back and some bridle trails running through part of the property. It was no accident that we'd ended up on that sort of land.

When Doug was twelve, his family was living in Lloydminster on the Saskatchewan-Alberta border, and he would walk into town every day and ask just about anyone he encountered if they had a horse for sale. All my dad had was fifty cents in his pocket, so even if the response was yes, the eventual answer was bound to be no.

One day, though, he approached an old guy in a wagon hitched to a few old nags, and posed his usual question.

"How much you got?" the guy asked.

"Fifty cents," Doug told him, expecting the usual rejection.

My dad got his first horse that day, an old black gelding he named Midnight. What he didn't learn until later was that the horse wasn't the man's to sell. It had wandered onto his property. Luckily, no one ever claimed it. Doug owned it lovingly for the three years he lived in Lloydminster. He once rode fifty-five miles on Midnight to visit an uncle on his farm in Heath. The trip took three days.

Around the same time, he became friendly with a man named Fred Howard, who tended horses on a big dairy farm. Doug would go and help him out, and became a skilled horseman, eventually getting good enough in the saddle to compete in local fairs on Howard's horses. The deal was that Doug kept whatever he won riding English style, and Howard kept the money he won riding western style.

My first memory of chores was shoveling the stalls and working around the barns of our house in Portland. I loved caring for the animals. We had a Shetland pony and an Anglo-Arabian mare. My brother and sisters and I used to play this game with the horses that gave me my first real taste of team-work and strategy. Paul and Jenny were one team, and Mary-Kay and I were the other. I was on the Shetland and Paul was on the Anglo-Arabian. We'd line up a hundred or so yards away from where our sisters were waiting, and then would gallop on our horses straight toward them. The point of the game was to collect your partner and race back to the start. The Anglo-Arabian was bigger and faster, so Paul usually beat me in the race to reach our sisters. But because the Shetland was closer to the ground, it was easier for me to collect Mary-Kay. We won our fair share. The game showed me there can be different systems or visions of winning, and you have to believe in yours. The race isn't always to the swift, nor the battle to the strong. Or put another way, as I like to say, there are many ways to the *one* way.

A decade or so later, I would have the best seat in the house to witness confirmation of the theory. In a physical game, a skinny kid from Brantford, Ontario, Wayne Gretzky, proved that skill and hockey IQ can be just as effective as brute force.

In the summers, our family would go to a small vacation cabin we had near the base of Oregon's Mount Hood, in the town of Rhododendron. It had three bedrooms and was made out of logs.

We hiked and fished and rode bikes. We played kick the

can and every card and board game you could imagine. We stayed up late talking and laughing. We got up early raring to go and do it all again. The only other entertainment we had was a record player. We had a total of two choices: *Abbey Road* by the Beatles or *Here I Am* by Dionne Warwick. We wore them both out.

When Doug stopped playing for the Buckaroos and our family moved back to Edmonton, these summer trips to the cabin would bring us even closer together—literally.

It would be the six of us, my grandmother Alice, and our 80-pound Old English sheepdog, Tootie, packed into our red Oldsmobile Vista Cruiser station wagon. We looked like the opening scene from that TV show *The Beverly Hillbillies* with all our stuff lashed to the top of the car and hanging out in every direction. It was a two-day adventure over a thousand miles. And sometimes, a couple weeks after we got to the cabin and set up camp, or maybe later in the summer, we'd jump back in the car and go another thousand miles to visit friends from our Portland days, Jack and Mavis Robinson, who lived in Malibu.

On the way down from Edmonton to Oregon, every year we'd stop in Deep Creek, Montana, and stay at the same little motel, all seven of us—and Tootie—piled into one room. The place didn't allow dogs, so sneaking our canine family member in was just another team-building exercise.

By that point, Doug was a schoolteacher with a modest salary, so we had to watch what we spent. One year, Mom and Dad came down to breakfast late to find we'd all ordered freshly squeezed orange juice. It nearly blew the budget for the entire trip. Needless to say, Doug was not happy.

Something we all learned early on was that when you're

close to people—especially when you're physically that close, and for many hours at a time—conflict is inevitable. Actually, the companion to closeness *is* conflict. It's unavoidable. Can you imagine how many disagreements seven people in one station wagon had on a seventeen-hour trip, *about the radio alone*?

But when it came to conflict, we had an ironclad rule: Get over it. You have a choice to either resolve your differences and live together productively, or you can ignore them and allow the toxin of resentment and anger to infect your relationships. When it comes down to it, these are the only two options.

That car was a rolling test tube that distilled patience, tolerance, understanding, and respect for other people's space and points of view. We all know people who are unaware of the way they affect others, who are too loud, too demanding, too uncompromising. My parents wouldn't let that happen with us. If they had, the windows might have exploded out of that Oldsmobile. Ultimately someone had to be in charge and that was always my parents. And one thing was certain: Once either Mom or Dad settled a disagreement, that was it. We knew not to argue, and they never contradicted each other.

I didn't know it at the time, but dealing with those dynamics prepared me to be part of a team, where you travel and live with the same people for months on end. Long before I skated around with the Stanley Cup, I learned valuable lessons about getting along with others.

In a family, like any team, there are always going to be different personality types. Not everyone looks at a piece of art and has the same response. Not everyone hears the same message in a speech. Each person is a unique combination of their genetic wiring and life experiences. As a leader, you learn to accept and appreciate that each of your teammates might react differently to the same situation. With that knowledge, you can resolve any conflicts that arise from a place of understanding.

During those summers in the cabin, Doug would drive on the weekends to the University of Portland, where he was working on his master's. On Mondays, he'd come back to his own little laboratory at home, where he would test his coursework out on the four of us, and teach us at the same time. It all felt like fun and games, but there were lessons being learned.

One time, he took two wide glasses of water, both filled to exactly the same point. Then he emptied one of them into a new glass that was taller and skinnier. Then he asked us each to tell him which glass contained more water.

Of course, the correct and obvious answer is that they both had the same amount of water. But a seven-year-old might look at that second, taller glass, with a higher water level, and not be entirely sure, while a nine-year-old may understand what's really going on immediately. The concept he was testing was called the "transfer of learning." He was both teaching us and also getting a picture for himself of how children's minds develop at different ages when it comes to abstract learning. He recognized a valuable corollary as well along the way: If you try to teach a person something before they are ready, it could not only be futile, but frustrating, and possibly diminish their self-image.

Dad thought very carefully about the way I developed. Although he steered me toward hockey from a young age, he also made sure my life was filled with all sorts of experiences—each with its own lessons to teach. Growing up, I didn't only play hockey, I played soccer, baseball, lacrosse, and a lot of the time I just played outside the structure of organized sports. The balance in my life made me love hockey even more. When the season came and it was time to play the game, I would be ready to go and run toward it.

Those days in Portland and summers in the shadow of Mount Hood were in many ways laying the foundation of who I would become. It might surprise some people that so little of it had to do with hockey. But my obsession with the sport wasn't far off. Just as every dwelling is more than simply a foundation, I was about to add some essential building blocks to what I had learned, and so much of it would happen on the ice.

CHAPTER TWO

PLAYING UP

When Doug retired from his professional playing career in 1969 to take a job teaching junior high in Edmonton, it was a big change for our family. We moved away from the horses and bridle trails and four acres of land, to my grandmother's three-bedroom, one-bathroom house in Edmonton—the same family home my mother lived in when she met my father. There were eight of us, altogether. Paul and I slept in the unfinished basement down by the furnace. Our parents and two sisters, along with my mom's mother, Alice, and her mother, Jen, had the bedrooms upstairs. It sounds like a lot, and it was, but I am tremendously fortunate to have had this time with my grandmother and great-grandmother. I had close relationships with them all.

The move to Edmonton was also a turning point in my relationship with hockey. Just as Doug seemed to be stepping away from playing, I started to take it more seriously. In Portland, hockey wasn't a sport that many people cared about, and I was interested mostly because of my dad. But in Canada, it wasn't an oddity, it was religion. This was the land of outdoor rinks and entire communities organized around the game. Kids skated after school on lakes. There were even little differences in the lingo to be learned—athletes wore sweaters, not jerseys, as we said in the United States. The bottom line was that in Canada, hockey was what you did. Period.

The idea that my dad was going to leave hockey behind and embark on a completely new phase of life was fine in theory, but back in his hometown, steeped in this atmosphere, it didn't take long for him to get drawn back to the sport. The $4,600 he made for teaching sixth-graders reading and math at the St. James School was considerably less than he'd earned playing for the Buckaroos. The solution, no great surprise, was hockey. For $2,500, Dad took a job coaching the Edmonton Monarchs, an amateur team that practiced three times a week and played on weekends in the Alberta Senior Hockey League (ASHL). On top of that, he was intent on making time to coach my brother, Paul, and me as well.

As a seven-year-old, I should have started youth hockey at the Mite level. Instead, that first year in Canada, I joined Paul on a team in the Pee Wee division of Edmonton's Knights of Columbus league. Pee Wees are supposed to be eleven and twelve years old.

Physically, I probably wasn't ready, but the choice was a necessity for our family, and one that would set the course of my journey through the sport. With all my dad had going on, there wasn't time for him to coach both me and Paul on different teams, or even if he wasn't coaching, to take us to separate games and practices. Recognizing my size and age disadvantage, he protected me by putting me in games against the other teams' lesser lines.

"Playing up" above your age, size, or skill level can be challenging. If you're always playing against competition that is bigger, stronger, and faster, it's hard to get involved in the game. That's no fun. It can kill your confidence and squash your potential. And if you don't have the strength to compete against older kids, there's even risk of getting injured.

But if managed properly, the benefits of playing up can be tremendous. I was practicing twice a week with kids whose skills were certainly more developed, and who were probably skating slower on line rushes just so I could keep up. But at the same time, they were not so far advanced that I couldn't compete. Since I couldn't rely on size, strength, or speed, I was forced to bust my ass and pay attention to the fundamentals of shooting, passing, stickhandling, and skating, building up those skills to match the level of play of the older kids around me. Growing up with Paul, I was used to playing with someone bigger and stronger than me, and I didn't worry about it. I was just happy to play with him on the team. I was never scared, and I slowly started to make real progress.

Once we were doing a shooting drill and I let loose a slap shot that hit my uncle John Dea, my mom's youngest brother, who was coaching with Dad, square in the shin. He went down like a sack of potatoes and yelled, "Holy cripes, your shot's getting really hard!"

I thought he might just be trying to make me feel good. Then again, he was saying this while lying on the ice howling and holding his leg. If it was an act, it was a convincing one. I remember thinking, "Really? I've got a hard shot?"

There were two youth leagues in Edmonton, the Federation league for the public school kids, and the Knights of Columbus (known as the K of C) league for those of us who went to Catholic school. There were a lot more kids who played in the Federation league, so their teams were deeper and often more talented. The K of C was a ragtag collection where Doug needed to do some creative coaching to work with what we had and get the most out of our team.

Traditionally, coaches keep line mates together and play all four lines in consecutive order, usually with the top forwards on the first two lines. Instead, Dad numbered his best forwards one through five, and then constantly juggled the lines so that at least one of those forwards would be on the ice at all times. Paul was the best player on the team, but by the end of that first year, I had improved enough to be taking a regular shift. And our team won the league.

As if teaching school and coaching both an adult and a youth hockey team weren't enough, Dad started playing hockey again the next year, too. He became not only a coach for the Edmonton Monarchs, but a player as well. With four kids at home, the family needed extra income. It may sound odd now, but at the time it wasn't unusual for coaches to also play on the team. Budgets weren't as high back then, and a player-coach might not skate every game but fill spots as needed. Coincidentally, Glen Sather, who would later become a huge part of my life in Edmonton as coach of the Oilers, may have been the last first-tier professional player-coach during the Oilers' 1976–77 season in the World Hockey Association (WHA).

There were only three clubs in the ASHL that season, so to fill out their schedule, the Monarchs played teams from similar leagues in other provinces, such as in Trail, British Columbia, 560 miles from Edmonton. One night that season they played a game against the local team there—the Smoke Eaters—and then jumped on the bus for the ten-hour ride back home.

Doug got back just in time the next morning to put on a fresh shirt and get to school to take attendance in his homeroom.

It was hardly a glamorous existence, but senior amateur hockey in Canada had a distinguished history. In 1955, a team from British Columbia, the Penticton Vees, not only represented the country in the Ice Hockey World Championships, but won the gold medal by beating the defending champion, the Soviet Union, 5–0 in the final game. A decade and a half after the Vees had been Canada's darlings, the senior amateur game in western Canada still had good talent, but didn't draw many fans—unless the Edmonton Monarchs were playing the Calgary Stampeders, as happened in the playoffs that first year when Doug was coaching and playing. That was a whole different story. The two cities could have faced each other in tiddlywinks and still generated the partisanship and passion of a Yankees–Red Sox game.

The intense Monarchs-Stampeders ASHL playoff series turned out to provide one of my most memorable lessons in team dynamics. It was a five-game series, and the morning after the fourth game, I got up and walked upstairs into the house's one bathroom. Dad was standing there with his buzz cut, looking into the mirror and shaving, like it was any other day. But in addition to the lather on his face, he had lumps all over his head, and his eyes were both black. That'll make an impression on an eight-year-old first thing in the morning. He looked like a creature from a horror movie.

As we stood there, Doug told me that in the third game of the series, he had run roughshod over the Stampeders and taken out a few of their players. The Monarchs had won that game to go up 2–1 in the series. So, when the two teams met for the potentially decisive fourth game, as he said, "they were waiting for me." A couple of Stampeders jumped him during the game. The beating that he took was bad, but it wasn't the worst part. Almost none of the guys who he'd been fighting for all year long—his teammates—got in there to help. Only the goalie came to his assistance, while other big, strong players stayed put on the bench. The Monarchs lost that game.

He then told me something like that had happened to him only once before. It was his rookie year with the Edmonton Flyers, and he'd been kicked out of a game after a couple of guys ambushed him and he'd fought back. No one jumped in to help that time, either. So he sat in the dressing room until the game was over. When the first guy from his team came through the door, he coldcocked him.

The guy looked up from the floor, dumbfounded. Doug was standing over him and said, "If we're not going to fight together on the ice, you're going to fight me in the dressing room."

The point, Dad explained, as he talked to me with shaving cream framing his two shiners, was you've got to stick together. If a team doesn't have true solidarity, that's a deep vulnerability. He didn't punch out any of his Monarchs teammates in the locker room this time around, since they still had another game to play, but he was "disappointed as hell" in his guys. "Divide and conquer" is one of the oldest competitive strategies there is. You can never let that happen and you have to trust that your teammates won't leave you exposed. There's nothing worse than lying in bed at night knowing you didn't take a punch in the nose to help your teammates.

Teams are like a symphony: If someone plays the wrong notes, it doesn't matter how good everybody else is. The music isn't going to sound right. That's the kind of mentality I grew up with: all in. It's no surprise that the Monarchs lost game five in their ASHL series against Calgary. They weren't playing for one another.

When it's done right in hockey, it looks like the Philadelphia Flyers "Broad Street Bullies" teams of the mid-1970s. They were an expansion club, trying to get respect, but they were losing. And there's nothing worse than losing *and* getting beaten up. That can tear a team apart. They decided to carve out an identity.

In 1975, Dave Schultz set the all-time record for most penalty minutes in a season with 472. But a lot of other teams had tough players. What made the Flyers different was the way they all stuck together. They became the perfect example of a team where everyone supported one another. The Flyers' coach, Fred Shero, instilled that "all for one, one for all" mentality. If Bobby Clarke was getting hassled on the ice, there wasn't one guy you had to deal with, it was the whole team. They rode that mentality to two Stanley Cups.

IN MY SECOND SEASON AS a Pee Wee, I was still playing up and learning how to shoot and skate, but I was also learning just as much about how to be part of a team, and how to win.

I ended up sticking around and playing at the Pee Wee level for four years. Doug likes to say I was the only kid who played Pee Wee long enough to collect a pension. But by those last couple of years, when I was eleven and twelve, and actually playing against kids my own age, I had grown really comfortable and was putting up some respectable numbers.

It was around this time I started to sense I had a chance

to be pretty good at this game. Paul was fifteen—three years older than me—and he started playing on a team called the Mets. My dad was the coach. This was tier-two junior hockey, one step below the top rung on the elite amateur ladder that served as a portal to the NHL. The players on this team were anywhere from fifteen to twenty years old.

In addition to playing in my last year for my Pee Wee team as a twelve-year-old, I also got to be the "stick boy" for the Mets—meaning a kind of coach's and equipment assistant, like a bat boy in baseball—as well as skate with the team in practice. It was an opportunity for me to witness success and absorb how it happened—riding the bus, sitting on the bench, my eyes and ears were wide open.

It was great being with Paul again. He was so much further along in terms of skills and physical development at this point. Because of our age difference there had never been much hockey rivalry between us, and now he was just someone to look up to. I had a long way to look up. Paul scored 101 points in his first season on the Mets. I remember doing drills in practice one day, and Doug was yelling at me, "Move your feet! Move your feet!" In my head I was thinking, "What the heck? I *am* moving my feet. I *am* skating hard." In retrospect, I realize that I just didn't have the strength to generate the power to keep up with these much older and bigger guys—yet.

After graduating from Pee Wee hockey the next year, I kind of treaded water when it came to my development. I played at the Bantam level and didn't have as good a season. I think we only won a single game. I wasn't playing at the level that I expected of myself, but wasn't too discouraged, either. I still loved just playing. But I was learning a ton in my second year tagging along as a stick boy for the Mets. They moved from

Edmonton to Spruce Grove that year (teams often relocated for better facilities or similar reasons). There was one experience in particular that gave me a good lesson in the importance of communication.

A big part of Doug's success as a coach was that his players had no ambiguity about what he expected of them, and about whether or not they were meeting that expectation. He was an absolute believer that people need to know where they stand. The message might not always be what they want to hear, but if a leader establishes that they are honest, and that they will always communicate, then the people they supervise or lead will be freed from wondering—and worrying about—whether or not they are doing a good job. That kind of anxiety is counterproductive and far too common.

Back then, and certainly in the Canadian junior leagues, hockey was a tougher game. When the puck went into the corner, every player knew what was expected of them: They had to go get it. That's what the sport requires of those who take it seriously. But the corner is also a place where some of the game's more brutish interactions occur, and so rushing in headlong meant you were likely to pay a physical price—much like wide receivers in professional football who run routes across the middle and subject themselves to savage hits. Someone from the other team was inevitably rushing in, too.

Dad had this one player with the Mets who was talented, but wasn't fond of some of the more physical aspects of hockey. When the puck went into the corners, he would always skate toward it, his face twisted in an apparent grimace of maximum effort, but somehow never quite get there. It was a sizable hole in his game. Doug viewed it as his job as a coach to figure out what was holding this player back—lack of commitment, or outright fear—but the truth is, not everybody is hardwired to play in a winning environment.

Spruce Grove was playing in Red Deer, Alberta, a notoriously tough place, with a tough crowd. The kid was doing his usual thing—avoiding the hit—but in this situation the team really needed everybody to do the dirty work. Doug had made that clear. So when this kid came back from a shift, Doug just told him—right there on the bench—to take his stuff off.

The kid never played for the team again. There were no theatrics or screaming. It was a very simple message, really to the whole team: Here's what I expect. Here's what's necessary for us to be successful. Perhaps there was a place in hockey for this particular player, but it certainly wasn't in this program. Sometimes, the difficult truth is that for an organization to be successful, not everyone will work as a part of it. A good coach is a chemist in search of the right formula. The next year, the Mets won the national championship. Dismissing this one player wasn't the main reason for their ultimate success, of course, but it wasn't insignificant, either.

I had a front-row seat for that Mets title run, and it made me eager to play for them, too. But as I worked my way through Bantam and then Midget hockey, and approached the age of fifteen, I wasn't in the same place as Paul had been at that age, physically or in terms of talent. I wasn't yet ready for junior hockey, which is a completely different level. Along with fifteen-year-olds, there are also guys up to twenty years old, with beards and full-time jobs. The year the Mets won their title, they played against a team from eastern Canada that had five players who were married! These were men.

The summer *after* I turned fifteen, though, things started to change for me. I had a growth spurt, and I started lifting weights. Most crucially, I made big improvements to my skating.

For so long, I'd felt like I was marching in mud. For a couple more years after Doug had shouted at me at that early Mets practice to dig in and speed up, as hard as I tried, I still couldn't seem to generate any real force as a skater. But then I started training with a former figure skater named Audrey Bakewell who was teaching classes in "power skating." She wanted to change everything about my form. She pointed out that my top was churning side to side, and my bottom going straight ahead—the two halves working against each other. Instead, she wanted me to think and move like a sprinter on the track, with my arms helping to power me forward, instead of moving laterally. Everything needed to move in unison down the ice in the same direction.

With the growth spurt, the weight lifting, and working with Audrey, it all came together that summer when I was fifteen. My stride got longer, I was generating more power, and I could actually feel myself moving faster on the ice. I felt like Forrest Gump when the braces fell from his legs and he just took off.

I was brimming with confidence, and I was determined to make the Mets at the age of fifteen, just as Paul—who had moved on to play college hockey at the University of Denver— had done. Doug was still the coach, and every day, we drove the fifteen miles together in the morning to the Mets' month-long preseason training camp, and back home again, without talking about hockey. I was adamant about making the team on my talent and effort. I didn't want to influence his decision by talking. We covered nine hundred miles that month going to and from the rink this way. Dad wasn't going to cut me any slack, either, and that was fine by me.

At the end of each training-camp day, we'd have these two-man, two-lap races. There was nowhere to hide. You got your matchup, took the starting line, the whistle blew, and you were off.

Doug always put me against this kid named Jay McFarlane, a lanky defenseman from Winnipeg who was a year older than me, but also really developed for his age. He had a strong stride and could seriously move in the corners. At first, the kid dusted me by half the ice surface. I knew what was at stake, and I wanted to show Doug that even though he'd put me up against a ringer, I wasn't giving in. I don't think I ever managed to beat McFarlane, but every day I closed the gap a little more, and in the end, racing him was a tremendous benefit. It forced me to skate faster, and give it everything I had, to avoid the sheer humiliation of getting pounded into the ground.

I don't remember how my dad told me I'd made the team. Maybe he mentioned it at home. There was no celebration—we just got down to work to make sure I stayed on the team.

I not only stayed, but was proud to have a pretty decent year with the Mets, scoring 55 points in 57 games. There were vets on the team with much more, and I would have loved to have been one of those players who puts up massive numbers, but I knew that points weren't the only measure of a player. Teams need all kinds of different players, and especially back then, when intimidation was so prevalent, you needed to have guys to protect the top scorers. In the era just following the Philadelphia Flyers' heyday, it was a game of physical domination, intimidation, and outright brawling—every night.

And so, when that first season in juniors started, I knew Doug was wondering if I could handle myself. I gave him the answer in our first road game.

We were playing in Taber, a town of near eight thousand in southern Alberta. Corn produced there is sweet, the hockey players, anything but. These small farm towns in particular were known for producing tough guys.

A twenty-year-old Taber player cross-checked me and skated away. I went after him, and when he turned around, I dropped my gloves. I don't think he was expecting much of a fight from some fifteen-year-old, but he was wrong. Doug told me that was the moment he knew that he didn't need to worry about me.

Everyone was young and kind of full of themselves, and the fighting was a lot about earning your spurs. You had to figure out a way to get respect, otherwise players would take advantage of you. If one team was bigger and stronger, they would often skate into the other team's end during the pre-game warm-ups and take all their opponent's pucks. The only way the first team could warm up was to go and take their pucks back. And so the brawl would inevitably start.

Once you were in the games, you had to finish every check. Players would look for opponents they could hit and who wouldn't do anything back to them. It's the law of the street: People will treat you the way you let them know it's okay to treat you. So you don't want to be someone who lets others take advantage. If you hit the wrong guy, you're going to have to answer the bell. As a junior player, the mission was to show everyone that you were the wrong guy. The thing is, when fights broke out, it would rarely end up being one on one. If you started to fight one guy, it soon became two, then three, and next thing you knew, the cavalry was coming. If it sounds like the movie *Slap Shot*, it was.

It wasn't an easy lesson in this environment, but Doug tried to teach me that in order to be a tough guy, you've got to be a smart guy. You've got to understand the circumstances, the odds, and what's to be gained. My second year on the Mets I had 194 penalty minutes and 30 fights. Was every one of those minutes spent in the penalty box a tactical decision, to give my team an edge? No, I can't pretend that I never lost my cool. But I always felt I was standing up for something, and competing hard for my team.

Ahead of that second year, there were two big changes: The Mets moved from Spruce Grove to St. Albert, right beside where we were then living, and for the first time in my life, I became the captain of a hockey team.

It's funny, but as much as my life has revolved around understanding leadership, I barely remember the very first time I was formally called to take the role. There was no big heart-to-heart sit-down, no presentation in front of the team. Before the first game that season, I got to the dressing room and hanging in my locker was my number 11 sweater—that had been Doug's number, and Paul's, too—with a big "C" embroidered on the upper-left part of the chest. The moment itself was utterly uneventful, but it was a big deal for me.

We'd lost a number of the vets before this season, but not all of them. In a way, I felt like a vet myself. I'd been working with the team as stick boy and soaking up the culture. I'd learned so much being in the locker room and watching Dad interact with the players. As a sixteen-year-old, I'd been around hockey at this level more than most, and while I couldn't have articulated this at the time, I knew I had to lead by example, on and off the ice. I'd watched Dad create a culture with the Mets, developing the camaraderie, and players who would skate and fight for one another. Maybe he thought that as captain I could extend that philosophy into the future.

All I knew was I was proud to be named captain and took the job seriously right from the start.

Doug loves to tell the story about a game that season when he was delayed getting back to the dressing room between periods to talk to the team. He was hurriedly making his way through the door when he ran into our trainer, Buck Buchansky.

"Don't worry, Doug," he told Dad. "Eleven's already talked to the guys."

Whatever the quality of my physical skills at the time, I was already tuned in to the concept that teams aren't successful because of talent alone. I recognized that strategy, cohesion, commitment, and so many more of what are commonly called the intangibles were critical components.

I was also at this point realizing why sports teams can be such a useful model of successful group dynamics. Every year in hockey, you enter with a defined goal: to win the title. The hope is everybody's pulling on the same rope to achieve that goal.

In a lot of jobs outside the world of sports, there may not be as clear or singular a goal, but I still think it's critical for leaders to create an environment where colleagues have a collective purpose they can strive toward. People are inspired when they work for organizations that have a shared vision. They're more passionate and productive, they take pride in their work, and a culture of trust and commitment is created. They also have a lot more fun.

Inspiring people is different from motivating them. Motivation requires constant reinforcement through reward and punishment. It can make people compliant, but it can also make them resentful. It's a short-term tactic that doesn't create lasting results. It also means leaders have to micromanage their teams, spending a lot of time and energy trying to get people to do their best work. This scenario can be challenging because it funnels responsibility up to the top of organizations and takes power away from the team.

If you create a great place to work instead, where people are inspired by a shared purpose and goal, they will motivate themselves.

It's still the leader's job to set benchmarks and sell the vision. The leader then has to convince people "we can do this," and help them understand "this is *how* we're going to do it." But each person on the team is still responsible for finding their own motivation.

People play hockey for different reasons. Everyone wants to win the Cup, of course, but some play because they love the challenge, some to make their parents proud, others for money or the lifestyle—there are lots of motivations. You can't lead them all with the same message. But you can steer them toward a common destination. That way, when the team reaches its goal, there's a sense of excitement and fulfillment, on both the individual and the collective levels. Whatever the organization and whatever the goals, the same logic probably applies.

That second season of juniors, my first as a captain, I had 25 goals and 49 assists in 54 games. Much more important, we made it to the league final, before losing to a team from Calgary.

Even though we were disappointed to lose at the end, I was proud of the team, and how we got there. It was a successful season, and while I'd like to think my captaincy was a factor, most of it was due to Doug's great coaching. He made people feel good about their roles, pushed them to reach their maximum potential, and held them accountable. He had an ability to get people to play for one another. By this time, Doug's philosophy was so ingrained in my nature that I didn't even think about it—the way we play the game for keeps. I just followed his example as a player and captain.

I was seventeen, I was playing well, and I felt that I was ready for a step up. That meant major junior hockey, which back then was where the vast majority of NHL players came from.

My rights were owned by the Portland Winter Hawks, a major junior team of the Western Hockey League that previously was based in Edmonton, which was how they knew me. Their playoffs were starting after the Mets' season ended, so I joined them. I was the youngest player on the roster, and just a bit anxious stepping into a team that had played together the entire season. It was also immediately clear that the level of play on the Winter Hawks was different than on the Mets. The roster was deep and talented and full of future NHL players, and the stars in particular—like the tall centerman Dale Yakiwchuk, Larry Playfair, the brothers Wayne and Dave Babych, and Perry Turnbull—were a step up in skill level beyond what I was used to.

But there was a certain comfort level, too. I was not only back in Portland, the town where I'd spent my formative years, but playing in the Coliseum—the very same arena where my dad had been a Buckaroo. Ten years earlier, I'd been playing shinny with friends in the building's vast hallways, using broken sticks and wadded-up tape as a puck while we waited for our dads to be done with hockey practice. How far I'd come.

We took the first playoff round to seven games, but ultimately lost. My time back in Portland was short, but I felt like

I had been up to the challenge. I had four goals and an assist in the series.

That summer I came home to St. Albert with a decision to make: Was I going to return to Portland in the fall and play a full season of major junior? Or was I going to stay with the Mets in tier-two hockey, which would preserve my amateur status, and give me a path to playing in college, like Paul was doing?

I was leaning toward college. Then everything changed.

CHAPTER THREE

GOING PRO

I n 1967, Dennis Murphy—whose most notable prior distinctions were attending high school with Marilyn Monroe and later becoming mayor of Buena Park, California—stormed professional basketball's palace walls. He and his partner Gary Davidson created the American Basketball Association. The upstart league signed big players, planted franchises in markets where the more established NBA was absent, and literally changed the rules—the ABA gave basketball the three-point shot, not to mention an iconoclastic red, white, and blue ball.

Murphy turned out to be quite the sports entrepreneur. He was part of groups that created not only the ABA, but World Team Tennis, too, and eventually set their sights on hockey. In 1972 the NHL was the king of the hill, but Murphy and his partners thought there was still a widespread and underserved appetite for the game. They created the World Hockey Association to meet the demand.

The new league needed players and started recruiting some of the best. The NHL had long operated with a restrictive rule known as the "reserve clause," which essentially meant that players' rights were owned by a particular team for life, unless the player was traded or released. The WHA boldly refused to honor that clause, viewing any player whose NHL contract had expired as fair game, and then started with a bang, signing the eventual Hall of Famer and Chicago Black Hawks icon Bobby Hull. He and the WHA made history by signing the first million-dollar hockey contract.

Scores of established players then followed the "Golden Jet" to the WHA. The great Gordie Howe came out of retirement and played with not one but two of his sons on the same team, the Houston Aeros. It was the first father-and-son combination to play professional hockey together. The league also welcomed a talent pool the NHL had largely ignored— European players, who typically had a slick and fluid skating style. Even with all this, by the summer of 1978, as the league's seventh season approached, it was struggling in its attempt to go head-to-head with the established NHL and needed to do something else to further distinguish itself.

In the spirit of the flair with which the league was founded, the next move was to go after young North American kids whose rights didn't yet "belong" to the NHL—to get the seeds before they flowered. The NHL had regulations against drafting and signing underage players, meaning players younger than twenty. But the WHA had no issue with it, allowing the league to access young prospects and talents that they may have otherwise missed out on.

And that's where I come into the story.

In the fall of 1978, I was seventeen years old and had pretty much decided I was eventually going to go to college. My brother, Paul, had gotten picked in the third round of the NHL draft that summer by the Colorado Rockies (who became the New Jersey Devils in 1982), and he'd done it after spending two years at the University of Denver. The year before, when I was sixteen, his college coach Marshall Johnston had told me that a scholarship was waiting for me when the time came, and that sounded good to me at the time. He was a Saskatchewan guy who'd played in the NHL and then came back to work at his alma mater. He'd been recruiting for Denver in western Canada for years. I had been figuring that I would follow Paul there.

Back then, if you played more than ten or so regular-season major junior hockey games, you were ineligible to play in the NCAA, and with college still being my plan, I left Portland and went back to St. Albert and the Saints at the tier-two level to keep my eligibility open. It quickly became clear it wasn't the right place for me.

In 17 games I had 33 points and 64 penalty minutes. Doug, who felt I needed a bigger challenge, saw all these young players coming and going to the WHA, so he called an old teammate.

Pat Stapleton and my father had played together as defensemen for the Buckaroos, and now Stapleton was coaching the Indianapolis Racers of the WHA. They arranged for me to have a tryout with the team lasting five games.

It was potentially a big step. Back then, not a lot of guys essentially went from tier-two juniors directly to the professional level—almost all of the underage players that the WHA had signed were highly recruited, heavily scouted big names in the tier-one major juniors. One team in particular, the Birmingham Bulls from Alabama, signed *seven* of these underage juniors in the summer of 1978. They soon came to be known as the "Baby Bulls." I wasn't 100 percent sure I could compete in the WHA, but I also knew there was only one way to find out. I saw all these other seventeen-year-olds playing well in the WHA and suddenly, college didn't seem so important to me. This was a chance to play professional hockey—the thing I'd always dreamed of. If the five-game tryout didn't work out, I would still have my college eligibility, but in all honesty, the more likely scenario is that I would have put college aside, gone back to the Winter Hawks in Portland, and worked as hard as I could for another chance at the WHA or the NHL draft. I was committed to the path ahead of me, unconventional as it was.

I felt good. In St. Albert, I was scoring and brawling with the best of them. Headed to my WHA tryout with the Racers, I wasn't intimidated. But Doug, in his own way, tried to tell me to keep my head up and be cautious. As I was getting ready to leave, the only thing he said about it was that it's good to have confidence, but don't underestimate other people. If you do, you can get surprised, and those surprises usually aren't the good kind. I should know that at the professional level, *everybody* is tough.

At the time I wondered why in the world he was telling me that. I could obviously handle myself. I'd just come off a run where I was having three fights a game. When I was fifteen, I was fighting twenty-year-olds. I grew up with it. But some things you have to experience to truly learn.

I got on a plane and joined the Racers in Winnipeg, where they were playing the defending WHA champs, the Jets, the next day. The two-hour flight was uneventful except for one twist of fate. As I was taking off from Edmonton, Wayne Gretzky was landing there. I'd heard of him—everybody had, he was a phenom—but we'd never met. Gretzky had just been dealt from the Racers to the Oilers—who got their start as one of the founding teams in the WHA—and he was joining his new team the same day. I was about to fill the Indianapolis roster spot he had vacated. We probably passed each other in the air.

ON NOVEMBER 5, 1978, I made my professional hockey debut. It's funny, but this game, the culmination of my dreams at the time, is something of a blur in my memory. I remember entering the dressing room and there were a bunch of veteran players there. Nothing much was said. I got dressed, went out onto the ice, "The Star-Spangled Banner" and "O Canada" played, and then, before I knew it, I was over the boards on the fly and got the puck up the middle for a breakaway.

The goalie was a twenty-one-year-old from Finland named Markus Mattsson. He would later go on to become the first Finn to play goal in the NHL. I snapped a wrister to his low stick side, but it hit the pipe. I was a pro for all of ten seconds before I got my first scoring chance! Maybe this was going to be easier than my dad had said.

Despite that strong start, I didn't score any goals that game, and we lost 6–2 to the Jets. There was a small story by Pat Doyle in the *Winnipeg Tribune* the next day that mentioned it was my first game, and that I "didn't look out of place."

I'm glad that was the case, and I did feel okay about the way I'd played in that first game overall, but at moments it had also felt like I was having an out-of-body experience. That continued over the next few days as my five-game tryout progressed. I was just two and a half years removed from my mom driving me to Bantam hockey practice, getting player stickers to put in my book, and collecting Esso rookie cards while my mom filled the car with gas. I knew every team from the California Golden Seals to the Montreal Canadiens, and just about every player. Now these guys from my sticker books were coming to life, sitting across from me in the dressing room or skating on the other team.

After that first game, it was clear that this was a step up from junior hockey. The guys in the locker room were pros. Some of these guys were playing when my dad was in the league. I was wide-eyed with excitement. It was a new level of competing. At the junior level, things can sometimes be a little helter-skelter. There are a lot of talented players, but they're not always on the same page, or playing the system the way it was designed. At the professional level, however, just about everything you do on the ice is meticulously organized—the routines for practice, the way guys work together. Of course, mistakes are made, but it's much more structured.

It was a little strange playing with guys twice my age, but I also admired them, and found that I got over the age difference quickly. In the end, it's just hockey, and these were teammates. Our goalie was Gary "Suitcase" Smith, who was thirty-four when I joined the team. Suitcase was a thirteen-year veteran who'd spent a life on the road playing for eight different NHL teams. In 1972, he shared the Vezina Trophy as the league's best goaltender with his Chicago Black Hawks teammate Tony Esposito.

I really enjoyed Suitcase. He was one of the game's great characters. He wore thirteen pairs of socks when he played! I have no idea if it was superstition, or ritual, or if he just liked the way it felt, but before he put on his skates, he'd sit at his locker and put on one pair after another. And if that wasn't strange enough, between periods he would come in, take off his uniform and equipment, shower, and then get suited up again, including all those socks. He did that twice a game.

On November 17, the fourth of my five tryout games, we were scheduled to play the Oilers in Edmonton. It would be my first time skating in my hometown as a pro, and I was really excited.

At the pro level, there were creature comforts I wasn't accustomed to. The way you're taken care of was nice. The night before our travel day, I ordered lobster thermidor from room service at the hotel in Indianapolis.

I got food poisoning.

I was violently ill the next morning. When it was time to go to the airport, I could barely get my head off the pillow. The 1,600-mile flight that followed was merely confirmation that Murphy's Law is real. I found myself, hot and sweaty, in a middle seat between two people who smoked the entire trip. Mom and Dad took one look at me when I got to Edmonton and I'm sure were questioning the wisdom of releasing their seventeen-year-old into the wild.

The food poisoning had knocked the hell out of me, but I wasn't about to miss out on playing in my hometown, and my parents understood that. Playing through pain and injury at this point in time was a badge of honor for me as it was for a lot of other players. If you gave anything less than your all, there would always be another guy ready to take your job. I rested as much as I could before the game, and hit the ice at Northlands Coliseum. We lost the game 6–1, but it turned out to be a significant game for me nonetheless. Glen Sather had stopped playing for the Oilers and become their full-time coach after the 1976–77 season, and he took notice of my aggressive style of play. He would soon become a huge part of my career.

We wound up losing all five of the games I played for the Racers. I didn't score or have any assists. Maybe the bigger surprise was that I didn't have any penalty minutes, either. My confidence had dropped pretty low.

The team must have seen *something* they liked, though, because a contract was being discussed. However, a couple of days after my run with the Racers ended, the team folded. Although I didn't make a mark on the stat sheet, I did distinguish myself by becoming perhaps the youngest player to ever help put a franchise out of business. I had earned $2,200 for my time on the team.

The check bounced.

I went back home to Edmonton and was trying to figure out what was next for me when Doug got a call from the Cincinnati Stingers, one of the WHA's six remaining teams. One of their scouts, Flo Potvin, had seen me play and thought the Stingers could use me.

I had yet to reach my eighteenth birthday and I was off to play for my second professional team. This time, there would be no turning back.

AT THE OLYMPIC GAMES, THEY always say the judges in skating or gymnastics never want to give the early competitors too high a mark because if they do they might not leave adequate room for a later competitor who offers a superior performance. I mention that because if playing alongside "Suitcase" Smith in Indianapolis had been a big deal, what awaited me in my first week in Cincinnati was next-level fantasy stuff.

On December 30, wearing sweater number 18 (the NHL veteran Darryl Maggs already had my number 11), I stepped out onto the ice at Riverfront Coliseum in front of 6,800 people to skate against the New England Whalers.

Playing center was Dave Keon, who, before joining the WHA, had spent fifteen seasons with the NHL's Toronto Maple Leafs. In his first—the year I was born—he'd been the league's rookie of the year. That might have been enough to overwhelm me had it not been for the man who lined up on Keon's right wing: Gordie Howe, Mr. Hockey himself.

Wayne Gretzky would eventually go on to become the game's undisputed GOAT, but before he did, the greatest of all time in hockey had, without question, been Howe. Here I was skating around with the Babe Ruth of our sport. He was an even bigger deal to me because he and Doug had briefly crossed paths in the Red Wings' camp years before.

And to top it off, I looked over during warm-ups, and there were my parents. They had flown in to surprise me.

I tried to keep my focus on my matchup. Johnny McKenzie was a five-foot-nine fireplug who'd won a Stanley Cup playing with Bobby Orr and the Bruins. Although he was now forty-one and in the final year of a long career, McKenzie was still a real agitator who needed to be watched.

But whenever Howe was on the ice, I couldn't help but pay attention to him as well. At fifty one years old, he was the oldest pro to ever lace up skates. He was six feet and 200 pounds, but he looked bigger than that. He looked bigger than *life*, but that might have had something to do with the way I always thought of him. And he could still really move.

I watched him with a mixture of awe and caution the entire game. It was partly because I was a fan, sure, but it was part self-preservation, too. He was three times my age and still mean as a rattlesnake. I knew all the stories about how lethal his elbows were. I gave him more attention than anyone I had ever played against.

His skill and feel for the game were unrivaled. Doug always said Howe was like some kind of magician who specialized in making something happen that nobody saw coming. He'd told me about a time he watched Howe put the puck between a defenseman's skates and when the guy looked down, he poked it through his legs, brought his stick over the guy's head, and then took the puck on the other side. Meanwhile, the guy skated off the ice with blood dripping from his head and his ear hanging partway off. When you have a reputation for making a move like that, you don't have to do it often. Howe commanded tremendous respect. It was the only time in my career that I took a gulp before lining up against someone.

Howe didn't fight often, and in thirty-two years of professional hockey, he averaged just 65 penalty minutes a year. But when he did fight, it was devastating. If you do an online search on the old Rangers tough guy Lou Fontinato, one of the first images that will come up is the chilling aftermath of his fight with Howe on February 1, 1959. Fontinato's face is covered in tape and dressing. Howe beat him to a pulp. Every time Fontinato went down, Howe would pull him back up and hit him again. The picture is from an article in *Life* magazine entitled "Don't Mess with Gordie." The pistonlike beating Howe gave that day was described in the magazine as like "a man chopping wood."

Dad later told me that when he and Mom got to the arena that night to see me play, Mom sat down, saw who was on the other team, and said to him, "What in the world did you get Mark into?"

It all turned out okay, though—better than just okay, actually. With the game tied at one halfway through the third period, I took a face-off and found my teammate Mike Gartner, who scored the winning goal. (He'd go on to have a tremendous NHL career.)

It felt good to come away from Howe's Whalers with a win, and with a goal I helped set up. My first week on my new team was off to a solid start. The Stingers decided to keep me on the team, and I played out my first full season of professional WHA hockey with them. But it was apparent that whatever talent I had could only be described—and charitably so—as raw.

Physically, I felt comfortable. I'd tagged along with Paul my whole life, so playing with and against older and more experienced guys wasn't an issue. In terms of skills, though, I had a long way to go. I was an unfinished product.

That entire season, I had only one goal, and it was far from a thing of beauty. I was coming off the ice for a shift change so I just dumped the puck into the zone. Next thing I knew the crowd was going wild. Somehow the puck had bounced into the net, and I didn't even get credit for the plus because by the time it went in, I had one foot off the ice!

I was hardly setting the league on fire.

People say I'm crazy when I mention this, but I've always looked at myself as a late bloomer. Even though I turned pro at an early age, I was nowhere near a finished product physically, or in terms of my skills.

But I was lucky. I could have gotten into an organization that didn't have the patience to let a young player mature, or couldn't afford a mistake. Often, organizations get clouded with the need for immediate success, so they cut short the process. In that scenario, they might have looked at me differently and not given me the opportunity.

Our coach with the Stingers was Floyd Smith. He'd been behind the bench in Buffalo, where he'd had "The French

Connection Line": Gilbert Perreault, Rick Martin, and René Robert. I really admired Perreault, so I knew about Coach Floyd. I had watched the Sabres in the Stanley Cup finals against Philadelphia.

When you're young—as an athlete or in any other career— you're really at the mercy of the people around you, whether it's a coach, an owner, your peers, or your boss. In Cincinnati, Smith might have chosen not to play me that much. It could have been a setback, but he supported my growth. He went out of his way to make me feel comfortable—making conversation, being generally kind—and it made a big impact at a critical time.

But skill development wasn't the only area where I needed work. There was the issue of maturity as well. I was seventeen. As you read these words, think about where you were at that age.

Considering some of the things I did, it would have been so easy for the Stingers to send me home. It was mostly innocent stuff, but when I look back, I cringe. One of our team flights got diverted to Phoenix due to bad weather and the decision was made to have an ad hoc practice while we were there. I treated a break in our schedule like a vacation. I had friends who lived in Phoenix, so for two days, I never went to practice. I didn't even know there was a practice. I guess I just never heard about where I was supposed to be.

Someone eventually got in touch with me and wanted to know if I was okay. It hadn't dawned on them, because it was such a ridiculous thought, that I didn't know about practice. During those two days when I was MIA I remember thinking, "Wow, pro hockey is great!"

What I failed to grasp at seventeen is that as much as "it's just hockey," at the professional level there's a lot at stake. There are livelihoods and families—a whole other level of responsibility. You're part of an organism, and in order for the organism to thrive, each and every person needs to do their part. The organization needs to be able to count on you.

One of the ways they count on you is by assuming you'll be on time. Hockey is almost like the military. There's zero tolerance for being late. If you're five minutes early, then you're late. I didn't think much about that until I was late a few times. What seventeen-year-old hasn't slept through an alarm? Then again, most seventeen-year-olds aren't playing professional hockey.

The bottom line is I was being disrespectful of everyone's time. When I was late, it was as if I was telling my team, "I don't care if anybody is inconvenienced."

I found out quickly that team buses don't wait for rookies. Unfortunately, you have to feel the sting for a message to sink in. My first road trip to Quebec, I had a late night and by the time I got back to my hotel in the morning it was too late to pack my bag and get to the bus before it left. I had to take a taxi to the airport. First lesson there, and one I took to heart from that point on: Pack your bag *before* you head out to enjoy your evening! Of course, the real lesson is there are actions and there are consequences, and if you're not going to change your actions, you are going to suffer consequences. I wish I could say it sank in immediately and that I changed completely before I went to the NHL, but that wasn't the case.

In Cincinnati I lived in a hotel with Bryan "Bugsy" Watson and Paul "Stew Cat" Stewart, which made things interesting. The three of us had to be the most unlikely trio you ever met.

Bugsy was a thirty-six-year-old defenseman from Ontario who'd played all over the NHL. He might have been the biggest antagonist the league ever had. In his fifteen-year NHL career, he had more than 2,200 penalty minutes and just 17 goals. His face was rough from all the battle scars, but that didn't dull the light in his eyes.

Stew Cat was a super-tough guy from Boston. He went to the University of Pennsylvania, but had anything but an Ivy League air about him. He bounced around the minors for a few years before playing in the WHA. He later played one year in the NHL, before he went out in style. One night at the Boston Garden he had four fights, including one in the warm-up. After the game, he walked out of the building, threw his skates into the Charles River, and retired. Later, he went on to have a long career as—of all things—an NHL official.

We were different ages, at different stages of our careers, and we came from different backgrounds, but all three of us had one thing in common: We liked to have a good time. I would say the hotel was like a frat house, but if it had been, we probably would have behaved better.

We never got into any real trouble, but there were a lot of late nights and laughs. When I first got to town, Stew Cat bought me a beer and introduced me to Pete Rose at Sleep Out Louie's, our home-away-from-home local sports bar. A few months later, when Stew Cat got sent down to Philadelphia in the American Hockey League (where he would be teammates with my brother), we had an all-night party at Louie's to send him off. We shut the place down at five in the morning and drove him right to the airport.

Was I wild? Yes, I was. I can say that much of it was that I was running at the speed of a league that was serious as hell, but had a "work hard, play hard" mentality, too. A lot of it was on me, though. I am naturally exuberant about *everything*: my family, my friends, my work, my interests—and my pursuit of having a good time. Ultimately, I believe that immersive personality trait was responsible for what I accomplished in the game. But it has its downsides.

My season in Cincinnati was an early lesson that life is a balancing act. If the nights were sometimes unhinged with guys like Stew Cat and Bugsy, the days were inspiring and productive, in many ways because of our captain. Robbie Ftorek made a big impression on me.

Robbie demonstrated what I would later come to understand is one of the essential qualities of a leader: empathy. He was stoic and all business, but he was really compassionate, too, and sensitive to the feelings of people around him.

I remember at one practice we didn't have the right number of players to evenly fill out the three-man lines for a drill. So Robbie did a rush with his line and then skated back to fill out my line. Nobody had to ask him to do it. Small gestures like that told us he was thoroughly invested in our success, whether we were on the first line or the last; veterans, or new to the team. He made everybody feel included and comfortable.

Robbie was ten years older than me, and as an American—he grew up in Boston and was a two-time Massachusetts League MVP—he was unusually successful. The American high school and college system just wasn't as clear a path to professional hockey as the Canadian junior league system back then, and while there were some Americans who made it, there were very few stars or leaders. At five feet ten he was on the small side, too, making it even more of an uphill climb.

He impressed enough people to be signed by the Detroit Red Wings, but never really got a chance to play in the NHL, so he jumped to Phoenix in the WHA. He flourished there, winning the league MVP award in 1977. Up until that point, no American-born player had ever earned that individual honor in a top-tier North American professional league.

In many ways, Robbie was the opposite of me and my partying friends. He carried himself with his back pretty stiff, like a little army sergeant. He commanded a lot of respect, not necessarily because of what he said, but because of what he did.

Robbie was our leading scorer by a mile. Nobody was within 45 points of him. Not surprisingly, he had nearly twice as many assists as he did goals. He was a facilitator in every way. His size and skill made him something of a target, too, in a league tumbling toward anarchy, making his accomplishments all the more impressive.

As it turned out, my year with the Stingers ended up being the WHA's final season. The players and organizations knew the league was struggling, and we turned to chaos and fighting to sell tickets. The Broad Street Bullies had legitimized mayhem in the NHL, and the WHA became a brawling circus. It was right in my wheelhouse, but it wasn't good for the game. Coach Floyd actually sent me out once just to get into a fight. We were playing against Winnipeg. They had an old veteran left-winger named Bill Lesuk. I don't know if Floyd saw some hesitation in me, or just wanted me to get involved. Maybe he just wanted to know what I was all about.

He came up behind me on the bench and said, "You gonna let that guy take advantage of you the rest of the game? Maybe you should go out there and do something about it."

I'd never been asked to pick a fight with a specific player

like this. But I was a rookie, and when they called your number, you just went and did what the coach wanted.

The end of the season was near bedlam. Four of the six teams were going to make the playoffs, and our back-to-back games with the Birmingham "Baby Bulls" would determine which of us went to the postseason. It got completely out of control. There were five bench-clearing brawls. In one game, John Brophy, then the Birmingham coach, somehow got one of our players on their bench and pounded him with haymakers. It was complete insanity.

Intimidation had always been a part of the game, and everybody had to "man up" at certain times—put a stake in the ground and let the rest of the league know you were going to be there for a while. When it became sheer violence, though, it wasn't good for hockey. A lot of kids got hurt.

We ended up making it to the best-of-three preliminary round of the playoffs, but on April 24, we were eliminated by the Whalers. It was disappointing. And yet things weren't all bad. It didn't seem that long ago I was in junior hockey, getting ten dollars for a win, seven for a tie, three for a loss (they called it "gas money" as a way around the rules for paying players), and trading in empty pop bottles to make a little extra cash. For my five months with the Stingers, I made $35,000. I felt rich. I had completed a season of pro hockey, I loved the traveling, and I knew there was no other kind of life I wanted to live.

While I had money in my pocket, the WHA didn't. The league officially folded, and four teams were absorbed into the NHL: New England, Quebec, Winnipeg, and Edmonton. As a Cincinnati player, my future was uncertain and not at all secure. There were to be two rounds of dispersal drafts for NHL teams of unclaimed WHA players later in the summer—one in

June, and one in August. The one in August would be my big chance to keep playing professional hockey.

I had been away from my family all year. We were all out of the house by this point, except for my younger sister, Mary-Kay, and I was excited to see them again after the season ended. Paul had just wrapped up a difficult first professional season after getting injured early on in the NHL and spending most of the year in the AHL and CHL. His season ended around the same time as mine, so he picked me up in Cincinnati. He showed up in a brand-new custom van, painted two shades of blue, tricked out with four powder-blue bucket seats, a big stereo, a refrigerator and little cooler bar, a small closet, and a back bench that could fold into a bed. We drove that van nearly two thousand miles back to Edmonton. It was like our old summer drives down to the cabin in Oregon, but this time we were controlling the music.

From there, I decided to use some of my own money to rent a condo on the beach in Malibu, and invite my parents and siblings, plus my grandmother, to move out there with me for six weeks. This California vacation was a time to reconnect with my family. We all played Frisbee and bodysurfed down at the beach for hours, and played card games at night, just like we did at the Oregon cabin.

It was also a time to get myself in physical and mental shape to play in the NHL. I worked out like a madman. I got a ten-speed bike and rode up Malibu Canyon until I literally couldn't turn the pedals. I was trying everything I could to gain strength and conditioning. My siblings and I went into the town of Malibu—where we'd see celebrities of the era like Johnny Carson and Jan-Michael Vincent casually going about their lives—and did studio aerobics, which everybody was doing, and yoga, which nobody in hockey was. No fitness idea was too wacky for me, and I'd heard that strengthening was connected to stretching. I was also doing a lifting regimen designed by Jon Kolb, the offensive lineman for the Pittsburgh Steelers and a World's Strongest Man competitor, three times weekly. By the end of that summer, I was an animal, and couldn't wait to get my shot at the NHL. I loved playing hockey, what a life, but it was just a game.

Until I found my tribe.

CHAPTER FOUR

THE EDMONTON OILERS

Edmonton has always been a great sports town. In the Canadian Football League's modern era (dating back to 1954), the Edmonton Elks, which is what it's called now, has won the Grey Cup for the league championship fourteen times. The team qualified for the playoffs in thirty-four consecutive years. Both are records.

Through the years and going all the way back to the 1880s, a parade of professional baseball teams has also called Edmonton home. And the city boasts one of the winningest basketball teams of all time. From 1915 until it disbanded in 1940, the Edmonton Grads, a barnstorming women's team, compiled the best winning percentage of any North American sports team ever—men or women. They played 522 games against teams from all over the world, including the United States, and won 502 of them!

When it came to hockey, when I was a kid, the Edmonton Oil Kings junior team was the biggest show in town. I remember taking the bus to the old Edmonton Gardens stadium to see them play. They were an institution with such great history. When the Oilers were founded as a WHA team, and ex-NHLers started playing in the Gardens, it legitimized us as a sports town and became an even bigger source of identity for the city.

So when folks opened their *Edmonton Journal* on the morning of March 14, 1979, what they read didn't seem out of place. Right there on the front page, next to news about the peace process between Israel and Egypt, was an editorial concerning another important issue: The paper was pleading with Edmontonians to stop drinking Molson beer.

The WHA was ending, and it wasn't yet certain which teams would merge with the NHL. The idea was to pressure the brewery, owners of the Montreal Canadiens, to stop blocking the proposed NHL expansion, which included taking in the Oilers, along with three other teams from the WHA.

There it was on the front page. The things that mattered most to our city: world peace and NHL hockey.

Whether it had anything to do with beer sales or not, a deal was struck on June 22, and the Oilers, along with the Quebec Nordiques, the Winnipeg Jets, and the Hartford Whalers, joined the NHL. This was beyond big: something that very few people in Edmonton ever thought could be possible.

Whenever a new franchise enters the league, there has to be an expansion draft to fill out the new rosters. But bringing in these four existing teams from the WHA required special circumstances. Each one got to protect just two players and two goalies (the Oilers obviously protected their eighteen-year-old phenom Wayne Gretzky). And players who had left the NHL for the WHA saw their rights revert to their old NHL clubs. After the initial expansion draft for the four new teams in June, the NHL then held its usual annual draft on August 19, during which any former WHA players whose rights never belonged to an NHL club were eligible to be drafted, along with college players, European players, and so on, as always.

Because my rights never belonged to an NHL club, and my WHA team was disbanded, this second draft was going to be the biggest day and opportunity of my life.

My family and I had returned from Malibu. Back then ESPN and TSN didn't exist, and the draft wasn't aired on live TV, but because everything connected to the Oilers and their entry into the NHL was such big news in Edmonton, there was actually local live radio coverage. That was the only way you could find out what was going on. My whole family was gathered together, listening at my parents' house in St. Albert.

My thinking was that, because I'd played a year of top-level professional hockey in the WHA, I had a huge leg up on other kids my age who had only played major junior. For that reason, I felt that I stood a good chance of getting drafted early on. So my ego was bruised when the first round went by and there was no mention of my name. I also knew how much more likely it was that you'd be given a chance to play if you were drafted in the first round. Those players get a lot more lee-way from their clubs, and more chances to prove themselves, while lower-round selections need to make more of a splash, and can face an uphill battle just to make the team.

After the second round passed without hearing my name, I was so disappointed. More than that, I was getting concerned that I might not even be drafted at all. I left my family inside and went out to the driveway to shoot pucks.

A little while later, someone—I don't even remember who—came out and said I'd been drafted by the Oilers in the third round with the forty-eighth pick overall. Despite being a lower pick than I'd hoped for, I'd been selected by my home team. I was about to get a chance to be part of the biggest thing that had ever happened in my town. It was also great for my parents, who would now be able to come see me play regularly. Any lingering disappointment I had at not being drafted higher seemed small next to that. It was a dream come true.

What I recognize now is that I didn't have the equity coming into the draft that I imagined I did. Having played a single WHA season, one in which I'd scored a single goal and had 10 assists in 52 games, no less, there wasn't enough evidence of who I was as a player. It seems obvious in retrospect that I was far from the conventional choice.

As it turned out, Edmonton's coach, Glen Sather, who would make a Hall of Fame career by doing things differently than everyone else, had ignored the advice of his scouts to take one of the young junior prospects in the WHL who was further along in his development than I was, and chose me. As a player, Glen Sather had a ten-year career in the NHL. He'd been an agitator and a role player. Decent skills, almost 200 points, pretty tough, good team guy. He'd come out of High River, south of Calgary, but forged a deep connection to Edmonton because it was where he started his playing career, in juniors, for the Oil Kings. He ended his playing career in Edmonton as well, serving in the last eighteen games of the 1976–77 WHA season for the Oilers as not only a player, but their coach, too. The next season, he retired as a player, remained the coach, and started building a dynasty. Peter Pocklington was the Oilers' owner, Larry Gordon was the president, but Glen *was* the Oilers. He did everything.

Glen knew our family, especially my dad. They'd played against each other once when Glen was a left-winger with the

Oil Kings and Doug played right defense for the Lacombe Rockets. During that game, Dad laid a pretty good hit on him, but Glen got right up, earning Doug's eternal respect.

So Glen knew what kind of hockey DNA I had. He'd also seen me play. When I was skating for the Mets, the team my dad coached in St. Albert, and Glen was coaching the Oilers, we practiced on the same rink, right before them. A few years later, Glen saw something in that one game when I was on the Cincinnati Stingers and we were playing against his Oilers in Edmonton. I got into a fight with one of his players, Dennis Sobchuk, who was a talented guy out of junior hockey. It was actually my first fight as a professional and I walked away unscathed.

Sather was quoted saying, "Mark wasn't a goal scorer, but he had the fire in his eyes."

Another connection was that Bugsy Watson, my old roommate from Cincinnati, was friends with Sather. They'd played together in Pittsburgh and St. Louis, and Bugsy had been claimed by the Oilers in the June dispersal draft. He didn't tell me he was doing it directly, but I knew that he was getting in Glen's ear about choosing me.

In short, Glen was banking on positive talk, gut feeling, my family hockey background, and what he saw watching me practice and play just a few games, more than any kind of hard evidence that I'd be able to make something of myself as an NHL player.

In the week following the draft, there was an article in one of the papers that got my attention—actually, it stayed with me like an itch I couldn't scratch, annoying and impossible to ignore. It insinuated that the Oilers were taking a risk on me.

But what stuck with me the most was that it characterized me as "wayward." The article made it seem like I was some sort of derelict. To me, it called my character into question and I was confused as to why.

The article sounded a trumpet: This team was serious business, and the object of a city's attention. I'd never felt scrutiny like this. Despite the fact that it was my hometown, or maybe even because of it, I was fair game.

Thankfully, there were seven weeks from the draft to the start of the season, so I had time to digest it. Then, just like that, I had reason to feel slighted again.

The Oilers had a big charity softball game at Renfrew Park, a stadium in town where professional baseball teams had played through the years, during which fans could come out, see the team, and get a look at the new players. It was heady stuff, my first appearance as an NHL player, and in my hometown. They had team jerseys for all of the players with our names on the back—with one exception. There was no jersey anywhere with the name "Messier" on it. They found a blank team shirt and gave it to me. I'm sure it was just a mistake, and I tried to enjoy the event, but all I could think was, *What would I need to do to be remembered?*

Everyone cared about the "other" eighteen-year-old on the team, Wayne Gretzky. Then again, Wayne was just different, and always had been. Even out west in Edmonton, where we didn't get a lot of hockey news beyond the basics, he'd been on my radar for a long time. When we were in grammar school, *Hockey Night in Canada* was already showing clips of his games.

I remember reading a big feature article about him in *The Canadian* magazine. We were both ten at the time. He'd scored something like 369 goals, or some other crazy number. He *averaged* four and a half goals a game. I was playing hockey, too, and remember thinking, "How is that even possible?"

Years later, as Gretzky's star continued to rise, I was driving to a junior practice with my dad, and out of nowhere I asked: "Do you think Wayne Gretzky is better than me?" Doug started clearing his throat—hemming and hawing—and finally said, "I think you've got to make a right here."

By this time, there was no comparing myself with Wayne. The previous year, when I'd scored 1 goal for Cincinnati, he'd had 104 points, scoring 43 goals and 61 assists for the Oilers in 72 games after being traded from the Indianapolis Racers. Here I was just trying to make the team. I'd been disillusioned by the draft, the article, and the team jersey, but all of it together gave me motivation and an understanding that I was going to have to do something about it. I would use it all as fuel, put my head down, and do the work. *Next year when we came back to the softball game,* I told myself, *they'll have my name on a jersey because I'll have earned it.*

BEFORE I COULD EARN ANYTHING on the ice, an agreement needed to be made as to what I would earn for my salary, and as training camp neared, my contract still hadn't been finalized. My dad and my agent, Gus Badali, were negotiating with Glen Sather.

Glen and the Oilers were proposing a "two-way" contract, which meant they would pay me one salary if I played for their NHL club, and a lower salary if they sent me down to their farm club in Houston.

It was actually my mother who first objected, based on what she'd seen my brother, Paul, go through just the year before on a similarly structured deal with the Colorado Rockies. In just the fourteenth game of the season, Paul's ninth appearance in the NHL, he got run into the boards by Bob Kelly of Pittsburgh and separated his shoulder.

The Rockies, who were struggling at the gate, didn't have much incentive to pay him his NHL salary, so, with a two-way deal, he was sent down to the farm club in Philadelphia. He languished there, and never got another chance with the Rockies, or in the NHL at all. My mom, dad, and Gus wanted to make sure nothing like that would happen again.

And as for the dollars on the table, they were proposing a four-year deal for $20,000 a season, which was low compared to most pro salaries. If you looked at it from the Oilers' point of view—and you always have to think of the other side's perspective when you're negotiating—it's easy to imagine what they were thinking: "What kind of a case can this kid make for more money? He had one goal and ten assists in a full year of professional play."

The facts *were* indisputable, but it was still a lowball offer—I'd made $34,000 the previous year in Cincinnati, after all—and so it became a matter of principle. I needed to feel the transaction was fair. This eventually became a guiding principle of leadership for me: If people don't feel they're valued, how can you possibly expect them to give their maximum effort? It's not terribly complicated.

We negotiated for a while and came to an agreement just in time for training camp: five years at $50,000 a season, and a one-way deal. Even if I didn't make the team, I'd still be paid that amount, which gave the team less incentive to send me down and meant my chances of staying in the NHL had improved.

Training camp was at the University of Alberta. It wasn't all that long after I'd come back from Malibu, so I had a bit of a tan. I pulled up to camp on a Suzuki 1000 motorcycle, all dressed in leather, my bleached-blond hair spilling out from under my helmet (yes, I once had hair). Nobody said anything that day, but Glen saw me ride up, and about two weeks later, he showed up at the house in St. Albert, where I was living with my parents, and declared he was putting a provision in my contract that I wasn't allowed to ride a motorcycle anymore. Glen clearly didn't want me to get hurt, but secretly, I always thought he liked the wild streak in me—as long as I could keep it under control. He knew my dad and had probably heard more about me than I knew, or wanted him to know. But I came to learn that what he wanted from me was—as contradictory as it sounds—a measure of reckless abandon.

In Cincinnati I'd joined the team after camp was over, so this was my first pro training camp, and I felt a mixture of nerves and excitement going into an NHL locker room for that first day. I knew one of the trainers, John Blackwell, which helped me feel a bit more at ease. There were young guys like me—Wayne, of course, and Kevin Lowe, who was the team's number one draft choice that year. Kevin had been the first-ever English-speaking captain of a Quebec major junior hockey league team, the Quebec Remparts.

But there were also a lot of vets. As with my first day in the WHA, I only knew these guys as stars from my Esso sticker book. Al Hamilton was an Edmonton-born guy and local icon. He'd had a great career with the Oil Kings and treated me like a son. Blair MacDonald was a skilled player who put up some strong numbers. Dave Dryden was an experienced goalie who gave us stability as we formed a team identity. Lee Fogolin was a tough guy from Buffalo. He didn't say a lot—he didn't need to. He was always on time, always prepared, and led by example. And our captain, Ron Chipperfield, was a total class act, solid player, and treated us young guys well.

We also had some big characters on the team in Dave Semenko, who'd become a key ingredient in our future success, and Bill "Cowboy" Flett, who was beloved by Edmonton fans.

Between scrimmage and practice and drills there wasn't much opportunity to get to know people on a personal level. But there were probably sixty players in camp to start with, from old pros trying to latch on, to new players like me trying to make it. A lot of guys who weren't under contract got cut altogether. Young players who were under contract but weren't going to make the team got sent to the minors and even back to juniors.

I got to play some exhibition games, and because no one ever told me I was being sent down, it was the same thing as being told I'd made the team. As elated as I was, I was also relieved. I'd seen the year before with my brother how guys would often get sent to the minors and then never be heard from again. The minor leagues back then weren't about developing skills, they were about warehousing players in case the big club needed some fill-ins. I had no intention of being a fill-in.

With camp behind us, things got off to a good start. I came in one day and there was a sweater in the locker room for me, number 11. I didn't ever request it—John Blackwell, who knew my dad, and his history, just took care of it. It even had my name on the back.

WE PLAYED MOST OF OUR preseason games in the Canadian northwest, places like Brandon, Manitoba; Saskatoon,

Saskatchewan; and Medicine Hat, Alberta. The atmosphere and energy in these small arenas didn't seem all that different from the year before in the WHA. But on October 10, the regular season started, and everything changed.

I'd seen Chicago Stadium on TV. I'd read all about it over the years, but I'm not sure anything could have prepared me for what we were walking into. It was a beautiful old building that looked like it was chiseled out of stone. The seats rose almost straight up from the ice, and even before the game started the arena was covered in a blanket of noise. The dressing rooms were a level below, underneath the seats. As we were getting ready, we could not only hear the cheering, we could feel it, too. The building literally shook.

When it was time to play, there were twenty-two concrete steps to climb to get to the ice, through a canyon of screaming humanity. Some fans had been known to rain down gravel and sand on the path to dull visitors' skates, or soft drinks and beer on their heads to dull their spirit.

I'd been skating almost as long as I'd been walking, but standing on the blue line that night in the "Madhouse on Madison," an original-six arena, and hearing the anthems coming from that giant pipe organ, I was so jacked up I could feel my pulse in my eyes.

The energy was incredible. Then the puck dropped, and thirty seconds into the game, there was a fight. I'll never forget that moment. As I watched from the bench, I literally said to myself: "Welcome to the NHL."

I don't remember much about the rest of the game, but we lost 4–2. I had one shot, but otherwise I didn't dent the scoresheet. My first real career highlight as an NHL pro came three days later, and I don't know that I could have asked for more.

Sixteen thousand people packed Northlands Coliseum on October 13 for the city's first-ever NHL home game. The Red Wings were held up by bad weather getting out of Vancouver, where they'd played the night before. The one-hour delay only served to ratchet up the energy.

Twelve minutes into the game, Blair MacDonald converted on our third power play of the night, and the place erupted like we'd won the Stanley Cup.

The game went back and forth and was tied with seven minutes left when Dale McCourt slipped one past our goalie, Eddie Mio, and all the air came out of the balloon. The Oilers seemed headed for a loss in our home debut.

But with just about two and a half minutes on the clock, I centered a pass that bounced off a defender's skate and past Detroit's Rogie Vachon. It was hardly a thing of beauty, but the record would show my first NHL goal came against a former Vezina Trophy and Stanley Cup winner who would end up in the Hall of Fame. And it was my mother's birthday.

I slid comfortably into the rhythm of the NHL. I knew what a life in hockey felt like, but the first thing I learned was how much I had to learn. Normally you look to older guys for an education. I was seeing hockey as a whole new game by closely watching the *youngest* guy in the league.

Nobody had ever seen anything like Wayne Gretzky before. Coming into this year, everyone knew he was skilled, but a lot of people were curious to see how he would stack up against NHL talent. Gordie Howe did it with strength and brawn. Bobby Orr did it with sheer skating speed and dynamic movement. Nobody had ever done it with cerebral finesse and guile like Wayne.

I watched him like a hawk, and what I saw was kind of odd. Wayne saw the ice in 4-D, where people were and where they were going. I think of that famous quote of his: "I don't skate to where the puck is. I skate to where it's going to be." The perception when Wayne came into the league was that he wasn't a great skater, but that wasn't the truth. He was an amazing skater—his edge work, and the way he'd change direction. He skated really bent over, and because he did, there was less of an angle between the shaft of his stick and the blade than I'd ever seen before. It was really unusual, but he knew what he needed to do to perform at his best.

People said he wasn't fast, but he never lost a race to the puck. Nobody could ever catch him, and nobody could ever hit him. He was like Houdini. I heard people say he didn't have a great shot, but you'd look at the scoresheet and he'd have two goals and four assists and you'd be scratching your head, wondering, *Did I miss something here?*

It was difficult to play against him because he didn't resist. He was like a guy practicing tai chi who fights by diffusing his adversary's energy. It was remarkable to watch. Even as a teammate, you had to make sure you didn't get caught flat-footed just admiring what he was doing. It was too easy to get mesmerized.

And then there was his iconic "office." Everybody would be chasing him and somehow he was able to hang on to the puck and set up behind the opposing team's net. He'd find his moment, come out, and lay it on someone's stick for a tap-in goal. Wayne did some serious work from his office.

Going into the season a lot of people had been asking if he

could handle the transition to the NHL. Wayne scored 51 goals and had 86 assists in 79 games that first year. He tied Marcel Dionne, a future Hall of Famer who was ten years older, for the league lead in points.

He was a different kind of player. His trajectory was like a rocket ship, and it was a good idea for anybody who was going to skate on this team to strap on and find a way to complement him. We all recognized he was a special talent, and his play elevated everyone's game. You'd see what he did on the ice, and, realizing it's possible, try to do it as well. His enthusiasm and joy for the game, and his competition level, were contagious. I was learning from Wayne on the ice, but I realized, nearly too late, there were things I needed to learn off the ice as well.

I made mistakes while learning to become a pro. The incident that seems to have followed me around all these years happened just nine games into that first season. I still cringe when I think about it.

I was living out in St. Albert with my parents and we'd lost a home game to the Washington Capitals. The next day we were heading east to play in St. Louis. My mom was driving me to the airport, and for some reason, I thought we were leaving from Municipal Airport, which is downtown. She dropped me off at the terminal and as I looked around I started to get a bad feeling. No one was there. I took out my itinerary and saw my mistake: The flight was actually leaving from Edmonton International Airport.

My heart sank. I got on a pay phone and tried to explain to a woman who answered at the team office. She told me, "Don't worry, Mr. Sather has phoned. Get over to Edmonton International and there'll be a ticket waiting for you at the Air Canada counter."

I finally exhaled and jumped in a cab, figuring I'd just be getting a later flight in, but it would be okay. I got to the other airport and my ticket was waiting for me, just as she'd said. I picked it up, but it wasn't to St. Louis. I was going to Houston, where the Oilers had a minor league team. I was crushed.

It was literally, up until that point, the worst day of my life. You can't miss a flight. It's not an unwritten rule, it's actually in the code of conduct. And as a rookie, it was especially bad.

I kept thinking about my brother and how hard it was for him to make it back up to the NHL after he'd been sent down. Actually, I had plenty of time to think on that flight, and I didn't like what else came to mind. I'd missed practice in Phoenix when I was in the WHA because I wasn't thinking like a pro. I'd been late getting to the team bus in the past. And I swore to myself after that softball game, before the season started, that I'd earn my place on the team.

Fortunately for me, my minor league spanking with the Houston Apollos lasted just four games. You would think after this I might have learned my lesson, but I was eighteen, and still had some maturing to do.

When I was back up with the Oilers, the team was in L.A. and we were all like kids on the last day of school: We couldn't wait to get out and have a good time. I was rooming with Kevin Lowe. After a big night out, the phone in our hotel room rang and I sprang out of bed to pick it up.

"Mark," the voice on the other end said, "it's Glen. You guys interested in practicing today?"

We looked at the clock and it was already 10:45. Practice was scheduled at 11:00, down at the Forum in Inglewood, twenty minutes away.

I'd never dressed so fast. We jumped in our suits and were still buttoning up our shirts as we ran down the hall and through the lobby. We got a cab, and as we were pulling away, Dave Semenko and Curt Brackenbury were yelling at us to hold the taxi. We weren't the only ones to get a call from Glen.

At the arena we rushed to get our equipment and hit the ice. We were half an hour late and the team was practicing without us. Glen blew the whistle and brought everybody to the middle of the ice. He said, "We're glad you guys could join us. We're gonna finish up practicing here, but while we do, Dave, you go up and take a seat up there." He pointed to the farthest corner of the building, the last row up. He then dispatched the other three of us to seats in the top row of the building's remaining corners.

Off we went. With our skates still on, we walked all the way up the cement stairs and watched the rest of practice from our assigned perches. After a while, he blew the whistle again and said, "All right, guys, c'mon down now."

Back down the stairs the four of us went. He told everybody else to go to the bench and he started making us do laps, and down-and-backs. But because we'd walked all the way up and down the concrete stairs, our skates were completely dull—no edges—and we were falling down all over the ice.

Overall, though, I was lucky. Glen understood that his young players, especially ones like me with a wild streak, were going to make mistakes. He knew that a teenager isn't going to have the maturity of a thirty-year-old, and he saw it as his job to help cultivate and nurture my growth. Fundamentally, what he taught me was that making mistakes affects everything and everyone else on the team, so you have to commit to doing better. These were hard lessons, and I wasn't going to become perfect all at once, but if a player has character, you can work with them to make sure they're on the right path, and aren't stuck repeating the things they've done wrong. That's the role of a good coach and organization.

As much as I had to learn as a pro, there were certain things I'd already learned, especially from my dad, that helped show my character, and that my heart was in the right place. A big one: It's critical to respect your teammates, and by teammates I don't only mean those who wear a sweater and skates.

The coaches are your teammates. The doctors are your teammates. And the trainers are, too. A dressing room is the trainer's domain, and it's a sacred place. I knew that it was unacceptable to disrespect the trainer by not hanging up my equipment after practice, throwing tape on the floor, towels on the ground, not putting laundry in the basket. Trainers are the most undervalued, underpaid guys in the locker room, and rarely get the recognition they deserve.

When you play eighty-two games in a season, you quickly realize the training staff is a critical factor in your chances of succeeding, and the right way to treat your trainers is to understand that they're not your servants. They're not there to clean up your messes.

My dad told me that when he was playing for the Buckaroos, if a player didn't respect the trainer, Burrel Hodges, and the way he organized the dressing room, he found his equipment in a pile in the middle of the room soaked in cold water. This was in the era of two-a-day practices. Getting through that second practice was *already* a chore, but to do it in cold, wet, heavy gear—that was a good teaching tool.

What you do off the ice is all about respect, and it helps build a team. You have to recognize that you're all one entity, pulling on the same oar to get to the goal of winning.

For the Oilers that first year in the NHL, so many of us came from different places—only fourteen guys had played with Edmonton the year before—so we had to *become* a team. That takes more than practicing and playing games.

On road trips, as soon as we got to the hotel, we dropped our bags and went for a "team beer" together. There was always something else you could be doing, but getting together in this way was important. It really didn't have anything to do with the beer: It was a commitment you made, a way to strengthen the investment in the collective, even if you could stay for only half an hour. In those moments, I think we each started to feel we were part of *a whole*. We were all connected.

Maybe forty different players went through the team that year, but we had a galvanizing force in Wayne. As a new team it was so important to have that catalyst, and we all united around the hope he brought. I knew my job was to play hard, and in the right way—be a team player in every sense.

Wayne did a lot of things for us, a lot of things that got attention, but he'd be the first to tell you that he didn't do everything. No matter how good he was, we wouldn't have had the success we had without the great players that surrounded him. I think of that famous old saying, and it's true: If you want to get somewhere fast, go by yourself. If you want to go far, go together.

Glen lived that philosophy.

He also gave us focus. At our first team Christmas party, he presented each player with a beautiful shearling coat. On the inside, there was an embroidered patch:

EDMONTON OILERS
198_ STANLEY CUP CHAMPIONS

The blank was for all of us to fill in. It told us that for everything we did we had to ask the question: Will this bring us closer to the Cup? We weren't there to play hockey. We were there to win. Period. And deep down, that idea never left us. It was a seminal moment for the organization that, I believe, set us apart from a lot of other teams. It charted the course of where we were going, and instituted the culture of excellence that would take us there.

Together, we went on a hot streak at the end of the season, winning seven of our last eight games to squeak into the playoffs. If I thought that first NHL game in Chicago Stadium had been an eye-opener, I learned that in the postseason the level of play and intensity magnifies tenfold.

We met the Flyers in a best-of-three first-round series (playoffs were a bit different back then). They were coming off a remarkable year in which they had seven guys with more than 65 points. At one stage in their season they had gone more than two and a half months without losing a game.

We put up a pretty good fight—two of the three games went to overtime—but in the end, they just had more depth. They swept us. Still, it was year one, and we had made the playoffs. The seed had been planted. It would soon flower.

CHAPTER FIVE

THE RIGHT CULTURE

When a child learns to ride a bike, that very first experience can determine how the next ride will go, and the one after that. If she falls and bloodies her knees, she's probably going to have a measure of self-doubt about bike riding. For us, the series against Philadelphia to end the 1979–80 season was as if someone had taken away our training wheels. That first playoff ride might have been wobbly, but we didn't fall down.

There was a lot to process at the end of my, and the Edmonton Oilers', first NHL season. My teammates and I didn't feel good about getting swept in the playoffs by Philadelphia. We carried a lot of disappointment in the weeks after the loss. On the other hand, there was reason for pride: We'd made a late regular-season push, making the playoffs in our first year, and competed all out against the Flyers. I wasn't satisfied with the result, but I could see how the season had been a crucial learning experience for all of us. Playoff hockey in the NHL was at a whole new level—the intensity, the competition. We had gotten our first real test in battle. And the next season, we would come back stronger. We'd played good hockey, Wayne was amazing, and as a team we'd quickly become tight, fast friends. I had good conversations with my dad about the season. All around, there was a lot of excitement for what was to come.

A few days after the end of our series, a bunch of us decided to go to Hawaii: Wayne, Kevin Lowe, Glenn Anderson, Doug Hicks, and Dave Lumley. It was a last-minute, spur-of-the-moment idea. I went from an all-night celebration straight to the airport in the morning with nothing but the clothes I was wearing and a credit card in my shirt pocket.

Living out west, Hawaii was the place to go, especially that time of year, but it was my first time. It was a very relaxing vacation. We spent a couple weeks in Honolulu, setting up home base in Waikiki, cruising around the island to take in the sights, and enjoying getting to know some of the locals.

THE REST OF THE SUMMER was uneventful in my personal life, and I eagerly awaited the team coming back together for training camp. But while it was quiet for me, the summer proved to be momentous in the long term for the Edmonton Oilers. Three players would be added to the team who would all make a major impact, and come to be part of the critical core that would change hockey in Edmonton forever.

In June 1980, with our first-round draft pick, the sixth pick overall, the Oilers selected the defenseman Paul Coffey. Coffey was a promising fellow Canadian coming out of major junior hockey, having played for the Kitchener Rangers. He was six months younger than me, also nineteen. With so many veterans in the league it can take a long time for new players to really get their footing, and that's especially true for defense-men. But the buzz was that he was a superior skater as well as an imposing scorer who could put up points.

Then, in the fourth round of the draft, we selected the right-winger Jari Kurri from Helsinki, Finland. He'd had a huge year for a team called Jokerit in the Finnish professional league, his second year playing pro, and there was a sense that he could give our team additional firepower to complement Wayne's prodigious talent. He had just turned twenty years old, a few weeks before the draft. Jari didn't speak much English when he arrived, but my line mate Matti Hagman was also Finnish so at least he had a fellow countryman to help him out at first, and translate for us. We had a Finnish defenseman, too, Risto Siltanen, who helped Jari's transition to life in North America.

And finally, there was Glenn Anderson. Anderson was from Vancouver, and he was nineteen, going on twenty. Glenn had been selected by Edmonton sixty-ninth overall in the 1979 draft, the same year as me. But the 1980 Winter Olympics in Lake Placid had been coming up, and Glenn was selected for the team, so he spent the year touring the world playing with the national team in preparation for the Olympics, instead of playing with us. The United States had wound up beating the Soviet Union that year in the famous Miracle on Ice game, while Canada finished in sixth place. But the high-level inter-national experience had helped Anderson sharpen his game.

All three would end up in the Hall of Fame.

While they added a lot of talent to our team, they were green, and you just can't rush experience. Ron Chipperfield had been traded by this time, but fortunately, we still had great veterans in Blair MacDonald and Lee Fogolin, and the two shared the captaincy that year.

The team came together quickly and everyone, including our new players, was buying into our culture. That really was the catalyst for the successes that were coming. Yes, there was talent, but without the culture, which was all about playing and caring for one another, it would have been hard for us to find our way. Paul, Jari, and Glenn were selfless, high-character players and they fit in with our team. We were all marching together.

Every team changes from year to year and new players bring a different dynamic, which can be fun and exciting. New players can change the personality of a team and keep things fresh. But the culture, if it's strong, remains intact. One of the reasons you see teams lose year after year is that they keep bringing in new coaches with new ideas, philosophies, or systems. That might be needed, but it takes time for them to work. With no continuity, it's hard to create a winning culture.

In the regular season, we finished fourth in our division again, but as the playoffs approached, it felt entirely different from the year before. Even if it was new to Paul, Jari, Glenn, and some of the other players, what lay ahead was no longer unfamiliar to me or the team. We felt ready to take on the challenge of the playoffs, and find our next gear.

That was, until our first-round matchup was announced: We'd be up against the Montreal Canadiens.

Any discussion of the great franchises in sports history should typically be broken down into two lists: one of teams that had dominant runs during a select, closely grouped number of years; the other of teams that have found success again and again over the span of decades, with a winning culture that finds ways to bring championships to the organization across eras.

In hockey, the Montreal Canadiens are the undisputed leader on *both* lists. The Canadiens, nicknamed Les Habitants, or the Habs for short, are the winners of a record twenty-four Stanley Cups. The Toronto Maple Leafs are in second, with *thirteen*. Twenty-two of the Habs' Cups had already been lifted by the time we were scheduled to meet them in the first round of the 1980–81 playoffs. To put a finer point on it, they had won *four consecutive* Stanley Cups, from 1976 to 1979, before having what for them was an off year and losing in game seven to Minnesota in a close second-round series in the 1979–80 season. Only one other team had matched or beaten that streak of four consecutive Cups in NHL history, and that was, of course, an earlier Canadiens team, who won five consecutive Cups from 1956 to 1960. The Montreal Forum, where they had played since 1926, was our game's Mecca.

It was a best-of-five series with the first two games in Montreal. So here I was, in my second year in the league, headed to the Forum to play against guys that I and my other young Edmonton teammates had grown up watching and idolizing, including the eventual Hall of Famers Guy Lafleur and Larry Robinson. This was the biggest moment of my hockey life, bar none. And according to all of the analysts, it was a total mismatch. The Canadiens had always been skilled, but after losing in the playoffs the year before, they'd muscled up and built a team that could play physically as well. Their thinking was that they could match the rough-playing Philadelphia Flyers, who had gone on to win the conference championship after sweeping us in the previous season, before getting beaten in the finals by the New York Islanders.

Not everyone would have considered this an advantage, but we had started to cultivate a reputation as a team of brash youngsters, and that got into our opponents' heads in a number of ways. It was something we could hold on to, and build a little bit of an identity around to push back against the idea that we were out of our depth against the Canadiens. And the Canadiens didn't take kindly to it. They wanted to teach us a lesson. Richard Sevigny, one of the Habs' goaltenders, came out before the series and said that Guy Lafleur was going to have Gretzky "in his back pocket." In other words: Lafleur would dominate Gretzky, just as the Habs would dominate us.

Anybody who knew Wayne, who thrived in high-pressure situations, could see that was the last type of material you'd want to give him to put up on his bulletin board.

We were fired up as we took the ice for the first game, and jumped on the Habs right from the start, going up 3–1 by the end of the first period. Wayne assisted on all three goals.

As the game progressed, it got more heated and physical. There was a scrum along the boards, and a number of players looked ready to fight. Me and Larry Robinson—who was a hero of mine, an iron-tough, towering defenseman whom I'd watched take on the Broad Street Bullies as a kid and who could put up big numbers—got separated from the pack and we started to trade words. Larry had nine years on me, and at six feet four, 230 pounds, about two inches and 20 pounds as well. I remember staring at him and thinking, "Oh my God, look at the size of this man." And mind you, he was also one of three Canadiens who still chose not to wear a helmet, along with Guy Lafleur and Bob Gainey. (In the 1983–84 season, the team finally made a rule forcing these holdouts to put on headgear.) Robinson wasn't a guy who was fighting every game, but he would go when he needed to, and he could do damage. The refs pushed us apart, and we didn't come to blows just then— which suited me just fine as there was no way I wanted to.

It wasn't long, though, before he was skating up the ice with the puck from his zone, and I raced toward him, ready to put a solid check on him. But he saw me coming, let go of the puck, and twisted around to hit me high with an elbow instead. We got tangled up, and we both went down to the ice.

Next thing I knew, we were back on our feet, and I had my stick raised over my head like a club. I feinted a little swing. He goaded me on, but kept his distance. It was clear that he thought I was capable of swinging at him. Some of my team-mates quickly came over, and then the refs, and we were sep-arated and escorted back to our respective benches, where we were both given minor penalties.

I think Larry was shocked I'd threatened him like that, and in the Forum, no less. He probably thought I was absolutely crazy. That's one way to get respect, to be sure, but it's not the way I intended to get it, and I won't hesitate to say it was not one of my finer moments. I'm glad he didn't come at me the rest of the way—if he had, I really might have swung. But it also scared me that I could have. For a long time afterward I had to wrestle with this idea: How far would I go to win?

When I look back now, it seems so strange, because Larry and I became good friends. Just a year later, we videotaped a skills clinic for the CBC called "Pro Tips," giving lessons on fundamentals of the game. It played between periods of *Hockey Night in Canada*.

We won that game 6–3. Guy Lafleur didn't have a single point. Glenn Anderson and Paul Coffey had a goal each, Jari

Kurri had two goals, and Wayne had assists on *five* out of our six tallies.

After the game, he skated around the Forum, patting his back pocket.

It was a sign of more good things to come. We swept the fabled Canadiens in three straight games thanks to a stellar team performance—twelve different Edmonton players scored goals across the three games—as well as an especially impressive individual effort from Wayne, who notched two more assists in game two, and then a hat trick back in our home Northlands Coliseum in game three. We'd found a way to harness our brash attitude and showed just enough experience and maturity to win our first playoff series.

FIVE DAYS LATER, WE WENT from disposing of one legendary franchise to playing another one in the making.

The New York Islanders were the defending Stanley Cup champions, had the league's best regular-season record, and had opened their 1980–81 playoffs by matching our sweep of the Habs and taking down the Maple Leafs in three straight games. They were a remarkable machine.

General Manager Bill Torrey had been the Islanders' first hire when they came into the league in 1972. From the start, he took the long view and built the club around promising young players rather than veterans who might provide more immediate results. The first couple of years were ugly. New York won a total of just eighteen games.

But those lean years yielded bountiful drafts. Denis Potvin in 1973, Clark Gillies and Bryan Trottier the next year. With the arrival of Mike Bossy in 1977, and the skill development of the goalie Billy Smith, who had been with the team since the start, the Islanders were now skating five players who would end up in the Hall of Fame.

Under the direction of the coach, Al Arbour, who would also eventually become a Hall of Famer himself, the Islanders made it to the league semifinals in just their third year. Three years after that, they had the league's best record and had been a force ever since.

In our second-round matchup against the Islanders, it would be a seven-game series. The first two would be in Long Island's Nassau Coliseum, which was one of the tougher places in the league to play. Fans were loud, passionate, and aggressive.

As scary as this Championship-winning Islanders team was by credentials, on the ice they were even more formidable. In game one, they scored five goals before we even got on the board. They dominated us again in game two. We headed home to Edmonton down two games to none, having been outscored fourteen to five. We played better in game three and got a comfortable home win, but then we lost game four in overtime.

Even though we were down three games to one, we felt we were still very much in this series. We had played well in the last two games. We were confident and went to Long Island ready to play game five.

The game got off to a rollicking start, with both teams scoring two goals in the first period, including Glenn Anderson netting his fourth goal of the playoffs with barely a minute left.

The second period was a back-and-forth stalemate, until, with barely a minute left again, Brett Callighen stepped up for us and scored his fourth goal of the playoffs.

Brett was a left-winger from Toronto, closing in on his twenty-eighth birthday, who had done a lot over the previous twelve months to teach everyone on our team about what toughness and resilience really mean. In 1979, he'd been having a great season, notching 23 goals and 35 assists for a total of 58 points, when in February 1980, in a game against the Boston Bruins, a Bruins player's stick clipped Brett in the left eye. He missed the rest of the season and underwent multiple surgeries. They couldn't repair the injury: He was declared legally blind in that left eye. Somehow, he fought his way back onto the ice, and in fifty-five games with us in the 1980–81 season—four fewer than he'd played the year before after his season got cut short by his injury—he scored 25 goals and made 35 assists, for a total of 60 points. It would be his career high.

Watching your teammate overcome this kind of hurdle is galvanizing. It takes so much passion for the game to work through an injury like that and come back. The team looked at his work ethic and commitment and was inspired to play harder, be mentally tougher. His presence and love of the sport showed us we were all playing for a higher purpose, not just for ourselves. When teams win championships, these are the stories that get told.

In the third period, five minutes ticked by, then ten, and no one else scored. Brett's goal was still carrying us, up by one. But the game was tight.

As I sat on the bench waiting for a shift, we started a cheer.

"Here we go, Oilers, here we go! Here we go, Oilers, here we go!"

One by one, everyone on our bench joined in. It was totally in line with who we were: a young, fun-loving team, exuberant and wrapped up in the moment. But more than that, it was a moment of team solidarity. It hadn't been intended to be a direct taunt to the Islanders players: It was just a way for our guys to vent some anxiety.

Nassau Coliseum was a tough place to play, almost like the Roman Colosseum, a madhouse packed with passionate fans. On top of that, with the springtime New York humidity, the air was literally thick and heavy. Honestly, it felt like we were alone in there, a bunch of guys on a twenty-foot bench looking for a flotation device in a heaving sea of fourteen thousand screaming fans rooting against us. For us, the chant was about survival and trying to accentuate the positive.

It was not well received by the Islanders' faithful. It was perceived as a "how dare they" gesture of arrogance and cockiness, or was at least used that way. Part of the psychological warfare in sports is to capitalize on moments like these to rally your team and find a reason to hold a grudge. Whether they actually cared about our chant or not, the Islanders were going to use it as fuel.

We won that game five, but the Islanders finished us off in game six back in Edmonton to close out the series. In the process, they taught us something important that we would have to take to heart if we wanted to be champions. We had talent, and we had many offensive weapons on our team, but their game was more evolved than ours at this point. Their team moved and functioned as a whole. They rarely gave up odd-man chances or high-percentage shots because they played so well together. It felt like there were ten of them out there. Everybody did their job. They played for one another, as one. As much as we wanted it to be, our team game wasn't at that level yet.

The Islanders would go on after beating us to win the Cup

again. In four playoff rounds, they lost just three games, and two of them were to us. We felt that, with a few bounces of the puck one way or another, who knows, maybe we could have beaten them.

Still, the playoff run we had was another critical juncture for us in terms of growth. For Wayne and myself, it was just our second year in the league. For Jari, Paul, and Glenn, it was their first. We had swept the most iconic franchise in the sport, and then taken the defending Stanley Cup champions to six games. It was a massive boost to our confidence, and furthered us along in the process of getting comfortable in the insane environment of road playoff games.

Most important of all, we were molding our identity as a team.

CHAPTER SIX

PLAYING AS ONE

After ten months of totally committed mental and physical grinding, and a grueling battle against the Islanders, I wanted to get away from it all for a little while.

Our family vacations in Oregon as a kid had taught me and Paul to understand the importance of resetting after a hard effort, and finding balance in life. Those trips had also instilled a sense of wonder in us: We saw that the world was vast and worth exploring.

With the memory of the previous year's trip to Hawaii fresh in my mind, Paul, Paul's college roommate Vince Magnan, a junior hockey buddy of mine named Darrell Morrow, and I set out on the first of what would become a tradition of postseason trips. We all had a sense of adventure, and some years, we would literally spin the globe. Wherever our finger landed, we would go.

The summer of 1981, my finger landed on the Caribbean island nation of Barbados. The fact that it was summer—Barbados's low season for tourism—made it an especially lucky spin.

The four of us arrived on the island with nothing on our agenda but exploring and enjoying. We stayed at a place called Boomer's Guest House, which is no longer around. Modest would be an overstatement. It was four cots in one room with no air-conditioning. But it was a great spot, a short distance from the beach toward town. And Boomer, the proprietor, was a big, welcoming, gregarious guy.

We rented bikes and hit the beach. At night we drank beer with the other guests back at a common bar and dining area at the guesthouse. A bunch of other people, traveling from all over, were staying there, too, and we all made friends.

One day, one of the other guests at Boomer's said: "C'mon with us, we're gonna go make some tea." I asked what he meant: "Why do you have to make tea? Can't you buy it?"

He told me this tea was special. It was *magic* tea, he said. They were going to go to a farmer's field to pick some mushrooms to make it.

I'd never heard of making them into tea before, but I understood what the words *magic* and *mushrooms* meant in this context. I knew people ate them and had mind-altering experiences.

Why not, Paul, Darrell, Vince, and I decided. I was eager for new experiences, enticed by the excitement of the other guests, and up for an adventure.

We went out to a field—Boomer, too: He had organized the whole thing, it turned out—and started picking mushrooms that were growing in the cow dung. I took my shirt off and tied it at one end so that it would hold what I was harvesting. It wasn't long before it was completely filled up with these skinny little brown mushrooms.

We came back to the guesthouse and dumped the mushrooms into a vat with a couple of quarts of boiling water and started mashing them down as they cooked until it became a super-dark liquid.

When it was ready, we took the brew and strained it, so we were left with only the liquid. We poured it into teacups, about halfway up, and drank.

Paul, Vince, Darrell, and I sat around with everyone at the guesthouse bar, waiting to see what would happen. The bar was on the honor system—you were free to eat and drink whatever you liked as long as you wrote it down. Almost right away, I started feeling loose. We were all laughing and having a good time.

And then, suddenly, the lid came off.

Seemingly all at once, my sensations became amplified and intense. The music was piercing. The light was bright. My head was spinning. It all became too much and we went back to our little room and tried to sleep it off, but there was a problem.

The geckos.

We had gotten used to these little lizard critters, which were plentiful on the island and were frequent guests in our room. The thing was, I wasn't seeing them as lizards anymore. I was seeing dragons, with horns and fangs.

It was like *Jurassic Park* projected on the walls. They were coming at me from everywhere, with their tongues darting out. I swatted at them, but it made no difference. I was terrified, and yet—it was also awesome.

At this point I knew I had ingested way too much of the tea—a few sips would have been plenty—and desperately wanted to sober up. I took a shower and tried to shrug it off. When that didn't work, the guys and I went outside and paced.

It was not a pleasant walk. Like weathering a storm at sea, there was nothing to do but square up and take it.

Finally, the fear and discomfort started to lessen. I began to feel better. Soon enough, I felt not only happy, but elated. What followed was an experience unlike any other I've had. For the rest of the night and well into the following morning, Paul, Vince, Darrell, and I were bonded together and riding the wave the mushrooms were taking our minds and emotions on. We laughed a lot. We cried, too—it was a wide range of feelings. I remember at one point we were playing Frisbee in a big open field and as the disk was coming at me, I truly believed it was an alien flying saucer.

When the mushrooms wore off, and after we got some sleep, we had a chance to decompress and look back. There was a profound sense of *what the hell just happened?*—and one comical, physical piece of evidence was part of that. At the bar where we jotted down our food and drink orders, we looked back at how our handwriting changed over the experience, going from clearly legible at the start, to barely readable by the end. But the journey we took went much deeper than that, and left me with the question: *How is what happened even possible?*

The only answer I could find was that our minds are capable of so much more than we understand.

And that realization changed me.

It's now well recognized, and becoming more so every day, that psilocybin mushrooms have medical benefits, even if the exact mechanisms are still to be discovered. Researchers at Johns Hopkins University and other top medical facilities have found it to be an effective treatment for psychiatric distress, depression, anxiety, nicotine addiction, and substance-abuse disorders. Cities in the United States such as Denver and Oakland and Washington, D.C., have begun taking steps to decriminalize psilocybin mushrooms. That being said, I'm not an expert, and it's a good idea to talk to a medical professional if you want to know more.

But what taking them did for me, at the age of nineteen, was profound. I was electrified with an appreciation for how vast the mind is, that there is so much we don't know. And that of course it wasn't just my mind, but *everyone else's* mind that was vast, too.

The result was a deep and lasting appreciation for the diversity of human beings. People cannot only act in different ways, it struck me, but they can *think* in different ways than I'd ever imagined. From there, I realized that intolerance is often due to a person not being able to recognize and respect this fact. Just because I wasn't familiar with someone else's perspective didn't make them wrong. Never again would I believe that someone was fundamentally mistaken because their mind worked in a way I was unfamiliar with. I saw that they could just be exploring different parts of this same huge landscape of possibility.

The mind is a powerful thing, and it can either help or hurt you. Talent can take you far, but ultimately what separates you is how mentally strong you are. I started to wonder how I could train my mind to make my body do something extraordinary. At the time in the NHL, 99 percent of the training was physical. Over my career I became increasingly interested in sports psychology and breathing techniques. I wanted to marry the physical with the mental, not just to improve my game, but also my life. I learned that the mind is a muscle, and you have to train it—like you do all the other muscles—in pursuit of excellence.

From that point forward, I was willing to be more open to where other people were coming from. It was the start of the development of an important part of who I would eventually become: a more curious person. That in turn helped me become a better athlete, and a better leader.

I was blindsided by the experience, but grateful, and still am to this day.

AFTER BARBADOS, I COULDN'T WAIT to get back to hockey. When training camp rolled around in 1981, I was twenty years old, but entering my third calendar year in the NHL already, and my fourth year as a pro. I'd had a pretty good season in 1980–81, scoring 23 goals and adding 40 assists. I was settling into the lifestyle of being a professional hockey player. The basics of it—the way of life, the travel, the time-management skills, the game preparation, the efficiency of practice—were all coming together.

With my increasing confidence, I was able to put attention into improving some of the finer details of my game, including the equipment I was using.

I spent a lot of time trying to figure out what kind of stick worked best, what kind of lie, what kind of curve. Paul Coffey and I also got deeply interested in improving the dynamics of our skates.

Nowadays, the boots of hockey skates are all molded and made of synthetic materials, but in 1981, they were made of soft leather that didn't hold up terribly well. Paul and I, like many other players at the time, were getting stronger and more powerful thanks to the intensity of our workouts, and the leather boots were no longer sturdy enough to contain the force we were putting into them. It was like trying to get going in a sprint off a starting block that wasn't nailed down.

So Coffey and I reinforced the boots of our skates up by the ankle with thick thread on a heavy-duty commercial stitching machine. Barrie Stafford and the Oilers trainers located a place that could do it. When we took a stride, the boot held firm and we got more power and response. We were among the first in the league to do this.

Blair MacDonald had left the team at the trade deadline the previous season, and Lee Fogolin took over as sole captain. As we went through training camp and started the season, we bought into an all-for-one, team-first mentality. It paid off. We took off on a hot streak and never looked back. We won nineteen more games than we had the year before and ended up with 37 more points. Our team scored 417 goals. No franchise had ever previously broken 400. Everybody knew their role and everybody was happy. There were no cliques. We were one.

The irony of figuring out how to play together as a team was that, in doing so, many of us racked up huge individual numbers. It was a breakout year collectively, and personally. I was on a line with Glenn Anderson and Matti Hagman that year. With their help, I found a way to use my speed on the wing, and get more comfortable with my particular skill set. Instead of being way up ahead of the play, standing still and being an easy check, as I'd been guilty of doing in the past, we worked up a strategy where Matti would jet ahead and use his stickhandling skill to buy some time. Then I'd come roaring up the wing and freeze the defenseman in the middle. Then Matti would hit me with the pass. I got a lot more chances that way. I had 50 goals and 38 assists in the 1981–82 regular season for a total of 88 points. I'd have more points in later seasons, but it was the only time I'd score 50 goals.

I was super raw when I turned pro, but by this time, I'd developed physically into a bigger and stronger forward. I was also getting to know the league better, figuring out how to play against different goalies, and where to position myself to be a more offensive player. And my skills were sharpening. Every day at practice was a learning experience as I'd watch the incredible talent on display from my teammates. You can't hurry experience but by my third full year I was feeling more confident. And playing with a centerman who could really distribute the puck didn't hurt.

I was chosen for my first all-star team. That was a huge deal for me. But more important, everyone on the team was excited by what was happening. Sather was pleased by the culture we'd embraced, and successes were everywhere, both individually and as a team.

I certainly wasn't the only one putting up good numbers. Glenn Anderson had 105 points—which would be his career high—Paul Coffey had 89, and Jari Kurri had 86. These were great stats for all of us, even if we didn't make too much of them or play them up in interviews and in our own team meetings. While I could say that this was completely because of our emphasis on team over individual performance, it's also true that it was kind of tough to beat our chests about scoring when we were playing with Wayne. He just kept on going where no one had even considered a player could possibly go. Wayne became the fastest ever to 50 goals that season, hitting the number in only 39 games. By the end of the season, he'd scored 92 goals, which beat the previous scoring record by a preposterous 16 goals. In total, he racked up 212 regular-season points—shattering his own record of 164 points from the season before.

We were on a roll, becoming a collective force of high-performing individuals. Each of the previous two years in the playoffs, we had taken a step forward in our development. So as this regular season came to a close, we all had big expectations for what we could accomplish.

The postseason started with a best-of-five series against the Los Angeles Kings. We were the clear favorites, and had home-ice advantage. The Kings had qualified for the playoffs with the fewest points of any team, 48 points behind us in the Smythe Division.

The series opener in Edmonton was like a video-game version of hockey: a bunch of flashy goals and not a lot of defense. We lost 10–8. But we didn't panic. The next night, things normalized, and we won 3–2.

Going into game three in Los Angeles at the Forum on Manchester Boulevard two days later, we were pretty loose. In the pregame, some of our guys thought it would be comical to cut the wire of the public address microphone, which happened to run in front of our bench. Sure enough, a few minutes later, out came the actress Gloria Loring, in high heels, waving to the crowd. She took her place in front of us to sing the anthems. She raised the mic to her lips, started to sing, and then stopped. No one could hear her. As she tapped the mic with her finger in the familiar "testing" exercise, everyone on our bench tried to hide their grins and stifle outright laughter.

The stunt kind of backfired, though, because as she was struggling, one of the Kings' defensemen, Jay Wells, skated out onto the ice and literally swept Loring off her feet and carried her over to the other side of the rink. There, the PA announcer,

Dave Courtney, handed her the penalty box microphone, and she sang to a now adoring crowd.

The game got underway. I scored the first goal about halfway through the opening period, and over the next twenty-four minutes, Wayne scored two goals, and assisted on two more, scored by our captain, Lee Fogolin, and Risto Siltanen. We were up 5–0 when the Kings' owner, Jerry Buss, got up to leave. The crowd in the Forum started booing. For some reason, we thought it would be a good idea to join in. Whatever maturity we had gained over the previous year seemed in short supply in that moment. Clearly, we hadn't yet learned our lesson. Don't poke the bear.

In the third period, the Kings roared to life and scored five unanswered goals. The last one, to tie the game, came with just five seconds left and with two of our men serving penalties. The young Canadian Steve Bozek backhanded a loose puck in front of our net.

Two and a half minutes into overtime, another young Canadian on the Kings, Daryl Evans, scored. What came to be known as the "Miracle on Manchester" was complete. It was the biggest comeback in NHL history.

We got too loose. We started making mistakes and taking bad penalties. I remember Garry Unger took a five-minute major for retaliation, but he wasn't alone. We lost our focus. The Kings started to believe again and we ended up on the wrong side of the momentum. The crowd got into it, and the next thing we knew, a house of karma collapsed on us in one twenty-minute period. The booing from our bench wasn't the right thing to do, and it made the aftermath a little more uncomfortable. Wayne would later say: "We thought we were God's gift to hockey." But we didn't leave there thinking we'd lost because we were disrespectful. We lost because we didn't execute.

Energy is so important to a team, whether it comes from confidence or a sea of fans. And anything is possible in hockey. After this game, we learned to never take a lead for granted, not until the final whistle blows.

I won't say the night got worse, but it didn't get any better. A few hours after this historically embarrassing calamity, we had to *share* a plane with the Kings for the flight back to Edmonton.

We had chartered a flight down from Edmonton—which was a rare treat in those days—on a big old prop plane. But there was a problem getting the same aircraft for the return trip. The good news was we ended up with a much larger plane, a jet. The bad news was it was considerably more expensive, so we needed to fill as many seats as we could to spread out the cost.

The Kings insisted they sit in the front of the plane. They were concerned that if they didn't disembark first, hockey-loving Canadian authorities might not be in a great hurry to process their paperwork, and the team would potentially be delayed at customs. That meant we had to sit in the back of our own plane, with thirty or so media members occupying the seats in the middle as a sort of demilitarized zone. We kept separate and weren't looking to start a fight or anything like that, but it was a very uncomfortable three-hour flight.

We won the next day to even the series, but lost game five the next night in Edmonton, and with it, the series. It was a massive disappointment. And that game three was, to this day, the most shocking loss I've ever been a part of.

We were certain we had figured things out. We were

convinced our playoff trajectory would be one-directional. We thought we were destined for success.

We still had a lot to learn. Thankfully, we proved to be very good students.

OVER THE OFF-SEASON MONTHS, WE regrouped, took stock, and earnestly set about learning the two most critical lessons.

Lesson one, the most obvious one: Never disrespect an opponent.

Doing so calls their character into question, which only increases their motivation. It doesn't matter if you're playing the lowest-seeded playoff team: These are pros, they fought their way to that spot, and there's a reason they got there. They rose to the occasion.

Lesson two, the most important one: We didn't execute. We underperformed. Period.

Just before training camp, the Oilers' management got involved in a sort of three-team trade that resulted in Risto Siltanen going to the Hartford Whalers, and Philadelphia's Ken Linseman joining us. The season before, Linseman had been among the league's most productive centers, tallying 92 points in 1981–82 for the Flyers. As the 1982–83 season got underway, this kind of depth was a massive weapon.

As our team was maturing, however, *culture* was a big buzzword and something we paid serious attention to, and folding Linseman into the culture of our team proved to be a mutual lesson on leadership.

Aside from being a dangerous scoring threat, he was known for being a real agitator on the ice who could put other teams off their game. But off the ice, he was perceived as something of a loner. The truth is, he was anything but. He just had an eccentric personality, and as teammates, we respected and embraced that: It was part of our culture to do so.

As a team, it was easier for us to bring in new guys. Most of us were single and had no family commitments, so we could spend time with him away from the rink and get to know him.

One time we were all out in a bar and I looked over across the room, and there was Linseman sitting on top of one of the speakers by himself, smoking a pipe. He was only three years older than me. You just didn't know anybody like this guy. He listened to Roxy Music and read Ayn Rand. He was a surfer. He'd bought an Andrew Wyeth watercolor when he was twenty-one, and went to check out art collections and museums when we were on the road. He set up his own pension plan and corporation ("Mother Hazel and Company"), named after his mom. He was certainly the only player on the team who had a briefcase—he was into real estate and was always carrying around all sorts of documents about properties he was interested in or involved with.

When he came to Edmonton, I think he understood right away that whoever he was, that was okay. Our dressing room was one that prided itself on diversity—letting people be themselves was a big part of the dynamic we were building. We wanted a room that was rich with culture, music, and ideas. Kenny was certainly helping to bring that. So was a defenseman that we picked up during the first month of the season named Randy Gregg, who was not only an actual medical doctor, but after playing four years of college hockey at the University of Alberta became the captain of Canada's 1980 Olympics team in Lake Placid. Then he played two seasons in the somewhat obscure Japan Ice Hockey League for a team called Kokudo Keikado Tokyo, before getting picked up by Edmonton. He was super talented and athletic, and was also married and the father of a couple of young children. Like Kenny Linseman, he was one of a kind.

And yet, in Kenny's case, while we celebrated his eccentricity, we also needed him to be willing to adapt to certain ways we did things in Edmonton. Just as we'd make room for who he was, we needed him to make room for us, and the philosophy that we had as a team. The fans were like a part of our team. At first, when Kenny went out, I don't think he felt that it was part of his responsibility to interact. But it was important for us to have a real, two-way relationship with the fans. As a team, we understood that if we didn't feel like engaging with them, maybe it was better to not go out at all.

To his credit, Kenny came to understand the importance of the team's relationship with the fans. He may not have ever embraced it wholeheartedly, but he got the message, and he started to come out with us more, and became more approachable and open. He would take the time to have a drink with fans and "bring them into the circle."

He became not just a great teammate, but ultimately a great Oiler. That season, he had one of his best years ever— 75 points in 72 games—and the highest shooting percentage, by a wide margin, in his career.

There's an easy lesson here: You want to make somebody productive? Make them feel comfortable first.

WE ARRIVED IN LOS ANGELES on January 16, 1983, on a mid-season hot streak. We had won three in a row and eight out of our last nine games. In two days, we would be playing the Kings for the fifth time already that season, so there wasn't much remaining tension anymore from the year before. We were all looking for something fun to do with our little bit of down time.

I got a call from my dad's brother Larry, who lived there. He had always been a real character, a mover and shaker who seemed to know everybody. Once, on a trip to L.A., he had arranged for me and my teammates to go and visit the set of the TV show *M*A*S*H*, which at the time was the number one show on the air.

But in 1983, he had the best connection of all, because he was working for one of my heroes: Muhammad Ali. Larry was one part promoter, one part souvenir sales supervisor, and 100 percent a part of the champ's entourage. He always seemed to be in the middle of everything with Ali.

"It's Muhammad's forty-first birthday," Uncle Larry told me. "Do you and the guys want to come out and visit with the champ?"

I said yes right away. I couldn't believe that I was going to get a chance to meet The Greatest. This was the guy I'd idolized as a kid, staying up late with the transistor radio on beneath the covers of my bed, listening to his fight.

Ali's house was a historic mansion in a famous gated community called Fremont Place in Hancock Park. We took our charter bus there—probably a rare and strange sight to see, in that neighborhood—and parked on the street at the bottom of Ali's long, gated driveway. Twenty-five of us hockey players piled off the bus and were greeted by Ali and his wife on the front steps of their home.

I knew I was meeting someone bigger than life, and he

was. He spoke quietly and carried himself so elegantly. He was beautiful, strong, and perfectly proportioned. He seemed to glide when he moved—still a godlike figure for me even as an adult.

He was a tremendous host, and provided the entertainment, too. Ali was really into magic tricks, which surprised us. He did a little performance, and he was really good—he could even make it look like he was levitating. Then there was a cake and he blew out the candles.

He was more than a year removed from his last fight, a loss to Trevor Berbick, and there was no boxing talk, but all of a sudden, he got very animated and said: "All right, who's the tough guy here?"

He then started to playfully spar with Dave Semenko, a big left-winger who played on Wayne's line and was known as his bodyguard because of his inclination to get physical with anyone who threatened our star. (Six months later, at Northlands Coliseum, Ali and Semenko had a proper exhibition fight for charity. Six thousand people were in the stands. It was called a draw and ended up being one of Ali's last fights.) It was all good-natured and a lot of fun with Ali and Dave. We were in disbelief just being in his presence and watching him joke around with the guys. There was no talk of what it takes to win or championships—just a special shared experience together. The Ali visit was a team-building exercise before such things really existed. Everyone could join in and contribute to the conversation because we were all there as equals. That's how team exercises work. On the bus ride leaving afterward, we were in awe from the experience.

We ended up with the best record in our division and conference again, but this time, as we approached the postseason, we were a very different team than a year before: focused, well-rounded, with depth and more maturity.

It showed. We rampaged through the playoffs, sweeping Winnipeg in the first round, then taking down Calgary four games to one, and then sweeping Chicago in the semifinals. We outscored our opponents by forty-three goals, and came into our first trip to the Stanley Cup finals with a 1983 playoff record of 11–1. We were on the doorstep of the holy land.

Waiting for us there was just who we should have expected: the New York Islanders.

You might say that there are four seasons in the NHL: the exhibition or preseason, the regular season, the playoffs, and then the Stanley Cup finals. We'd seen how the intensity, the anxiety, the level of play, and competitiveness ratcheted up for each one, but this last season, the Cup finals, was brand-new to us. It wasn't new to the Islanders. They had figured out how to consistently navigate all four in a way few before them ever had. They were coming off their third Stanley Cup in a row. They were only the fifth team ever to do that, dating all the way back to 1927. Winning it all is hard. Repeating is harder. Mentally, it's a grind   eighty-two games just to get back to the playoffs. And, throughout that season, there are no easy games because every team uses the defending champs as a benchmark for where they are: The champions are coming to town.

It hadn't been the Islanders' best regular season in 1982–83—they finished tied for the league's sixth-best record—but they'd been here before, they knew how it was done, and we had no choice but to respect them.

Still, respect wasn't the same as liking, and we'd seen enough of them to not like them. It was clear they felt the same way about us.

During the season, they'd beaten us in all three of our games, but they were close. Our first finals game was at home, and everything about it was electric. My whole life had pointed to this moment. My dad had been a professional hockey player before me, and now the highest level of competition had finally come to my hometown and I was in the middle of it.

I remember standing on the blue line for the anthem and being beyond excited. Here I was living a dream: I was in the starting lineup for the Stanley Cup finals. When I got out on the ice, I lasted something like fifteen seconds before my vision got blurry and I started seeing spots. I had never experienced anything like that before. Have you ever been so amped up that you couldn't see straight? I had to go back into the dressing room for a moment to try to get a hold of myself.

I had a little water and regrouped, but it wasn't the last of my problems that night, or the team's. The Islanders took our biggest strength away—our speed through the neutral zone— and exposed weaknesses that we thought we'd put behind us. They shut Wayne out. The more we pushed to get on offense, the more we revealed our defensive shortcomings. We were impatient, and instead of waiting for opportunities, we tried to force our hand and as a result gave up far too many odd-man rushes. The Islanders were the perfect counterpunchers. They had the talent, brains, system, and experience to take advantage of our mistakes. It was a 2–0 loss, but in short, they just dismantled us.

This was a wake-up call for all of us: We had to tighten up defensively, paying more attention to our play without the puck. We'd have to start winning games 2–1 or 3–2, and not rely so much on our ability to score goals. We had to pay even more attention to the fundamentals than we'd been doing.

We were still overreliant on our skill and our high-energy, high-scoring, run-and-gun-style offense. That had served us well in the regular season, but in the playoffs, every minute and every goal is a grind. Nothing comes easily. Also, when you're playing the same team night after night, they can break down your style and dissect your system and tendencies in a way that regular-season opponents don't get a chance to do. Like the Islanders had, we still needed to learn a type of game that was more about structure, discipline, and focus. It was a resilient style that could withstand the inevitable moments when the tide turned against a team. We needed to be more well-rounded, play a more complete game, and minimize mistakes. But it wasn't something we could correct overnight.

The pattern continued. Game two, we lost again, at home, 6–3. Game three was even worse—a 5–1 destruction in Nassau Coliseum. And then the nail in the coffin, a 4–2 loss in Long Island. They beat us in straight games to win a fourth consecutive Cup. I could put all the blame on our own self-inflicted wounds. It was unquestionably true that we needed to play much harder. We needed to start blocking shots. We needed to push ourselves to do all the little things right. But that wouldn't be the full story, or the true one, because the Islanders were a team at the peak of their maturity and brilliance, who pounced on every opportunity, and played like the champions they were.

When we left Nassau Coliseum after getting swept, we walked past their dressing room expecting to see a big celebration. Instead, we just saw a bunch of guys with ice bags strapped all over their bodies, drinking beer like they were sitting around a campfire.

I think four Cups in four years took its toll. They were

beaten up, but the lesson was clear—there's a huge price to be paid in order to win. I don't think we left that series having paid the same price they did. Until that moment, I'm not even sure we knew what it meant to pay that kind of price. We tried to understand what they'd shown us. They were like a tank. They kept moving forward, no matter what was in front of them. We had to be that way, too. As far along and advanced as we thought we were going into that series, we realized after it, walking past them wearing their ice packs, what the difference was between being champions and being the runner-ups.

CHAPTER SEVEN

THE WINNING PLAN

With the summer upon us, it was time for Paul, myself, and our traveling crew to spin the globe and find a new destination. Without these restorative getaways—weeks on end with no schedule—I would never have been able to play twenty-six years in the league.

In the summer of 1983 we took a four-week trip to Thailand. When we arrived, we rented motorcycles with no plan and hit the road. In one town we made friends with locals who invited us to eat with them in their living rooms. Sometimes the people we met didn't speak a word of English, but you find ways to communicate. It was a month of complete freedom, the opposite of hockey, no structure.

One afternoon we stopped at a roadside bar, and these guys came in wearing military gear. They'd all jumped off the back of a truck and had big machine guns. They piled into the bar and started pounding drinks, all the while looking over at us. But we just kept to ourselves. We were peaceful travelers. "Peaceful warriors," we used to call ourselves.

The next thing we knew, these characters all ran out the

door and jumped on *our* motorcycles and took off. There wasn't much we could do about it. We figured we'd just tell the rental company that the bikes had been stolen—which was true. We had a few more drinks and then followed what seemed to be a rolling party down to the next bar, and then to a few more after that. Hours later, we found our bikes outside another bar. Our gun-toting friends had apparently abandoned them. We picked them up and just went along our way as if nothing had happened.

It was all part of the grand adventure.

I always like to think that, as I'd once heard someone say, life is a great big treasure hunt, and the grand prize is ourselves. These adventures always gave me a better understanding of myself.

WE COULDN'T WAIT TO GET back together for training camp in the late summer of 1983. We were still kids, and impatient to get the season underway, make use of the lessons we'd learned, and finally bring home the Cup.

On the morning of October 4, one day before the start of our season, we found out that our captain, Lee Fogolin, had come up with a plan to help us get there.

We had just wrapped up our last preseason practice and were messing around in the locker room as usual when Lee stood up and asked all the members of the media present to leave the room.

Lee was from a hockey family. His father, Lee Fogolin Sr., had played in the NHL and won the Stanley Cup with the Detroit Red Wings in 1950, then finished out the rest of his career with the Chicago Black Hawks. Lee had been drafted in the first round by the Buffalo Sabres in 1974, then came over to Edmonton in the 1979 expansion draft, so he'd been on the Oilers from the start with me and Wayne; a mature twenty-four-year-old in our eyes, when we were nineteen. He was a defenseman, not a big scorer, and he was quiet and reserved, but he made a point of sticking up for young teammates, which meant the world to us. For the 1980–81 season, he and Blair MacDonald were co-captains, and in the 1981–82 season, Lee had become the sole captain. He had served admirably in the role for these two pivotal seasons of our team's growth.

But when the media left the locker room on that October morning in 1983, Lee announced that he was giving his captaincy up, and granting it to Wayne Gretzky. He did it with selflessness and grace. We didn't know this was about to happen, but the truth was, it was Wayne's team already. He had been named the league's MVP in every one of his first four seasons. Though he was still only twenty-two years old, he went about his business with a focus and a seriousness that belied his age. Players both older and younger than him looked up to Wayne, recognized his greatness, and took what he said to heart. So Lee, at twenty-eight years old, realized the best thing for our team was to codify the reality that already existed, and voluntarily give his captaincy to Wayne.

He came out of the dressing room after he had talked to the team and made the announcement to the media.

"Maybe a change like this will help us win the Stanley Cup," he said.

It was the perfect example of how effective leadership is absent of ego, with only one thought in mind: the collective. Lee embodied the selfless nature that's required all the way down the roster. A person can have great pride, but no ego. It only made us look up to Lee even more than we did already.

With Wayne ensconced as captain—the official "C" serving as proof of the way he was already looked at by the team—we won our first seven games of the season.

What a leader does is get the best out of the people he or she leads. And Wayne's way of doing that was to lead by example. He was driven to win. His passion for the game was off the charts. His mental preparation and commitment were beyond imagination. My teammates and I saw that. It made us want to play harder, and follow in the example he set.

This had been true for me, personally, for years already. Early in our careers, I went to Wayne's apartment one day to pick him up for practice. I was waiting for him in his kitchen and I noticed he had our game schedule tacked up on his refrigerator door. No big deal, I thought—I had one on my fridge, too.

But then I took a closer look. In the box for each date on the calendar, I saw that Wayne had marked down what he wanted to accomplish, scoring-wise, for the corresponding game: November 15 vs. Calgary—2 goals/2 assists; November 17 vs. Boston—3 goals/2 assists; November 19 vs. Philadelphia—3 goals/3 assists.

He was thinking about the games, and I was maybe too often thinking about where we were going to go *after* the games. The moment was like a cold slap in the face for me. The amount of attention he was paying to his craft was way above what I was doing, *and I was already an all-star*!

It made me think: *How am I going to maximize my potential?* Watching Wayne go about his business—how he prepared, how he handled the media, how he handled the pressure, and how he worked on days we didn't have a game—gave me the answers.

There was absolutely nothing casual about the way he approached even the simplest, most mundane tasks—he always conducted them with intention and purpose. For instance, when we would do two-on-one drills, it was important for him that the play end in a goal, whether he scored it or not. He was focused on making sure that he and all the players around him put in the effort to get the most out of each repetition, each go-around, of each and every drill. But that doesn't have to come at the expense of a smile. He had a way of keeping things light and fun without losing that deadly focus.

On the ice, Wayne was always one step ahead of the play. When it came to thinking about people, he was the same way. If there ever was someone who could get away with "big-timing" people—being conceited—you'd think it would be someone whose nickname was The Great One. And yet Wayne was, and continues to be, kind to the people around him in a way that isn't only sincere—it's contagious. He just had this way of being able to get outside of himself and have compassion for others. This was not only a great characteristic in life, but the type of thing that made people look up to him. I don't think Wayne would consider himself an overly spiritual person, but considering the way he treated people, I'd say the karma around him was very good.

Early in his career, he was dating a woman named Vikki Moss, and became close to her whole family, including Vikki's younger brother Joey, who had Down syndrome, and was working earnestly in a bottle depot. Joey was a guy who was living with the type of circumstance that society sometimes might not treat kindly. But Wayne made Joey a priority, and wanted to help give him purpose by inviting him to be a part of something everybody loved. He went to Glen Sather and asked if maybe the Oilers could give the kid a job to help him feel good about himself and be part of something?

For nearly four decades, Joey worked for the team as an assistant locker room attendant. One of our trainers, Lyle Kulchisky, who we all called Sparky, really took him under his wing. Joey was a fan favorite who sat behind the bench at every game. It wasn't unusual for visiting players and coaches to stop by the Oilers' dressing room to find him and say hello. Sadly, Joey passed away in 2020. The compassion and love that Joey displayed was the embodiment of the culture we had, and was a big part of what made Edmonton special. He had a way of reminding you what was really important; he kept you grounded. He made such an impact on the players and the team for many years.

Wayne also helped to start a foundation called Joey's Home, which continues to raise money to support independent living for adults with developmental disabilities.

Committed, compassionate, and focused. Setting an example, and inspiring people to follow it. That was Wayne's leadership style.

Glen Sather modeled another.

Since the end of our first season in 1979, Sather had straddled both the coaching and general manager roles, giving him a lot of power. And he could be cold when he had to: He traded our first captain, Ron Chipperfield, to the Nordiques as Ron's mother lay dying in a hospital bed. She passed away the day he got to Quebec. That's the business side of hockey: It can keep GMs removed from the players.

However, he was relatable, too. He had played ten full seasons in the NHL—739 regular season games and another 77 playoff games—so he knew as well as anyone what it was like to be on our side of the bench. And he was still young. At the start of the 1979–80 season he was just thirty-six years old. Dave Dryden, one of our goalies then, was thirty-eight! Two of our other players that year, Bill "Cowboy" Flett and Poul Popiel, were the same age as Glen. He'd played against some of these guys himself. He even had a mischievous streak that made it easier for the younger guys like me to think of him as one of our own. I remember he would put shaving cream in the towels, then refold them so we wouldn't notice. Nothing like a face full of foam after a shower to get a laugh.

He did unusual things with us as a team. On the road, he would take us to art museums. In New York, we'd go to Broadway plays. He said he wanted us to broaden our horizons. I believed him, but part of me also thinks he just wanted to keep us out of the bars and clubs.

Our second year in training camp, he had this guy come in and give a three-day course, six hours a day, on the power of positive thinking. I was just barely out of the classroom myself, and the idea of spending eighteen hours over three days in a hotel ballroom was not something to look forward to. A bunch of us were taking the ink cartridges out of the pens and shooting spitballs across the room at one another, but despite myself, in the end, I got a lot out of it.

One of the big takeaways from the seminar was the importance of setting goals, both short- and long-term. It was critical to set a long-term goal, like winning the Stanley Cup, but it was also valuable to have short-term goals, something to make you feel like you're progressing. These successes add up to bigger victories.

Another crucial lesson that day was the importance of good "self-talk." People often talk to themselves in a negative way: "I'm so bad, I should quit, I can't do this!" Actually, they know they can do it, but for whatever reason, now and again, they don't accomplish that goal, and they *listen* to their own negative self-talk. It's so destructive.

I learned that when things were not going my way, I had to put on the mental brakes and say: "Wait a minute. I can do this. I've done it before and I can do it again. Whatever it is that's holding me back, it's *not* that I'm not capable." You need to change your inner dialogue, and have undying and total self-belief. That can never waver.

You have to hardwire a process into your game or your brain until it becomes second nature, like the 10,000-hour rule Malcolm Gladwell discusses in his book *Outliers*. But after you've performed a skill countless times, and then you don't do it at a *certain* time, the question becomes: *Why wasn't I able to hit that shot under pressure? Why did I make that mistake in the dying seconds of the game?*

We get distracted by the consequences of failure—the what-ifs. The hardest thing for any athlete is to get your mind out of the way and let your body do what it's trained to. We have to learn how to maintain confidence, and trust in ourselves. Being curious about how your mind works is a good place to start. It takes trial and error, but you want to get to a point where you're eager to be in those big moments, even with the pressure. It's a really important skill to learn because everybody struggles at one time or another.

Glen was really on the cutting edge, always searching for a new way to approach the quest for success, whether it was with mental training or physical.

On the physical side, he looked for opportunities for us to increase our fitness in ways that wouldn't overly stress our bodies. We used stationary bikes as a way to maintain fitness without taxing the rest of the body. And we were using dietary supplements—a vitamin drink a doctor made up for us to help bolster the immune system. The grind of a full season wore everyone down and it was important to find any advantage we could to stay healthy and strong.

We were one of the first teams to start with VO_2 testing— a test performed on a treadmill or bike where you're pushed to your absolute limit while connected to a machine that tells you how much oxygen you use. Our first year, four days after the end of the season, they decided to call us in to get on the bikes and measure our blood oxygen. It was brutal, but the testing was designed to give us an edge.

Our practices were different, too. Back then, as I understood it, the norm was for NHL teams to hold two-hour practices, during which they would often pause the action to go over things on a chalkboard. Our practices were only about forty minutes long, but they were conducted at a furious pace. As they say, practice the way you play. Our practices were always at game speed, and our passing and movement were expected to be precise. Glen was religious about that. The idea was that when we got to a game, it would be easy to play and concentrate with all of our energy for twenty-minute periods, because we were used to going twice that long without rest in practice.

This style of practice also helped us stay mentally fresh, especially during the dog days of winter, smack in the middle of the season, in January and February. During these short, cold days, guys were often fighting through injuries. The start and the end of the season both seemed so far off. Trudging through two-hour practices between games could really dull the edge when it needed to be sharp, so this forty-minute approach was a perfect prescription to accomplish what we needed to get done, efficiently, and give us more time to reset mentally.

OUR TEAM FLOURISHED DURING THE 1983–84 season. We kept on pressing after our hot start of seven straight wins. Our offense was off the charts. For the third year in a row, we set a new record for the most goals in a season by an NHL team. And we were having fun, too. We weren't traveling by charter back then, so we stayed the night when we played away games. We'd have morning skates the next day in small rinks and people would come out to watch. With Wayne and Glen's shared commitment to going all out in practice, the result was often quite the show for fans. We enjoyed giving that to them. We enjoyed the attention, too.

We were sailing along in first place in our division, when we hit a mid-season skid in February. Wayne injured his shoulder and had to miss six games. We had some other injuries, too. We lost five straight games, capped off by an 11–0 embarrassment in Hartford. After the game, Glen went berserk, kicking over garbage cans in the dressing room and screaming in outrage. Coaches need to keep players focused, but anger won't always get it done. Fortunately for us, Glen had an instinct for when to push and when to have some fun.

The next morning, we were supposed to travel early to Winnipeg, but got notified that instead we would have a morning skate in Hartford before we took off. We got up early and were all out there on the ice, waiting for Glen to show up, when some strange guy came walking up the tunnel in full equipment. We were grumbling to one another, wondering if maybe they'd called somebody up from the farm club, because we'd been playing so poorly. Or had they made a trade? Who the hell was this guy?

When he got onto the ice and started skating around, we realized it was Glen. By this time, it had been seven years since he'd played, and he was a long way off from NHL condition. He looked awkward—his pants were a little too long, his shoulder pads a little too big, everything mismatched. We couldn't figure out what the hell was going on.

Practice started, and after a few minutes, he blew his whistle, called us in, and launched into a lecture on "the right way" to do things.

Then he called Paul Coffey over to join him.

Paul Coffey is one of the greatest skaters to ever play the game. He was famous for coming around his own net and just exploding in an effortless burst of power and speed down the full length of the ice toward the other team's goal.

With all of us watching, Glen proceeded to show Paul the correct way to make his signature behind-the-net move. Of course, while he was giving the live tutorial, his ankles were scraping the ice like a novice skater. We weren't yet sure if we should be laughing or not.

We started practicing again. Wayne, who was feeling better and getting back on the ice, made a pass to Jari Kurri, which Jari, one of the deadliest shooters of all time, then "one-timed" with a great slap shot into the net. Glen blew his whistle again. We all gathered up, Glen called Jari forward, and demonstrated "the right way" to take a slap shot. He barely got his blade on the puck.

The trend continued. It just went on and on, like a *Saturday Night Live* skit. At one point, he showed Dave Semenko how to get in there and square off against a guy in a fight. The capstone was probably Glen showing Wayne—the greatest passer of all time—how to lift a saucer pass.

I've heard some people say they think he did it for the media, who were all there watching this bizarre practice, to give them something to write about other than our losing streak. But I think it was an odd and calculating move that was more designed for us, his players. Glen had survived in professional hockey all those years mostly by being a creative thinker. He knew we were putting a lot of pressure on ourselves and I think he was trying to introduce a little bit of levity into the situation, to break the tension. It was also a comical way to remind all of us not to overthink what we were doing. Just get out there and do what we know! It was the power of positive thinking, Glen Sather style.

After this, we went on to win eight in a row. Maybe that was due more to the fact that Wayne was back, but we closed the season winning eighteen of the last twenty-two on the way to notching the best record in the league.

In the playoffs, we continued to play well and with focus. By this time, we were seasoned, strong, and in our prime. We swept the Jets; won a tough series in seven games against the Flames; and then swept the Minnesota North Stars (who became the Dallas Stars in 1993) to put us back exactly where we were a year before: matched up against the defending champion Islanders in the final for the Stanley Cup.

It was the third time in five years we had faced them in

the playoffs. The rivalry had reached nuclear levels. We had won the Presidents' Trophy for having the league's best record (by a mile), but the Islanders had swept us in the regular season by scoring seventeen goals in three games. They had a lot of firepower, but also an ability to hinder our strengths. They could take away our speed through the neutral zone, effectively shrinking the ice for us. We knew from the previous year that we had to buckle down defensively, play more patiently, and not chase or fight the game when it wasn't going our way. That's easier said than done against such a powerhouse team. But by the time the finals started, we were ready.

The series opened in Long Island, and it was hardly what some might have expected from the two highest-scoring teams in the league. We won the first game 1–0, which affirmed what we had been trying to do all year: win games even when the things that normally went right for us were going wrong. We'd learned that we couldn't always play wide-open hockey, and had become comfortable being uncomfortable in games that became seesaw battles. We knew that when we had chances, our great players would capitalize on them.

To win the Cup opener, on the road, in a tight game, was critical. Sometimes it isn't how many you score, but how few you give up. We had won with our defense. Champions have balance. We had arrived. The only goal scored in the game came from Kevin McClelland on our third line, who was our fourteenth-leading scorer.

They thumped us 6–2 in the next game but we still felt good. It was one and one.

I always believed that in a seven-game series—aside from a game seven if it happens—game three is the most important. If you're up 2–0 and you win, you've got a stranglehold. If you're down 2–0 and you win, you're back in it. If it's even and you win, you seize the momentum.

Game three in this series was a real tug-of-war. We were doing a good job on defense, but we were having trouble maintaining our speed and playing the type of free-flowing offense that was so much a part of our success.

It was tied at one early in the second period when Clark Gillies scored on a power play to give the Islanders the lead. Then everything changed. I was back-checking and picked up a loose puck just inside our blue line, and I turned back up the ice with Denis Potvin and Gord Dineen defending me, one against two. I went to fake to the outside of Dineen, and he bit. I pulled it inside and shot. Tie game, again.

It was the first time in the series that we had scored a typical Oilers goal instead of a gritty rebound or a deflection, or a "mucky" goal. It was the first time we had shown a flash of speed up the ice and scored. The Islanders played such a suffocating style of defense, but this goal made us realize we *could* play our game against them.

We scored six straight goals and shut them out the rest of the game to win 7–2. Fourteen different guys were on the scoresheet. I ended up with two goals. Semenko had only had six goals that year, but he scored our final goal of the game. Our offense was in full swing.

We brought it again in game four. Wayne scored less than two minutes into the game, and by the end of the first period, we were up 3–1. We scored three more goals in the second period, and ended up winning again, 7–2.

On May 18, up three games to one in the Stanley Cup final, we had an off day to sit and think. We had a morning practice, then spent the rest of the day resting and getting good nutrition and hydration.

There wasn't much else we could do. Every emotion, every image in my mind all day long, was about the Cup. We needed only one more win to seal the deal. To accomplish the goal for which these guys, who had become my brothers, and I had been fighting so hard over a five-year journey. A lifetime dream.

I was living with Kevin Lowe, and the night before game five we were just sitting around listening to music—Tina Turner's "The Best" reinforced that good self-talk for us. We also talked, and somehow the conversation would always drift back to what we needed to do on the ice.

I must have played that game ten times in my head. It was a day filled with giddy anticipation. *What will winning a Stanley Cup feel like?* I wondered. *What will it mean to the fans? To our families? To us?*

I think it's important to allow yourself to imagine all of the positive things about to happen in connection with accomplishing your goals. You can't get carried away, but, especially on the days off, give yourself permission to dream a little. It's only human. To deny yourself those moments is unnatural. And it's healthy to imagine it going the other way, too: a crushing defeat so you can face your fear of failure. You just can't dwell on that. Then you have to compartmentalize, and put the thoughts aside, so you can be present and execute when you're on the ice. All day, I couldn't wait for night to come so I could go to sleep and get to that moment. But it was hard to sleep.

We started the game well, with Wayne scoring two goals in the first period. Jari Kurri assisted on both of them, and then scored one of his own. Late in the game, with a 4–2 lead and just thirteen seconds left, Dave Lumley got an open-net goal. Some fans started running onto the ice to celebrate, and there were balloons and ribbons, even though the game wasn't technically over yet. But we all knew.

We'd won the Stanley Cup.

And with 8 goals and 18 assists, I won the Conn Smythe Trophy as the most valuable player in the playoffs. That was a surprise. I was having a good run, but I wasn't really thinking about the Smythe Trophy until I was actually holding it. I had never won many individual awards, and where I came from, it was never about them anyhow.

It's true what they say, though: You make your money in the regular season. You make your name in the playoffs.

When I look back on that final series, I see that we were younger and healthier than the Islanders, and we had the best record in the game. Still, it's amazing how difficult it is to beat a championship team like them—guys with so much pride, experience, and heart.

We were battle-hardened rivals. We denied them a fifth consecutive title. I'm sure that was a bitter pill to swallow. Only once before in Stanley Cup history had a team been able to win five straight: the mighty Canadiens of the 1950s. But we owed them. If it wasn't for the Islanders pushing us and showing what kind of sacrifice was necessary to win, I don't think we would have ever become as good as we eventually did.

As you can imagine, Edmonton was delirious. The closest city to ever win a Stanley Cup was Chicago, 1,600 miles away. Growing up where we did, the NHL was basically a TV show. It was so mythic and grand it might as well have been a fairy tale produced on a soundstage. Many people in the area, including my extended family, spent their childhoods as Montreal Canadiens and Toronto Maple Leafs fans before the Oilers joined the NHL. Hockey fans in the Canadian northwest plains had always been like kids with their noses pressed up against the ice cream store window. In Edmonton, the NHL was a dream that fans felt so far away from, for so long. Now they finally got to taste just how good it was.

It was a sweet time for the team, too. There was a parade down Jasper Avenue, the main road through downtown Edmonton, on a beautiful early-spring day. We all rode in the back of open convertibles, confetti everywhere. The fans were so close as we slowly rolled by that I was afraid some of them would get their toes run over as they reached out to touch the Cup. The whole city was packed onto this one street.

In all the other major North American professional sports—baseball, football, basketball—you play for the championship, and there is a trophy *associated* with that championship. Hockey is different. You will never hear anyone who knows the game referring to the "NHL Championship." It is the Stanley Cup playoffs, and as much as you play for the championship, you first and foremost play for the Cup. It was first awarded in 1893, named for Lord Stanley of Preston, the governor general of Canada, and, unlike the championship trophies of most other sports, a new trophy isn't manufactured every year. There is one, onto which each year the names of the players on the winning team are engraved.

The tradition is that everybody on the team gets the Cup for a few days, and they can take it wherever they want. Some of the stories of where the Cup has traveled over the years and what guys did with it are wild. It has traveled the globe to small towns and big cities and been celebrated in every way. The Penguins winger Josh Archibald baptized his son in it.

Because the Cup is so sacred and singular, today there is a "Cup keeper"—an escort who shepherds it when and where its public presence is called for. He handles it only with white museum gloves. But back then, there was no keeper. That didn't mean the reverence that people showed for it was any less incredible. You would have thought it was the Holy Grail, which I suppose it was.

When it was my turn, I planned to just low-key it and take it to St. Albert, that little area north of the city where I grew up, where my extended family would meet me at my parents' modest house.

Before we got to the house, Kevin Lowe and I stopped to pick up a few cases of beer at a place called the Bruin Inn near the old barn where I grew up playing. We couldn't really leave the Cup in the car, so we brought it in with us. There couldn't have been more than three or four people in the place. It was pretty quiet. There was this old guy behind the bar who'd worked there for a long time, and if you could only have seen his face when we walked in and hoisted the Stanley Cup onto the bar.

He caught his breath and then headed right for the pay phone. Before we knew it the place was packed. It turned into a massive party with people drinking beer and everything else the bar had in stock from the Cup. We were there for hours. A bunch of my extended family actually ended up coming by because we were at the bar for so long and they wanted to join in the fun.

We eventually made it back to my parents' house, where my parents, siblings, and whole extended family joined us. It was a trip for my relatives to walk in and see the Stanley Cup in our living room: It just didn't seem real. It was something they never would have thought to imagine. It was just about as conceivable as coming over after church for a cup of coffee and sitting down next to the Pope. It was an especially powerful moment for my parents. Doug had the same dream as a player and now he got to see the Cup for himself. All of our parents were so invested in our success, and became like parents to everyone on the team.

My mind flashed back four and a half years earlier to my first Oilers team Christmas party, when Glen had presented each player with that beautiful shearling coat that had the embroidered patch inside.

EDMONTON OILERS
198_ STANLEY CUP CHAMPIONS

We had filled in the blank: 1984.

I don't want to say the days after were depressing, but what I quickly realized was that the soul of the experience was in the journey. Waking up and knowing I didn't have to go to the rink was a reward, but it left a void, too, because what made this special and meaningful was all the shared hours with teammates. The Cup was the symbol, but the real magic was in the day-to-day commitment, passion, and camaraderie with my teammates.

As hard as I'd worked, as long as the journey had been, as much as it meant, it didn't take long for another thought to enter my mind and refuse to leave:

This feels so good. How do we make it happen again?

CHAPTER EIGHT

CANADA CUP

Not long ago, someone asked who I thought was a bigger deal in Canada: Gordie Howe or Paul Henderson. Without thinking—just gut reaction—I blurted out Henderson. A minute later I switched and figured it had to be Howe, right? Mr. Hockey?

Ultimately, I'm not sure I know the answer, and that makes it a good place to start talking about the fall of 1984. For the first time, I had been named to Team Canada, representing my country against the world's best, just like Henderson had done.

Hockey fans, especially Canadians, have always had a hunger to see the very best players from their country compete on the international stage. But because of a complicated set of rules about amateur status, NHL players were barred from competing in the two premier international hockey tournaments—the World Championships and the Olympics. This only started to change in the late seventies, though there were still scheduling difficulties. Since the NHL was so disproportionately Canadian, this affected Canada more than other countries. The league was very nearly 100 percent Canadian in 1960 and it was still more than 80 percent in 1970.

Until the 1960s, with the NHL players sidelined, Canada's top amateurs admirably stepped up and competed well against the rival Soviets. But then the increasingly highly trained, professional Soviet teams began to dominate the international tournaments. They won gold at the World Championships every single year from 1963 to 1971, and gold at three consecutive Olympics, in 1964, 1968, and 1972.

To Canadians, it was salt in the wound to consider the Soviets amateurs. They weren't a bunch of plumbers and lawyers who played hockey after they came home from work, or college kids who were juggling classes and practice. The Red Army team, which represented the USSR, was fully underwritten by the government. The players' *jobs*, ten months a year, were to be on the team. It was how they earned a living! And we were considering them amateurs how?

So, by the early 1970s, Canadian hockey fans were fed up. It was a matter of pride about something that in Canada was more than a sport. Hockey was a part of our identity. We were certain that Canada's best players, all of whom were in the NHL, could easily take down the Soviets in a fair fight. Thus, the Summit Series was born.

The Summit Series would be a new, eight-game matchup between the two countries' top players, to be held in September 1972. Four games played in Canada, followed by four in the Soviet Union, in Moscow. Each game in Canada would be played in a different city—game one in Montreal, two in Toronto, three in Winnipeg, and four in Vancouver. (If the series ended in a tie on games, goal differential would be the deciding factor.) Even though the Soviet team had just come off an

Olympic win in the 1972 Sapporo games six months earlier, the sense in Canada was that we had nothing to fear. Politics and ideologies were a big part of the equation, too, and ice seemed the perfect place for the Cold War to continue. It felt like the whole country was all in on the Summit Series. I know that, at age eleven, I certainly was.

The expectation was that we were going to bulldoze them. It didn't happen. In the first four games at home, Canada won only once, and had one tie. When the Soviets then took the first game in Moscow, they were just one win away from claiming the title. With its back to the wall, Canada won the next two games, and so it all came down to the final game, in Moscow, on September 28.

By one estimate, more than two-thirds of Canada was watching. That included me in my fifth-grade classroom in St. Albert. My teacher wheeled a television in. The same was happening in classrooms all over the country.

Intense doesn't begin to describe it. The Soviets scored first. Then the legendary Hall of Famer Phil Esposito tied it up for us. The Soviets scored another, and the Canadians matched again: 2–2. But in the second period, the Soviets started to pull away. They went up 5–3. In the third period, Esposito scored again. We were now down by just one goal, 5–4. A scrum ensued on the ice. Extra soldiers were deployed to the stadium in case things got out of hand.

With ten minutes left in the third period, the great Yvan Cournoyer, who played sixteen years with the Canadiens and won the Stanley Cup in half of them, evened the score. But the goal judge didn't put on the light. One of our team officials, Alan Eagleson, who had been seminal in putting the series together, tried to approach the timer's bench to protest, and the Soviet police blocked him. In the classroom, we couldn't believe what we were seeing as we watched the drama unfold. *What was happening?* we collectively wondered. One of our players, Peter Mahovlich, jumped over the boards, with his stick, and got into it with the police officers. Eventually, the goal was granted. It was 5–5.

Play resumed, and my classmates and I were glued to the screen for every rush down the ice and close call either way. It was a referendum on what we took as an article of faith, that Canadian hockey was the best in the world. Those last ten minutes were agonizing to watch. This had come to mean everything for us.

Most Canadians of a certain age can tell you exactly where they were when it happened.

With thirty-four seconds left, Paul Henderson fought his way to the front of the net, recovered two consecutive rebounds, and put the puck in the goal. Henderson had a nice NHL career. He was never an all-star and never won a Stanley Cup, but when perhaps the most sacred pillar of Canada's reputation was on the line, he rose and made it safe for us all to proudly say what we always believed in our hearts:

The best hockey in the world *is* in our country.

And so Paul Henderson is as big a national hero as we have ever had. Howe had a legendary career. Henderson had a good career and a legendary moment.

The Summit Series was played just once more, in 1974, and was won by the Soviets, before it morphed from a bilateral grudge match into a six-team international tournament in 1976 called the Canada Cup. In addition to Canada and the Soviet Union, teams from Czechoslovakia, Finland, Sweden, and the United States would play every few years for the right to claim true international hockey supremacy.

Canada won the inaugural tournament in 1976. Then the Soviets took it in 1981. Which brings us to September 1984.

To play for Canada and defend the country's hockey legacy, to follow in the footsteps of Paul Henderson, was the greatest honor and privilege I could imagine. But the post-1984 Stanley Cup celebration had been unrelenting: equal parts exhausting and exhilarating. I took my annual trip with Paul and the boys, this time to Greece, and when I came back, everything was accelerated even beyond the normal grind of the run-up to an NHL season, to get ready for the Canada Cup. It was like going from one pressure cooker into another.

And there was a complicating factor. The two teams most heavily represented on the Canadian roster were the Edmonton Oilers and the New York Islanders. We didn't like the Islanders, and the Islanders didn't like us. Ultimately, we loved our country and the game enough to get us to a state of hockey détente.

It wasn't easy.

GLEN SATHER WAS CHOSEN TO be the coach of Team Canada— no surprise, given that he'd just won the Stanley Cup. Glen turned right around and picked his Oilers assistants John Muckler and Ted Green to be on his staff, along with three of the team's trainers, and the Edmonton PR director, Bill Tuele. In addition to me, seven other Oilers players were selected for the team. Wayne was of course one of them, as were Paul Coffey, Glenn Anderson, Kevin Lowe, and our goalie Grant Fuhr. It was shaping up to be a very comfortable operation for us Oilers.

Just the opposite was true for the four Islanders who were

chosen for the team: Mike Bossy, Bob Bourne, Brent Sutter, and John Tonelli. They were our bitter rivals, and outnumbered. Think about how they must have felt. The Islanders came into the league as an expansion team in 1972, and they had to survive and develop in the rough days of the Philadelphia Flyers' bruising Broad Street Bullies teams. The Islanders had to scratch and claw every step of the way. They weren't flashy. They had a lunch-pail mentality and they were able to succeed in a historic way.

Then along comes this raucous bunch of happy-go-lucky kids in Edmonton in 1979 who don't follow that script, and win anyway. As the great Montreal goaltender and broadcaster Ken Dryden said: "The Islanders were a great team. The Oilers were an important team." In other words, we broke the mold.

So we were Ali and Frazier, two champions with different styles. It's human nature that nobody likes to be told that *their* way isn't the *right* way. There was a real vibe from the Islanders players of *Fuck these guys. Who do they think they are?*

The rift ran so deep that people theorized it was the reason the Islanders center Bryan Trottier, who was an all-star that season and was born and raised in Saskatchewan, chose to play for the United States in the tournament instead of Canada, an option for him because he had Native American ancestry.

The times were different, too, and that didn't help. Nowadays, guys compete hard against one another, but there's much more civility between players before and after games. Back then, there was no fraternization between players from different organizations. If your coach caught you talking to a guy on the other team during warm-ups, it was looked at as a betrayal. You could count on someone else replacing you in the lineup that night. Suffice it to say that Team Canada's first meeting in

Montreal for training camp was odd and uncomfortable. There were no incidents, just a massive chill in the air.

We didn't like one another, but despite our differences, when it came down to it, we also had respect for one another. Ultimately, we knew our work was cut out for us and we couldn't let our internal divisions tear us apart. In 1984, the Soviets were back to being international hockey's dominant team. In the four and a half years since the Miracle on Ice game, when the team of American amateurs improbably beat them in the 1980 Lake Placid Olympics, the Soviets hadn't lost a single game. The Canada-USSR rivalry had become even more rancorous after the Soviets dominated Canada in the final game of the 1981 Canada Cup, beating us 8–1 at the Montreal Forum, no less, to win the most recent title. The tournament organizer Alan Eagleson—the same guy who had scuffled with the Moscow police back in 1972—had been so upset that he didn't allow the Soviets to take the Cup back home.

The goal for our ten-day training camp was to reach a truce with the Islanders players. This is the process for any all-star team of this type—since you have such a short amount of time to practice, you simply have to do your best to drop your baggage, drop your ego, and find a way to come together. We might never become pals, but we needed to at least tap into the level of respect that was layered in there beneath the animosity, for the sake of our country. In little more than a week, we would be going up against European teams that had been together so long they probably knew how their line mates took their coffee.

We didn't achieve the harmony that we were looking for in training camp. As a result, the pool-play round went poorly for us. We opened by beating West Germany, which had replaced

Finland for the 1984 tournament, 7–2, but that was hardly a great accomplishment. The Germans came in expected to be at the bottom of the standings, and ended up conceding 29 goals in five games to finish with a record of 0-4-1.

The sign of trouble came in our next game, against the United States. Though the Miracle on Ice team had inspired a generation of American kids, and Team USA would eventually become an international hockey superpower, in 1984 they had a lot of talented players but hadn't reached that elite level yet. So our 4–4 tie against them in the pool-play round of the Canada Cup was an undeniable tip-off that something wasn't right. We—and our country—expected more.

One of the things I'd learned from winning the Stanley Cup is that successful teams find harmony and balance. It's a matter of everyone playing their part, bringing their energy to the circle. It's about being awake, and tuning in, and it doesn't happen overnight.

Are people conversing and connecting? Is everybody included at team meals? Is there laughter at the dinner table? Is the music on in the dressing room, for everyone to enjoy? When things are going right, there's an easiness that permeates every aspect of the collective team experience.

Throughout my career, when I walked through a dressing room I was attuned to people's energy. A teammate might have made a play he wasn't proud of, or the coach had sat him out a game, or maybe a bad article had been written about him—it could be anything. If left unaddressed, problems can grow to affect the whole team. And if someone has a positive attitude, picking that up and helping to amplify it can be good for everyone. Either way, a leader needs to be aware and open.

We had found ways to be cordial to one another on that 1984 Canada Cup team, but it didn't seem to be enough. There was still a dysfunctional undercurrent blocking positive energy from flowing, like an artery that had started to clog. Even though the guys on the team would talk to one another, there was tension in the air. When we lost to Sweden 4–2, three days after tying with the USA, the situation became more serious.

"There were too many Oilers on the team," Brent Sutter's father, Louis, told the Toronto *Globe and Mail.* One anonymous Team Canada player told James Lawton of the *Vancouver Sun*: "There is a problem in thinking of yourself as part of the team. The fact is, there are the Edmonton Oilers, and the rest."

The pressure was really ramping up. You could picture a grandmother out in Moose Jaw, Saskatchewan, sitting in front of her TV, believing in us, all in, with all of her heart. In a way, she was just as much a part of Team Canada as we were. It felt like the country was peering into our locker room, and we were letting them down. The circle was so much wider.

There'd be no way to recover from a bad performance in a spot like this. Paul Henderson had become the forever hero. Surely those who let the country down would be remembered just as vividly. For us, the people responsible, it would live on in our souls forever.

When a team hits a rough patch, leaders earn their stripes. They step to the middle of the room and grab everyone by the lapels to deliver whatever message is necessary. We had a team full of "middle of the room" guys. The problem was most of them were Oilers or Islanders.

One wasn't, and he figured the middle of the room might not be the best place to start the discussion. With all the hardware you could possibly imagine, including at that point five Stanley Cup rings, the Canadiens' Larry Robinson was one of the oldest guys on our team, and a Canada Cup veteran, winning it in 1976 and losing in 1981. Neither Oiler nor Islander, he was Switzerland, big as the Alps in both size and stature, neutral and respected by everyone.

He got a bunch of guys together at a bar in Calgary called Yosemite Sam's.

When the Canadiens were struggling with anything, Larry would round up the guys and head to this little tavern right across the street from the Forum in Montreal. The idea was to get everybody talking about anything *but* hockey. Usually, after a few beers, people would loosen up and get things off their chests if they needed to.

There was nothing headline-making that happened at Yosemite Sam's that night, though Larry later said he maybe had a few too many beers and fell over in his chair. It was just a good night to take a deep breath.

The team seemed to respond when we notched a 7–2 win over Czechoslovakia. But the Czechs were a weak squad and would finish tied for last with West Germany.

The real test came two days later. It was our last game in the pool-play round. We were up against the Soviets. There was a chance we could lose and still move on in the tournament to the medal rounds, but we needed the win for ourselves. To heighten the moment, we were playing at Northlands in Edmonton.

We lost that game 6–3. Afterward, a reporter asked Mike Bossy, the Islanders' great forward, if the result would have been different if the Islanders' coach, Al Arbour, had been in charge of Team Canada, instead of Glen Sather.

"Yes," he said.

With one word, the fuse was lit.

BOSSY WAS A VERY OUTSPOKEN and opinionated guy. His comment brought the situation to a head, which was the right thing to do. It forced us to confront the elephant in the room, and it was one big-ass elephant.

Glen was seething, not only about the loss to the Soviets, but about the way we'd played.

"If you guys don't start getting along," he said after the game, "we have absolutely no chance."

He told Wayne and Larry that they needed to have a players' meeting. Not a "let's have a few beers and get to know each other better" meeting, like at Yosemite Sam's. A mandatory-attendance, all-hands-on-deck summit, to clear the air.

In a meeting room in our hotel in Canada, Bob Bourne of the Islanders, a good role player with speed and scoring ability, but not a marquee name, got up to speak. Addressing the Oilers in the room he said:

"I'm not gonna sugarcoat this. I don't fucking like you guys, not one of you. But I want to play for my country and we've got to win."

There was a lot of quiet in that room. It felt like Bob had finally verbalized the thing on which we could all agree. The flag was more important than anyone's individual vendettas, agendas, or feelings.

When we got to the arena, there was a new locker configuration. Instead of the Islanders all bunched in one area and the Oilers in another, the trainers shuffled the deck and put Oilers and Islanders players next to one another, particularly players who might not have gotten along naturally.

Bourne and Kevin Anderson, Lowe and Tonelli, and Gretzky and Sutter.

It's never good to have cliques on a team. The new seating meant that when we were all getting dressed before or after games, we didn't have a choice but to talk to the guy next to us even if it was begrudgingly. Often, it would have nothing to do with hockey, but it opened up a line of communication. It changed things.

Glen mixed up some of the lines, too, trying to find the combinations that worked best. Every team that comes together for a tournament goes through a process of figuring out who's playing with who, how to work together, how to have clear and concise roles. The quicker you can do it, the better, and we were getting there late, but we were getting there.

We squeaked into the medal round as the fourth and last qualifier. Our reward was a rematch with the top-seeded Soviets, who had come through the pool-play round undefeated, and had outscored their opponents 22–7. We had always imagined we'd be meeting them in the finals, but here we were, needing to find our best just to make it there. Whoever won the game would go on to the final against Sweden, which had routed the United States in Edmonton the night before, 9–2.

Our game was at the Saddledome in Calgary. The opening period was a tense draw, 0–0. We played pretty well but didn't have anything to show for it because Vladimir Myshkin, the Soviet goaltender, was having the night of his life. In the second period, we outshot the Soviets 17–6, and the Islander John Tonelli came through for us and finally managed to break

Myshkin. But in the third period, the Soviets fought back. They scored two goals in the first seven minutes, and suddenly we were on the ropes, down 2–1. With six minutes left, the Chicago Black Hawk Doug Wilson took a pass from Wayne and tied the game for us. When the horn sounded, it was still 2–2. We were going to overtime.

The minutes ticked off the clock in overtime. We had a power play, but we couldn't score. Neither could the Soviets. Then, about twelve minutes into the extra session, Vladimir Kovin came flying up the right side with Mikhail Varnakov on his left and Paul Coffey between them. It was a two-on-one break for the Soviets. I distinctly remember sitting on the bench and thinking, *This could be it, and if we lose, this is going to be devastating.*

Kovin slowed to let Varnakov get out in front and then tried to slip him a pass, but Paul—one of the best defensemen of all time, even though he's remembered today primarily for his offensive prowess—laid out and poked the puck away. That move, in this game, at this crucial moment—it was one of the greatest defensive plays I have ever seen.

Like lightning, Paul was somehow up on his feet with the puck on his stick, transitioning the other way, on the counter-attack. He passed to John Tonelli. Tonelli passed back to him. Coffey was then at the point, inside the Soviet blue line. Mike Bossy was taking up position in the slot, right in front of Myshkin in goal. Paul ripped a slap shot, and Bossy, like the pure goal scorer he was, stuck his stick up and deflected it into the net.

That was it. We'd done it. Oiler, to Islander, to Oiler, to Islander, for the win.

The final against Sweden was an anticlimax in the best possible sense. We played two games, the first in Calgary, the second in Edmonton, and won them both, meaning there was no need for a third, tiebreaking game. The 1984 Canada Cup was ours.

We were thrilled to have won, but even more than that, I think, we were relieved. It was hardly a warm and fuzzy experience for everyone. Bossy later said in his autobiography: "I felt obligated to accept Team Canada's invitation, but let's just say I didn't enjoy that Canada Cup." Personally, I loved the experience, and learned a lot from it. I was a better player afterward. I was lucky to spend the majority of my career on tight-knit teams that had the vibe of a family. Perhaps that wasn't the case for everyone on this Canada Cup team. But we came away from it with a lot of pride. We'd aired out our feelings and refocused on our common purpose. In a hard-fought must-win game for Canada, we got the job done.

Though it's true that the '84 Canada Cup team didn't ever fully gel, I don't attribute that entirely to the Oilers-Islanders rivalry. It takes years for teams to go from a bunch of individuals to a family, and all-star teams never have the time to build that kind of camaraderie.

To have long-lasting success like we did on the Oilers, you've got to feel that everybody in the dressing room is your brother. You'd sit with them at lunch or hang out with their kids. You'd do anything for them. If you've got a guy on your team you don't feel that way about, you need to make an effort to get to that point. The first step has to be looking in the mirror.

My dad's younger brother Victor, who has a PhD in psychology and has studied human behavior his entire adult life, always says anytime you have a problem with somebody, it has nothing to do with the other person. It all comes back to you. It's not actually about what they're doing or how they're treating you, but how you're internalizing it. Once you've taken the time to understand your reactivity a little bit and identify what the other person is doing that's pushing your buttons, then you can begin the process of fixing the problem. Instead of being reactive, you can take the time and effort to get to know the person, learn about his upbringing, his relationships with the people he grew up around, and in doing so, get a sense of why he makes the decisions he does. The end result of this is the discovery of two of the most important characteristics on an effective leader's tool belt: empathy and compassion. You can put forward an olive branch, and start a conversation to bridge the gap of how to coexist.

On the '84 Canada Cup team, though, we didn't need to have long-term success, and we didn't have the time to get around to any of this. It was two and a half pressure-filled weeks. In this case, having a common goal of defeating the Soviets and not letting our country down was enough to overcome the challenge. We buried the hatchet just deeply enough to make it through.

The divide between the Islanders and Oilers on that team in many ways mirrored the situation that existed initially on the 1980 U.S. Olympic hockey team that won the Miracle on Ice game. The roster was dominated by players from the University of Minnesota, where the man who led the Miracle on Ice squad, Herb Brooks, had been the coach. A small but important part of the team, including the captain and eventual hero, Mike Eruzione, and the goalie Jim Craig, was from Boston University.

Four years before the Lake Placid games, in the semifinal of the NCAA championship between BU and Brooks's Minnesota team, what is widely regarded as one of the ugliest incidents in college hockey history occurred. Just minutes into the game, a melee erupted between the two teams. The brawl went on for thirty minutes, even as police officers were out on the ice trying to break it up. Officials finally had to turn off the lights so the players couldn't see who to fight.

What Eruzione said about it was: "Once we all got together as the Olympic team, we just buried all that. That's just the way hockey is."

Just like the 1980 U.S. Olympic team, our 1984 Canada Cup team did what it took to achieve our shared objective. As the great golfer Johnny Miller likes to say: "A man shouldn't be judged by what he accomplishes. A man should be judged by what he overcomes."

Our name is on the Cup. That's what matters.

CHAPTER NINE

NO EASY WINS

Coming back to the Oilers for the 1984–85 season after the challenging but triumphant Canada Cup experience felt like rejoining a family. It would be an insult to the rest of the league to say that the season was a breeze, but we were in peak form, and we couldn't have played much better.

We opened the season on October 11 against the L.A. Kings. Exactly one month later, on November 11, we lost our first game, against the Philadelphia Flyers. We had gone 12-0 over that span, with three ties.

The Flyers ended up having the best record in the league, but we won just about everything else. Paul won his first Norris Trophy as the league's best defenseman. Wayne won the scoring title and was named MVP (again). And the team won the most important prize of all. We motored through the first two rounds of the playoffs against the Kings and the Jets without dropping a game, mirroring the start of our season. Then, after taking down the Black Hawks in six games, we beat the Flyers in five in the final to win the Cup for a second straight year.

Three decades later, an NHL fan survey to celebrate the league's centennial voted our '85 Oilers team the greatest of all time, edging out the 1991–92 Penguins and 1976–77 Canadiens. Wayne had set new NHL records for assists (30) and points (47) in a single postseason. Jari had scored 19 goals and tied the NHL record for goals in a single postseason. He also had four hat tricks, breaking the record for most in one playoff year, which had been held by me, with three in the '83 playoffs. We were no longer insurgents. We had become the establishment.

The summer after that second Cup, my family all went to visit my brother, Paul, in Germany, where he had moved to play professional hockey in Mannheim. The German season started earlier, so his training camp began in mid-July. When we came back, I still wanted to get away before my own training camp, but with Paul tied up in Germany, instead of spinning the globe to come up with a random destination, Kevin Lowe and I decided to go someplace familiar—back to Hawaii for the first time since our impromptu trip there after our rookie season.

We stayed with my uncle Victor, my dad's younger brother, who was spending the summer in a small house he'd rented in the Manoa Valley on the island of Oahu. He married a woman he met there, Wendy Kim, and later bought a house in the same area, where he'd go for the summer after each school year teaching at the University of New Hampshire, where he was a professor of psychology. The valley was truly paradise. This wasn't a touristy area by any means; Vic lived in and among the local Hawaiians, who were his friends and neighbors. Kevin described the house as having been decorated in a very minimalist way.

While Doug is a former professional hockey player who

married early, raised a family, and stayed home in Edmonton to teach school, Vic was a free spirit and took a different path. He was, and always has been, open-minded and a total searcher.

He left home after college and studied psychology at the University of Alberta and Penn State. He spent time practicing transcendental meditation and out-of-body experiences with Michael Murphy, the author of the novel *Golf in the Kingdom*, about a young traveler who encounters a mystical golfing expert in Scotland. He went to lectures given by the Harvard psychology professor turned psychedelic drug advocate Timothy Leary. I remember being with Vic in Oregon one summer when I was a kid, and looking up as I was cooking a hamburger over an open fire to see him doing this odd, slow dance. He later explained to me that it was tai chi.

The first time that Vic ever put on a suit was when he was interviewing with the dean for his professor of psychology job at the University of New Hampshire. For years, he lived in a converted milk truck, which he'd refurbished and outfitted like a small Winnebago. He later upgraded to a Volkswagen van, which continued to serve as his primary residence during the school years in New Hampshire.

He had always lived a different lifestyle from anyone I'd ever known, and had what I considered to be a very evolved perspective. He believed that to limit consideration of the mind's function to conventional theories and models was to limit true understanding of what it was or did. For him, life had always been about exploring what we really meant by "the self," and it made a huge impression on me. There weren't a lot of boundaries to the way he thought about things.

After a few great weeks in Oahu, Kevin headed back home, but I stayed behind to spend a bit more time with Vic. I had just come up from the beach one afternoon, and Vic and I were sitting on his small deck, having a few beers. He went inside the house and came back with a set of slides, holding the transparencies up against the sun to show me. They were paintings by a man named Alex Grey, from a series called Sacred Mirrors.

Grey is a so-called visionary artist who once worked as a medical illustrator at Harvard. He believes the body's energy is a very real and powerful force. The slides that Vic showed me were Grey's interpretation of how that energy might *look* when represented in visual form. You might have seen some of his best-known paintings: glowing, brightly colored images of human bodies in intricate anatomical detail, often doing things like praying, embracing, or meditating. The idea is that body, mind, and spirit are all brought together in one image. On the surface that might sound pretty far out, but seeing those slides on the deck in Hawaii, it completely made sense to me.

I was pretty open-minded from my travels each summer, but thanks to Vic, mostly, I'd become increasingly interested in Eastern philosophy over the previous couple of years. I did things like yoga and acupuncture, which at the time were still relatively exotic. But he also gave me a book that affected me greatly, the *Tao Te Ching*. I found it so interesting in the simplicity of its teachings: how to live with goodness and integrity in a world that makes that challenging. It made me think about my own actions and how they're perceived. *How can I be more sensitive to others? What kind of energy am I emitting?*

I was always in search of ways to grow and improve, both as an athlete and as a person. I figured that these practices had been around for thousands of years and there must be something to them. The understanding in Buddhism and other

Eastern religions of the connection between the mind and the body made perfect, intuitive sense to me.

When it came to what was behind Grey's drawings, I couldn't get enough of what Vic was telling me. The physical was one thing; the metaphysical, though, was something I had never considered. There's an energy source in all of us. We can harness that source, and use it to motivate, inspire, and lead the people around us. Maybe the reason I was so receptive was because the concept seemed vaguely familiar.

I'd had the sense at times while playing sports of being filled with a powerful energy—a sense that I could do anything. I felt invincible and like nothing could stop me. I knew that the source of this feeling was ultimately in the mind, but that only made me more in awe of how powerful and mysterious the mind really is.

Think about it. How many times have you not been able to fall asleep or woken up in the middle of the night because your mind was racing with worries about personal or professional issues? You're exhausted, but you can't sleep. Your mind has taken control of what your body can do. Why should we expect that the effect would be any less profound when we're fully awake and trying to make our bodies do something athletic?

Seeing these paintings by Alex Grey, it was as if someone had drawn a picture of a vivid and intense thought bubble that was already lurking somewhere deep within me, but I'd never been able to describe or give physical shape to. Grey had drawn a picture of an idea, and a philosophy, that I already understood and believed in, without exactly knowing it. The feeling would stay with me in the back of my mind, but it wouldn't be for another five years that I'd suddenly know what exactly to make of it or do with it. The seeds were being planted for another epiphany.

As we sat there in the sun above the Pacific Ocean drinking beer and considering life's existential mysteries, all I knew for sure was that the world seemed impossibly good. I was playing in the NHL, doing the only thing I ever wanted to do, succeeding at the highest level, and getting paid handsomely for it. I'd just helped bring a pair of Stanley Cups to my hometown, and skated to win something sacred for my country, too. I was twenty-four and it seemed like nothing could go wrong.

Until it did.

GROWING UP, I WAS REALLY into cars, and though I always had wheels—I think I was driving by the time I was fourteen—they were never anything elegant. Who had that kind of money?

One night after a game for the Stingers in Cincinnati, Darryl Maggs, who was kind of a cowboy, invited me to go grab a beer with him. He had this old Porsche, and my eyes got as big as saucers. All I could think was, *One day, I'm going to get one of these.*

In March 1984, I'd signed a new contract with the Oilers, and part of the signing bonus was this beautiful charcoal-black 930 Turbo, which Glen Sather arranged for me to get from a friend of his. It was my dream car, a "pinch me" moment every time I got behind the wheel.

There was an art to driving it. Those old turbos had a bit of a lag from the time you stepped on the accelerator until the car responded. And they would understeer a little because the engine was in the rear.

One night in early September 1985, I was with a buddy and coming around a traffic circle. I downshifted and hit the gas but then the boost kicked in. The car fishtailed up onto the curb and did a 360 onto a narrow street with cars parked on both sides.

We came to a stop and I was really spooked. Thankfully, we hadn't hit any car head-on. Instead, I realized a moment later, I'd scraped down the sides of a number of them.

I caught my breath and thought: "What the hell just happened?"

I was really in a state of shock, so we found a pay phone and called my mom. She came and picked us up and we drove out to St. Albert.

When I got to my parents' house, I called Glen, who called a lawyer, Gary Frohlich, and I gave a police statement. There were a couple of minor charges, but I got off pretty easily and paid a fine.

It hit the papers and I was angry at myself for making such a dumb mistake, both behind the wheel and after the fact. That said, I was very, very lucky. I didn't hurt myself or anybody else. Somebody could have been walking across the street. It wasn't the right place to be driving fast. I should have known better.

The accident made me think about how our actions affect others. I was so thankful that no one got hurt, but even if I had only injured myself, that could have affected our team. In a winning culture, you understand and accept that other people are depending on you, and you behave accordingly. If I crashed my car, what does that have to do with anybody else? The answer was sobering. Humbling, too.

Getting rid of the motorcycle early on was a blessing. Glen's instincts were dead-on. Life talks to you in whispers, but if you're not paying attention, they get louder and louder. I got the message.

We all make mistakes. How we handle them defines who we are and how others look at us. It's something I would remember the rest of my life.

In the fall of 1985, we stood on the brink of a dynasty. Only five teams had ever won at least three straight Cups, and we were a clear-cut favorite to be number six.

We had the best player on the planet, we had speed, we had toughness, we had checking, we had goaltending, we had leadership—we had it all. We were so confident that when the journalists and documentary filmmakers Bob and Terry McKeown approached Glen Sather and asked if they could bring a film crew to spend the season with us, Glen agreed.

All of us immediately took a liking to the brothers, and their crew, especially cameraman Mike Bolan. They were really cool guys, and we embraced them like teammates. We gave them total access to our locker room, and our lives—a fly-on-the-wall view of our team on what we all thought would be our march to another Stanley Cup victory, and our coronation in the selective club of three-peat champions. The film would be called *The Boys on the Bus*.

We cruised through the season and won the Presidents' Trophy with 119 points, matching our highest total ever. We won 56 games and lost only 17, the fewest in franchise history. Wayne had 215 points, setting the record that still stands today. We never had a losing streak longer than two games. For the fifth straight year, we led the league in scoring. We were a machine, and we felt like one.

The playoffs started on the right foot against Vancouver—
we outscored them seventeen to five in a three-game sweep.
Then the tenor of things changed dramatically because our
next opponent was Calgary.

There are a lot of great rivalries in sports—the Yankees and Red Sox, Ohio State and Michigan, North Carolina and Duke—but I think Edmonton and Calgary is the
most intense, and perhaps underappreciated, of them all.
Alberta's two largest cities have been at each other's throats
since long before sports had anything to do with it. The
rivalry goes back to the 1880s when the Canadian Pacific
Railway chose Calgary over Edmonton as the hub to run
its western route through. Since then, it has been game on.
Edmonton got the Canadian Northern Railway in 1905,
then was named the capital of Alberta in 1906. In 1908, it
became the site for Alberta's university. Historically, Calgary
has been conservative, Edmonton more liberal. Residents of
the two cities derisively refer to the other as "Deadmonton"
and "Cowtown." Sports gave the residents of the cities a
framework in which to yell at each other.

My own dislike for Calgary hockey was personal and pre-
programmed all the way back to childhood. I could never forget my father's bruised face as he shaved the morning after he'd
been pummeled by those Calgary hockey players when he was
the player and coach of the amateur Edmonton Monarchs.

The Atlanta Flames moved to Calgary in 1980, a year after
the Oilers joined the NHL, and since 1981 we'd been pitted
against each other in the Smythe Division. So far, Edmonton
had consistently come out on top. In the five years we'd been
in the league together, Calgary had gone further than us only
once in the playoffs. We'd beaten them in our single previous

head-to-head playoff series, and of course, won the Cup twice. They couldn't open a newspaper without reading about how great and successful we were. That had to hurt.

The Flames knew that they weren't going to be able to have a chance at a Cup without figuring out a way to get through us. So they started to put together a team and a system to do just that.

Today, there are limits on the numbers of players NHL teams can carry on their rosters, but in the mid-1980s, that wasn't the case. The Flames started using an innovative strategy where they carried a significant number of extra guys on the team—usually around ten to twelve. This allowed them to essentially dress two completely different teams depending on who they were playing. They could dress a fast, skill team, or they could dress a big, strong, solid checking team. (Today, even without roster limits, teams wouldn't be able to pay that many players as a result of the salary cap.)

Against us, there was no doubt which strategy the Flames would employ. For years, our opponents had decided that they couldn't match us in speed or skill, so the only way they could hope to stop us was through physical play and intimidation. During the 1984–85 season, the Flames brought in the six-foot-five, 220-pound undrafted free agent Joel Otto at center to try to neutralize me physically. They also got the tough guy Tim Hunter and the defenseman Neil Sheehy, who would antagonize Wayne all game long. Late in the 1985–86 season, right at the trade deadline, they picked up the Rangers tough guy Nick Fotiu. They also got our former Canada Cup teammate John Tonelli from the Islanders. Tonelli had been Team Canada's MVP in our hard-fought win over the Soviets, he'd lived through the contentious Islanders-Oilers battles, and he had been right in the middle of one of the nastier local rivalries with the Islanders and Rangers. "I lived that Islanders-Rangers rivalry," he now says. "I didn't think anything could be thicker than that, but I was wrong. Calgary and Edmonton was another level."

The formerly bitter rivals, Fotiu and Tonelli, became roommates who made each other pancakes and ironed each other's laundry. A pair of oil-and-water guys now had something they completely agreed on: Beating the Oilers was all that mattered.

The problem with the Calgary strategy to intimidate us physically was that our skill players were super gritty. It's something that had come to define our Oilers teams—our ability to win at either type of game. If things got really rough, we also had our "nuclear deterrents," Dave Semenko, Kevin McClelland, and our newest enforcer, Marty McSorley, who we'd added to the team in a trade with Pittsburgh at the start of the season. McSorley led the Oilers in penalty minutes in his first season with us, though to be fair, by the thinnest of margins— he had 265 minutes to McClelland's 264.

Still, the physical deterrent seemed to be the best strategy our opponents could come up with, and in particular they tried to deploy it against Wayne. Eighty-two games a year, Wayne played with at least one dedicated guy shadowing him on the ice at all times. The guy would have his stick in Wayne's stomach the entire game. Sometimes there would even be two guys on him, a forward and a defenseman.

It got to the point where Wayne would pretend to come off the ice, the guy who was shadowing him would skate over to his own bench in response, and then Wayne would bolt back into the play. When teams figured that one out, there started to be these moments where Wayne and his shadow would be standing over by the boards, just looking at each other, trying to fake each other out. It was quite a dance.

One other component was that back then, there was no obstruction rule. Going on a routine forecheck to try to get the puck in the other team's zone was like running through a gauntlet—there'd be hooking, holding, slashing, and interfering. It didn't intimidate us, though, that's where our grit came in. We never lost a game in the alleys.

The Flames also had a smart and accomplished coach. "Badger Bob" Johnson was in his third year in Calgary after a legendary career at the amateur level. He'd coached the U.S. Olympic team in 1976 and won three NCAA championships at the University of Wisconsin.

Because the Flames had so many players, Johnson devised a strategy to make use of all the extra men on his roster at practice. He would put the nonroster players on the ice and have them mimic Oilers plays and playing styles. Then he would get his core guys to go climb the stairs and sit all the way up in the arena to watch. The idea was to give the players a bird's-eye view of the proposed strategy. Nowadays, NHL teams have sophisticated video systems to film their own practices and evaluate game tape, often shot by cameras suspended directly above the ice, but at the time, this was the next best thing to animating a chalkboard.

So against the Flames in the second round of the '86 playoffs, we knew what was coming. Their plan was to take away our speed through the neutral zone, shut the boards off, drive traffic toward the middle, and hit us. It was going to be a very physical series. We were okay with that. In the 1985–86 regular season, we had pretty much spanked them, amassing an 8-1-1 record, including exhibition games. In a year when the biggest margin between first and second place in any of the other three divisions had been five points, we took the Smythe by thirty points over the second-place Flames. We had our documentary film crew with us, and our destiny. The Flames were an innovative team who were committed to beating us, and we knew better than to take them lightly, but at some level I think we felt they were just another step to get through on the way.

The series kicked off, and like a couple of heavyweight fighters, we slugged it out. The first two games were in Edmonton. They won the first. We won the second. The next two games were in Calgary. We won to go up 2–1 in the series, then they evened it up at 2–2. We lost game five at home, then won the sixth, away. All of a sudden, we had arrived at game seven, in Edmonton. We had played 18 periods of hockey in this series and each team had scored exactly 22 goals. People wondered if we'd made a mistake and gotten overconfident.

In game seven, with all that was at stake for both sides, the air was pretty thick. We gave up a goal in the first period, and then another a little more than two minutes into the second. Glenn Anderson brought us back within one about eight minutes later, and then with less than a minute left in the second period, I scored to tie it up.

Just about five minutes into the third period, Perry Berezan, a center on the Flames' third line, dumped the puck around the boards into our zone and skated toward his bench. Our goalie Grant Fuhr corralled it and left it behind the net for our rookie defenseman Steve Smith to bring out.

Smith was public enemy number one in Calgary. Two nights earlier, in game six, he'd speared the young Flames star Carey Wilson. Wilson ended up in the hospital and out of the series, needing to have his spleen removed.

No matter what people say, overconfidence had nothing to do with what happened next. An overconfident team is one that doesn't put in the work, because they don't think they have to. One that gets easily distracted. Overconfidence isn't what decided things between us and the Flames that year. In a highly contested seven-game series, as it often does, it was going to boil down to one great play. Or one terrible mistake.

Steve Smith got the puck from behind the net and tried to make a stretch pass up ice. Instead, it hit the back of Grant Fuhr's leg, and went into our goal.

Smith collapsed on the ice in despair.

Norman Mailer once wrote that in boxing, the best moves lie very close to the worst. The same was true for Smith that day. His intention was great. Firing the puck up the ice might have led to just the type of transitional situation that paid off. Instead, the Smith mistake, credited as a goal to Perry Berezan, ended up being the game winner. Neither team scored again afterward.

As bitter as the rivalry was with Calgary, what hurt the most wasn't the thought that the Flames might win the Cup (they ended up losing in the final to Montreal)—it was the fact that we *wouldn't*. The Cup was ours. We owned it. We'd started this year with a film crew to document our third Cup and this dynasty in the making. The fact that someone else was going to win was the worst feeling in the world.

After the game, the longtime *Edmonton Journal* writer Jim Matheson said that walking into our dressing room was like walking into a funeral. Smith was crushed. But he didn't run away. He sat there at his locker in a daze. We tried to shoo the media out, but one of the most shocking incidents in hockey history had just happened, and for us to think it wasn't what people wanted to hear and read about would have been naïve. Smith sat there for ten minutes and answered questions. "It was human error and I guess I'll have to live with it," he glumly said. "I don't know if I'll ever live this thing down, but I have to keep on living." It was his twenty-third birthday.

The easy, low-lying fruit would be to say that mistake cost us the series, but as a team we didn't react that way. We all felt blame, because we knew that we never should have gotten to the point where one unlucky goal in the third period of game seven would be the difference maker. We felt there were a million other mistakes along the way that led us there. It wasn't all about Steve Smith.

Our mantra always was that we win as a team and we lose as a team. It sounds cliché, but we lived it, and this was the perfect example. There were zero recriminations. I think we all put ourselves in his position and imagined how we would have felt. You could say that in the history of a franchise that is defined by winning, one of our finest moments was in a loss.

It hurt that we weren't going to win the Cup, but we felt that the blame fell on all of us, not just one. When you get to the third period of a game seven, you're already on a slippery slope. It could have been Wayne, or me, or Glenn Anderson, or Jari, or Kevin Lowe, who made what looked like the deciding mistake. As it happened, it was a guy who was new to the team, but nobody cut him down like a tree and counted the rings.

As I've said, mistakes happen. How you handle them determines who you are. Maybe without the empathy we felt, and the collective belief we had in supporting one another, things could have gone from bad to worse.

They didn't.

CHAPTER TEN

REDEMPTION

The essentials of storytelling are pretty simple. You need a good beginning, and you need a good ending. As we saw it, the end of the story about the Oilers that Bob and Terry McKeown and their crew had captured during the 1985–86 season wasn't what anyone had in mind. The narrative arc would show two-time Stanley Cup champions losing, not in the Cup final, not even in the conference final, but in the *division* final. That sounds like a tale about a bunch of underachievers, and not much in sports is worse than being an underachiever. It means you don't care enough to work hard, or your team is dysfunctional and can't get out of its own way. We didn't believe that was our story. We were beaten by a talented Calgary team who had a plan and a coach who made them believe.

There is, however, another essential of storytelling: Everybody loves a comeback. So, when Bob McKeown managed to raise enough money from investors to return for the 1986–87 season and follow us again, extending the scope of the narrative another year, we were excited to have them back. We'd become very comfortable with them and the cameras. They were almost like teammates, and became really good friends. There was something special happening in Edmonton and we wanted to help them capture it. Mostly, we wanted to earn a better ending.

Our season had ended on April 30. It felt like we were standing at the bottom of a steep hill and getting ready to run up it, knowing how long it was going to be before we had a chance to win the Cup back, and what it would take to get there. We were fully aware of the sheer distance ahead, how much effort it would take, and the physical toll it would exact. Before setting off, we needed to lick our wounds and reflect.

But we hardly got a chance. On May 12, while the play-offs were still underway for the four remaining teams, we were knocked off our feet again. *Sports Illustrated* published an article with the following headline.

THE JOYLESS END OF A JOYRIDE

Until Their Ouster from the NHL Playoffs, The Edmonton Oilers Were Flying High— Off the Ice as Well as On

The 2,500-word article detailed an assortment of allegations about the team's collective after-hours misbehavior. It did not paint a flattering picture.

The timing and tenor of the article made it easy to presume that we lost to the Flames because we were more focused on having fun than on winning. Nothing could be further from the truth. We didn't get shortchanged on fun, but it never rose to the level of interfering with our performance. You simply can't have the kind of sustained success that we had without an extraordinary amount of discipline.

There's no question that I had made choices as an eighteen- and nineteen-year-old that affected my play. What kid of that age *doesn't* sometimes do things that are questionable? You've got to make mistakes in order to evolve. It's also important to realize that you have to evolve as a person first, in order to do so professionally. It doesn't work the other way around.

I'm not suggesting that as a twenty-five-year-old, which is how old I was when we lost to the Flames, I had all of life figured out or had achieved anything close to perfection as a person. But I had done a lot of maturing, and I knew a lot about winning. Wayne, Jari, Glenn, and Paul, who were around the same age as me, had each done the same. We knew how to take care of ourselves in order to maximize our performances, and support our team. We'd spent years already learning to arrive at a place where we understood what healthy balance in professional sports looked like. A key piece of that included allowing ourselves to have a good time and reset when the schedule allowed it.

Our start to the 1986–87 season didn't help silence the critics. We opened with a loss to the Flyers, and by December 7, we'd lost 11 of our first 28 games. It was the Oilers' worst start in six years.

Five days later, we were on an east coast trip in an airport terminal when we found out that Dave Semenko had been traded to the Hartford Whalers in exchange for a future third-round draft pick. It was a cold slap in the face, and really hard on all of us, including the fans. He was a protective big brother to me and so many others. Respected by everybody on the team, he was probably the most universally loved guy in the locker room. He had a brilliant, understated sense of humor. We'd seen him at his best and his worst, which is the way it goes with family.

When the Oilers joined the NHL, he was probably the toughest guy in the league, but the job he was doing for us—basically being our resident nuclear deterrent and Wayne's bodyguard—had a shelf life. When you come in as a tough guy, you've got to maintain that reputation. Year after year, young guys come in and challenge you. It can be exhausting. Dave never really loved doing it—he was a gentle, softhearted person at his core—and it put a lot of stress on him.

I can't think of something much more symbolic than all of us together in that big airport terminal, with Dave going one way to his gate, and us going the other way to ours. It was an emotional moment, with a lot of tears from everyone. Did you ever have a really good friend who moved away when you were a kid? Did you see them pack up with their family and disappear from your day-to-day life? It's jarring, and it really hurts. Beyond the memories of our good times, the camaraderie, and the two Cups that Dave had been pivotal in bringing to Edmonton, I couldn't help wondering: *Did my performance have anything to do with this? If we'd played better together as a team, would he have gotten to stay?*

Those are sobering and uncomfortable thoughts, and they're the kinds you have to get used to in the NHL. And yet, as painful as changes can be, they are not only something you have to endure, but something that must be embraced. Teams are living organisms and need to adapt.

Our roster was in flux all season. Before losing Semenko,

we had picked up Reijo Ruotsalainen, a smooth-skating Finish defenseman, along with three other players in a trade with the Rangers. Later, around the trade deadline in March, we would get Kent Nilsson, a forward from Minnesota, who was arguably one of the top five most talented players in the league at the time. We also lost our former captain Lee Fogolin in a trade to Buffalo. That was another incredibly tough moment. Lee was the rock that our entire foundation had been built on—so steady, with such strong character, on and off the ice. He'd taught us about preparation and fitness and loyalty and selflessness; our captain who gave up the "C" to Wayne for the good of the team.

A hockey roster dresses just twenty or so guys. If you switch out four players, you've changed 20 percent of the team that people see on the ice each night. So, while our core was still the same, with all of these trades and changes, our roster as a whole was dramatically different.

That's why, while our 1985 Cup team would later come to be voted the best team in NHL history, I always say that our '87 team was our most resilient. With Reijo and Kent Nilsson eventually added, it also turned out to be our most talented. After our somewhat lackluster start to the season, we righted the ship. When we got to the all-star break in February, we'd lost just 4 of our last 29 games.

Except this year, there *was* no all-star game. Instead, we had Rendez-vous '87: a two-game series to be played in Quebec City between the NHL's best players and the Soviet Union national team. The Cold War was still hanging over everything, so the rivalry with the Soviets hadn't diminished, but there was a more relaxed atmosphere. Mikhail Gorbachev was now the general secretary, and these were the early days of glasnost.

I was honored to be selected for the team, especially considering that unlike a typical all-star game where there were two teams of NHLers playing each other, this time there was just one, so the number of available spots was halved. It's funny, the event was simply an exhibition, but it was one of the most memorable hockey experiences of my life.

It was the middle of February, during Quebec City's annual winter carnival. That's a spectacle even in a normal year, but millions of dollars had been invested to make the Rendez-vous '87 experience exponentially more elaborate. We arrived in Quebec on the heels of a snowstorm, which made the old city like a winter postcard come to life. Along with the snow and the setting, there was this festive sense of collegiality in the air. The restaurants around town were full, and all sorts of dignitaries and celebrities were wandering about, including Pelé and Wilt Chamberlain. There was a parade of floats of NHL teams. The Soviets brought over the Bolshoi Ballet as well as the Red Army Choir and did a concert up by the Parliament Building. It was otherworldly to be there with all the hockey players from both teams and our families—I'd brought my parents and Uncle Vic with me to enjoy the event—shoulder to shoulder, listening to the music in this quaint and historic town. The whole experience was like a party in a snow globe.

In the middle of it was some incredible hockey. The games were beautifully played and supercompetitive, but without the hostility and animosity of the previous Canada Cup.

We had a formidable team, led by Mario Lemieux, Wayne Gretzky, Paul Coffey, and Ray Bourque. But the Soviets matched us in size, strength, and skill. This was the time of the blossoming of one of the greatest lines in hockey history: the famous K-L-M line of Vladimir Krutov, Igor Larionov, and Sergei Makarov. Also on that team were Slava Fetisov and Alexei Kasatonov. Among the five of them, they'd won ten Olympic gold medals, twenty-eight World Championships, and they would later go on to earn five Stanley Cups. They felt that they could match up with us in every way.

Despite the obvious pedigree of our NHL all-stars, we were at a profound disadvantage. We were pulling a bunch of players together from different teams without so much as a practice. We somehow needed to play connected against a team that had played together all year long, that knew where one another were on the ice with blindfolds on. They were like a philharmonic playing a beautiful and complex symphony, and we were jazz artists, jamming. So, against an opponent like that, the result of our two-game Rendez-vous '87 series wasn't at all unacceptable: We split the two games, winning 4–3 in the first, and losing 5–3 in the second. Not the best hockey "Team Canada" ever played, but it was a great experience.

I admired the Soviets' game, and had ever since watching them play in the Summit Series back in 1972. They didn't play traditional up-and-down, stay-in-your-lane, tabletop hockey. They changed positions more and had a strong possession game: They would circle back in the neutral zone to regroup, instead of dumping the puck in. It was more like what we see in soccer than the shot-rebound type of mentality we mostly played in the NHL. Of course, in hockey, the field of play is much smaller, and a puck moves around faster than a soccer ball, so to me it was even more impressive.

I had patterned much of my game after some of their players as I was growing up, and continued to after the '87 series. What kid *hasn't* tried to imitate the big-time players they look up to? I was no different. In fact, eventually in North

America, we incorporated a lot of the Soviet style of hockey into our game. Hockey as we know it now is a blend of the Canadian meat-'n'-potatoes, hard-forecheck approach melded with the puck-possession beauty of the Russian game.

One player I really liked was Valeri Kharlamov. He would take a shot off the wrong foot, shifting his weight to the same side he was shooting from. It's a little less balanced, so harder to get power, but it has the element of surprise. I thought it was genius, and it kinda became my trademark when I was skating down the right side. He was only five feet eight, but he was incredibly fast and it was hard to take your eyes off of him. His own goalie, the great Vladislav Tretiak, said he was like a slalom skier on the ice.

Like the Soviets, I also used a straighter blade that didn't curve until the end—a "toe curve," as it's called—as opposed to the more classic "heel curve" shape in North America where the blade is curved all the way along. It was about feel and personal preference. So much of sporting equipment comes down to feel. Sticks used to come in batches of twelve, and they were all supposed to be made exactly the same, but often there'd only be three in the bunch that I liked and felt just right. If you're really tuned in, you can feel the difference in your equipment. Give Tiger Woods a dozen golf balls that aren't all the same and he can absolutely feel the difference in the compression of the balls. It's the same thing in hockey.

THE OILERS HAD COME INTO the Rendez-vous '87 break on a hot streak, but we emerged from it sluggishly, losing five of our first six games. Things changed after March 2, when we acquired Kent Nilsson from Minnesota. I don't think it was a coincidence. We beat the Canucks 8–5 in his first game with us, during which he teamed up with Paul Coffey for an assist on Wayne's third-period goal. After that win, we got six more in a row.

Kent's nickname was the Magic Man, because the only explanation for what he did on the ice was supernatural. It was incredible the amount of skill the guy had; his skating, stick-handling, shooting, and hockey IQ were all off the charts.

The thing with Kent, though, was that he came with a reputation. He'd always been known as soft, and he gave the impression to some that he didn't really care about the game. Neither of those things was true. The guy took an incredible amount of physical abuse on the ice before he got to Edmonton—he was whacked, hacked, speared, and maimed. As for the charge of laziness, I just think he was so naturally gifted that it seemed at times that he wasn't trying. He was so talented that he made the game look easy. When he came to the Oilers, everything was different. Our style of play suited him perfectly. In Edmonton, he stepped into a situation where everybody felt it was our duty to make one another better. We had our eye on the Cup, and he thrived when he had something to play for. Him coming to the Oilers was like when Kevin Durant left the Oklahoma City Thunder and joined the Golden State Warriors. We already had a great team, now we were gonna add somebody like this?

As a leader, you have to be very careful about buying into labels about people. Kent was not soft, lazy, or uncaring, as he'd been labeled. Kenny Linseman had unfairly gotten a reputation as someone who didn't fit in. Even Paul Coffey, one of the greatest skaters to ever play, had a coach in junior hockey who'd been in the NHL and said Paul was never going to make it because he wasn't a good enough skater. These guys had to change the narrative that had been created about them. I had to do the same when I entered the league as an unconventional draft pick with a limited and not very impressive track record in juniors.

The lesson is: Don't believe what you've heard. Judge for yourself. Be humble about all that you don't know, and have an open mind. You have no idea what the mitigating factors are, the circumstances that have conspired, or how the message has been filtered and through whom.

You don't know what the culture was like on the team someone came from. You don't know if they accepted him, and if they didn't: What was the backstory? It could have been something petty or personal. Somebody else could have felt threatened and had their own agenda to marginalize or ostracize him.

There are a million things that can go on in a team that can hurt or help a person in his own journey. From the outside you really have no idea.

It should be your goal to elevate people. After Kent got to the team, we won thirteen of our last seventeen games, and charged into the playoffs with the best record in the league for the third time in the previous four seasons. We dropped just two games during the playoffs on our way to the doorstep of the Stanley Cup, where we desperately felt we belonged.

The doorstep, though, is still out in the cold. Stepping into the warmth was all that mattered.

We started the final series against the Flyers with a 4–2 win,

When I won the Hart Trophy in 1992, I celebrated with my family. From the left: my brother, Paul, my sister Mary-Kay, me, my mother, my sister Jennifer, my father. As kids, Paul and I spent hours playing hockey together. Here I am (on the right) experimenting with a different position.

Hockey Hall of Fame

Playing pro hockey as a seventeen-year-old for the WHA Cincinnati Stingers, facing off against Wayne Gretzky (above), who would become the greatest player of all time. My dad played a year for the Nottingham Panthers in the UK, where my brother was born in 1958.

Hulton Deutsch/Getty Images

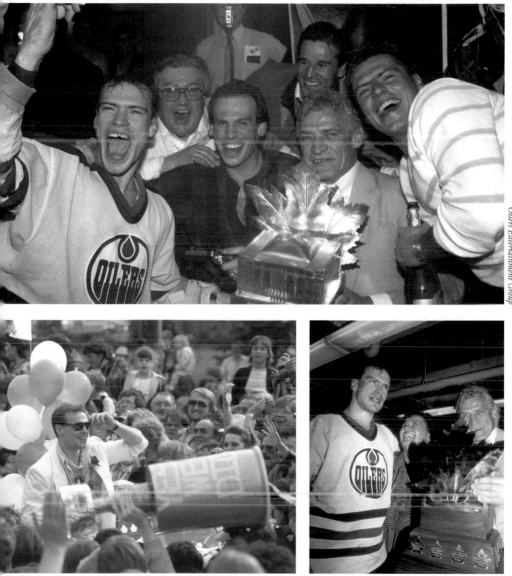

Celebrating the 1984 Cup with family friends (from the left) Jack Reid, Darrell Morrow, and Vince Magnan, and Dad and Paul (top). I also shared a special moment with my mom and dad who were so proud that I'd won the Conn Smythe Trophy (bottom right). I bought this white suit the day before the parade through Edmonton and felt like a rock star.

Nine Oilers players were selected for the 1986 all-star team (plus Glen Sather coaching). From the left: Andy Moog, Wayne Gretzky, Glenn Anderson, Paul Coffey, Kevin Lowe, Glen Sather, me, Lee Fogolin, Jari Kurri, and Grant Fuhr. The Battle of Alberta was tense in the 1980s, and we had a great rivalry with the Calgary Flames. Here, I exchange a few pleasantries with Joel Otto.

Jan Novak/JDN Photography Canada

I loved spending time at the lake during the off-season and water-skiing. It was also a great way to stay conditioned. And I've spent many great moments playing golf around the world with my three best friends: Uncle Vic, Paul, and my dad.

Playing for Team Canada was one of the greatest experiences I ever had,
not only for the pride of representing my country but also for the chance to play with some
of the best in the world. Wayne Gretzky and Mario Lemieux (above left) combined to
score one of the most iconic goals in hockey history (that's Paul Stewart between
them signaling the goal). All of us knew we'd been a part of something special.
Here's Dale Hawerchuk (below) making sure Rick Tocchet stayed hydrated.

Not enough can be said about what The Great One means to the game.
We didn't realize in 1988 that this would be the last Cup we'd raise together.
When Wayne came back to Edmonton, this time in an L.A. Kings jersey, it was
to break Gordie Howe's point record.

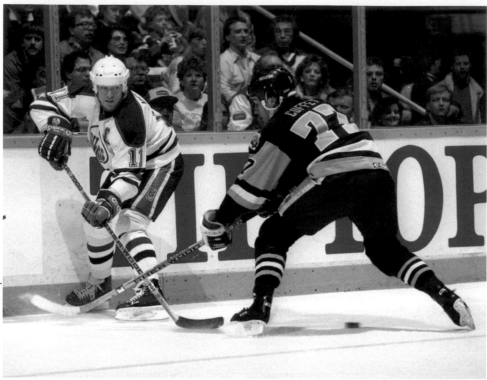

The reality of professional sports is that championship teams rarely stay together. Paul Coffey (above) left Edmonton for Pittsburgh and Marty McSorley (below) joined the Kings along with Wayne. But they remain my brothers.

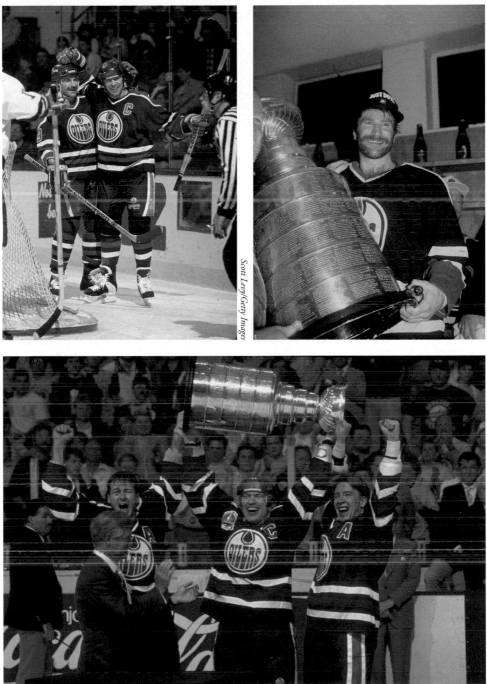

One of the greatest competitors I ever played with was Glenn Anderson. We won six Stanley Cups together with him on my right wing. After trading away the greatest player of all time in 1988, the team struggled to find its footing. But in 1990 we won our fifth Cup in seven years. It was a testament to the character, grit, and determination of the players that remained. Kevin Lowe, me, and Jari Kurri raise the Cup (bottom).

I couldn't wait to get to New York and put on the jersey. Here I am celebrating with two of my favorite teammates of all time, Adam Graves and Brian Leetch.

Brian Winkler/Getty Images

Bruce Bennett/Getty Images

Our team fought hard to beat the New Jersey Devils. Some people say it's bad luck to touch the conference trophy, but I don't believe in bad luck. We worked hard to earn the Prince of Wales Trophy and we wanted to celebrate our achievement.

Ending the fifty-four-year Cup drought in New York was incredible, not only for us but for the great fans of that city. I'll never forget the parade through the Canyon of Heroes.

In the aftermath of 9/11, we paid tribute to the brave first responders who worked tirelessly to save lives. In our first game that season, I was asked to wear a helmet honoring Chief Ray Downey (left). It was one of the most powerful and emotional moments of my career. It seemed fitting that I should retire from pro hockey in New York, the city that had given me so much. Before my last game there, my family was close by. My son Lyon and nieces and nephews joined me at Madison Square Garden (below). My younger children, Douglas and Jacqueline, never got to see me play, but they have been by my side ever since (bottom).

I've watched my banner be raised by two NHL franchises and both times I got to share the moment with my family. It's times like these that make you understand just how many people have been a part of the journey.

Being inducted into the Hockey Hall of Fame was a reminder that no one wins alone. Giving a Hall of Fame speech is not easy. I was filled with gratitude. At an event in Edmonton not long ago, I got to spend some time with Joey Moss. He was a huge part of our Oilers team and has five Cup rings to show for it. When he passed away in 2020, everyone who knew him grieved.

Anyone who ever met my mom always commented on what an amazing woman she was. I can't remember her without a smile on her face. We miss her every day. Christmas is never a dull occasion with this many characters all in one room. And I'm fortunate to have so many great friends. Jimmy Roberts and I had the pleasure of spending a day with Jack Nicklaus on his boat.

Sandra Mayer

and then a 3–2 overtime win in game two, with Jari scoring the definitive goal. After a loss in Philadelphia, we won game four, 4–1, meaning all that was left was the clincher at Northlands Coliseum, where we had the league's best home record.

The Flyers didn't seem to care about that. They got great goaltending from Ron Hextall and came back after being down two goals to win game five. Back across the continent we all went for game six at the Spectrum, and all of a sudden, things got tight.

Coming to Philadelphia, I couldn't help but remember a moment from the finals two years earlier, in 1985. We'd flown in the day before game one, and on the way to practice in a suburb of Philly, our bus broke down. We spent the better part of an hour hanging around in front of somebody's house in Cherry Hill, New Jersey. The people actually couldn't have been nicer. They let a bunch of us use their bathroom. Can you imagine what their neighbors must have been thinking? Thirty young men lounging on a nearby front lawn and occasionally taking turns going into the house. Eventually, our equipment truck showed up and we all piled into the back. The whole thing couldn't have appeared more absurd.

Then, after practice, we went to our hotel only to find out that our reservation had somehow been canceled. The hotel scrambled to make do, but some guys had to sleep on cots that night because there weren't enough rooms available with two beds. The next day, we had to pick up and move to another hotel. All of it was hardly the way you wanted to get ready to play a game of the Stanley Cup final, a game we ended up losing.

Gamesmanship is a big part of professional sports for a

reason: Distraction is a very effective tool. I don't think that Coach Mike Keenan of the Flyers canceled our hotel reservation or got the bus company to screw with us, but he was a great gamesman, and thoughts like that certainly crossed our minds. Either way, it doesn't matter. Whether it's mysterious 3:00 a.m. wake-up calls, or canceled reservations, psychological warfare is a part of the game. You're always looking for an edge, especially during the playoffs. Anything to make a difference, because doing something that causes even a small lapse in the other team's concentration can be the deciding factor in winning the Cup.

Therefore, anytime you can get in the way of your opponents' focus, you try and press your advantage. You're always kind of "working it" in this way.

Practice times were a big opportunity for gamesmanship. Let's say the visiting team would have plans to practice at a certain time. But they'd show up and the ice hadn't been resurfaced and there was a problem with the Zamboni. Or instead of an empty rink, they'd find our team's extra guys skating. You couldn't do that these days, when practice times are protected and league-mandated, but back then there was a lot of room to "loosely interpret" the rules. If a team thought it could give them an advantage, they might choose to interpret them very loosely. Everybody did it. And to be honest, I enjoyed this part of the sport, maybe because of how strongly I believed in the importance of the mental game and not just the physical one.

When we got to the Spectrum ahead of game six in 1987, we learned that the Stanley Cup—which was in the building because it was a potential series-clinching game for us—had been hijacked by Coach Keenan and taken into the Flyers' dressing room. He was working it in every way he could. Of course, we couldn't expect any different, as truth be told, we'd done the same thing to the Islanders back in '83. Similarly, we'd somehow gotten the Cup into our dressing room. I don't think it sat too well with them.

We jumped out to a 2–0 lead in game six, but the Flyers' goalie, Ron Hextall, was extraordinary again. He shut us out for the last forty-five minutes of the game, while the Flyers scored three goals of their own. They were determined. Momentum is an amazing thing, and the Flyers' crowd was blowing the roof off. They beat us 3–2. Which meant, for the first time in fifteen years, there was going to be a Stanley Cup game seven.

The stakes were incredibly high. It was so important to us to prove that what had happened the year before was a blip. To lose game five at home had been really tough. Then to go all the way back to Philly and lose that as well—the pressure was reaching an unbelievable crescendo.

There's such a fine line when the pressure ramps up in a situation like this. Teams can get a little too careful, a little too rigid. And that's the exact opposite of how we needed to play.

There's no better example of this dynamic than golf, which is such a mental game. You can easily lose all the fluidity in your swing and your touch because of the pressure. Hockey's the same, in that the pressure can lead to mistakes on the ice—mental mistakes, not physical ones, which are what the game comes down to at the highest level.

As the famous golf teacher Harvey Penick once said: "Sometimes the answer is to try *less* hard."

We were at our best when we played freewheeling and fast. We'd learned how to be a much better defensive team, but that didn't mean we had to sacrifice the offensive style that made us so dangerous. We couldn't become afraid to lose. We had to play with confidence, to show our self-belief by trusting that if we played in keeping with our identity, it would work out. We needed to relax in order to find that sublime state of execution you reach when you're playing at your highest level.

We didn't find it at the start of game seven—quite the opposite, in fact. We were called for two penalties in quick succession and, just 1:41 into the game, Murray Craven scored to put the Flyers ahead.

Talk about skating on thin ice. We'd won two straight Cups. We'd been on the way to a three-peat dynasty and felt comfortable enough to invite a film crew into our inner sanctum to document the journey. We then got derailed by our bitter rivals in Calgary. Now, we'd made it all the way back to the finals again, with the film crew in tow once more. We'd gone up three games to one, and yet here we were, in game seven, behind.

This could have gone two different ways. We had the opportunity to win and show that the previous year was an aberration; or we could have lost, ingloriously, and been the worst possible thing in sports: underachievers. We'd won two Cups, but we knew we were capable of more than that.

Thankfully, as high as the stakes were, we had enough experience and talent that we didn't panic. We felt deep down that we had the better team. We scored a few more goals to take the lead, but just as important, we shut the Flyers out for the final fifty-eight minutes of the game. We had truly grown. We won our third Cup by becoming a multidimensional team, matching our offensive skill with tighter, more connected defense.

We'd completed the comeback. And we'd done it all on film. Now *The Boys on the Bus* had its satisfying ending.

Hockey is a sport with a lot of tradition, and part of that is a pretty much inviolable pecking order. It's all about seniority. It's the ecosystem that keeps things in order on a team. When a team wins the Cup, it's just the way that it's done that the commissioner first presents the trophy to the captain. The captain takes a turn around the ice, then passes the Cup to the most senior team member, and so on. When Colorado won in 2001, the first person the captain, Joe Sakic, gave the Cup to was Ray Bourque. Even though Bourque had been on the Avalanche for only two seasons, he'd played twenty years with the Bruins before that, and it was his first Cup. He was undeniably the most senior member of the team.

After we won game seven at Northlands, the NHL commissioner, John Ziegler, came out onto the ice to present the Cup. He gave it to Wayne, who skated around to the roars of the Oilers' home crowd. And then Wayne came back to the gathered team and passed the ninety-five-year-old trophy to a twenty-four-year-old who was only in his second year in the league. When he lifted the Cup above his head, the noise in the stadium was astounding.

A year after having the worst night of his life, Steve Smith was hearing something he never thought would happen in Edmonton again: cheering. For him.

It was a chilling moment that resonated with everyone, because who among us hasn't failed, and how powerful is it to see that kind of redemption?

You need a lot of self-belief to move on from something like what happened to him the year before, when he scored the own goal. It could have ruined him. Unless of course you just don't give a shit—then you just brush it off. But that wasn't Steve. He was invested. And he'd been carrying a heavy burden.

Thirty years later, he looked back on that terrible moment as a blessing.

"I teach my kids on a daily basis about humility," he told ABC News. "I really believe that incident had a lot to do with making me a much humbler person. From that day forward, I cheered for people. I didn't want to see people fail. I didn't want to ever see people have that type of day."

AFTER A YEAR OF CHALLENGES and changes, we'd accomplished our goal. The *Sports Illustrated* article was a distant memory. In the end, I think it was just another log on the fire to fuel our comeback. And instead of the 1986 Stanley Cup being how *The Boys on the Bus* came to a close, it became the story's emotional fulcrum.

Looking back on it now, *The Boys on the Bus* has become something of a cult movie. My son Douglas, named of course for my father, is eighteen now, and he started watching it a few years ago.

When Tiger Woods came back to win the Masters in 2019 after not having claimed a major championship in eleven years, he was uncharacteristically emotional, he said, because his kids were finally able to be there and watch him do what they'd only read about or seen on the Internet. Mario Lemieux said he came back after he'd had cancer, in part, so his son could watch him play. Being able to share those experiences with your family is a very powerful thing for an athlete.

I am lucky that my son Lyon was there to see some of my playing days, but Douglas and Jacqueline weren't old enough. It's amazing how they can relive the experience thanks to all the footage out there. They've basically been able to experience my playing days through YouTube.

That's not always a good thing. Sometimes Douglas will flip open his laptop and show me clips of me playing, and especially if it's the big hits and fights, I'll kinda cringe and say: "Aw, well— It was a different time back then." His response: "Dad, you'd be in jail now."

But then we talk about what it was like then, and how things have changed. That's how kids really learn, from this kind of open dialogue around the kitchen table, about the successes as well as the mistakes. I'd like to think the mistakes I made and lessons I've learned have made me more empathetic, tolerant, and compassionate, especially toward my kids. I can try to help them without shoving a bunch of moral-high-ground stuff down their throats about what they have to be, what they should be. I've always told them they can't do anything or tell me anything that is going to shock me, because I've been there, I've done it, I've seen it, so there's no point in trying to hide it. Let's just get it out on the table and talk about it. That's how you become a good teammate and person, no matter what the context. It's the way that I learned from my own father, and that's how I've taught my children.

CHAPTER ELEVEN

A CHANGING TEAM

I played hockey because I loved the game, being part of something with friends, and competing. But at a certain point, for any professional athlete, money comes into the equation. Contracts have to be negotiated, and when you've had success, you want it to be recognized. In the late summer of 1987, I was about to start my tenth season as a pro, and was staring down the barrel of my twenty-seventh birthday. I wasn't a kid anymore—I understood better my value as a player, and the business of pro hockey—and that changed things. The same was true for Glenn Anderson and Paul Coffey.

In March 1984, I'd signed a five-year contract that took me from $50,000 to $300,000 a year. So in 1987, there were two years still remaining on it. But Glen Sather's words were ringing in my ears. From the time I was drafted, he told us: "Win a Stanley Cup, and you'll get paid." Winning would take care of everything. I'd signed that contract when we had yet to accomplish anything other than make people talk about what might be ahead. During the term of the deal so far, though, we'd won three Stanley Cups and become the most dominant team in the game.

It soon became clear that it wasn't that simple, win and get paid. I decided to renegotiate my contract, and my dad supported me completely. He always told me what I needed to hear, not what I wanted to, and he never tried to dissuade me. I needed to get away mentally and physically while he negotiated with Sather, and also get into shape for the season, so I'd be ready to come back into camp as soon as a deal was struck. I took off to visit and train with my brother, Paul, in Mannheim, as I had done before in the summer. It was an unforgettable time.

Paul's coach was an old Czech player named Ladislav Olejnik. He carried around a bible of skills he used to guide the team through a high-tempo skate each morning that went for about ninety minutes. Then, after a light meal and some rest, we went over to the track. We did sprints—100s and 220s—and took long runs in teams of five, where each person would take turns running from the rear and then surging to the front to set the pace. Sometimes we'd go down by the river and run in gravel that was a foot and a half deep. God, it made your thighs burn!

In the afternoons we did circuit training in the gym and played soccer, which was not only great for conditioning but footwork, too. The day ended back on the ice with an inter-squad game at 6:00 p.m.

The approach was one of total immersion, much like the way the Russians trained. On the physical side, it got me into extraordinary shape. On the mental side, Germany was the perfect place to go to exercise my wanderlust and get away from the pressures of holding out from camp. Sather was calling all the time, but I never talked to him. That was Doug's job. Besides, I wasn't easy to get hold of in Europe.

One night I was out at a club in Mannheim with Paul and some of his teammates, and some of the guys were talking about how Ibiza, Spain, was an incredible place, the party capital of the world. It sounded convincing enough to me. When night became morning, some friends and I went right from the club to the airport and hopped an early-morning flight to the Mediterranean beach island eight hundred miles away. All I had with me was my credit card. I stayed for four days, bought a pair of shorts, rented a motorcycle, and toured around. It was great, though that first day back in Mannheim picking back up with Olejnik's immersive training didn't feel very good.

But the training paid off when, late that summer, I was again honored to join Team Canada for the 1987 Canada Cup, along with my teammates Glenn Anderson, Paul Coffey, Grant Fuhr, and, of course, Wayne. But it was a totally different experience from that 1984 team. This year, for the first time, the world got to see Wayne Gretzky and Mario Lemieux—arguably the world's two greatest goal scorers—play together on the same line. Though we tied a couple of games, we didn't lose any, and won the Cup, beating the Soviets in the final. And Wayne and Mario? They were the number one and two point leaders, respectively, of the series.

Throughout this time, Doug and Glen Sather continued negotiating, but new contracts weren't being proposed by the organization. Our two newest European players, who had made such a difference in the 1986–87 championship season, Kent Nilsson and Reijo Ruotsalainen, pulled the rip cord before the start of the new season and went to play in Europe. Glenn, Paul, and myself, on the other hand, had no interest in leaving the Oilers. But we did think that we were worth more than we were currently being paid. So we held out for new deals, and didn't go to training camp. In a time before free agency, it was the only leverage that we had. Waiting two years for my contract to expire wouldn't have changed anything—I still would have needed to hold out for a trade or new contract if I wasn't happy with the deal I was offered.

Speaking for myself, I knew that if I didn't believe I was getting paid fairly, I wouldn't have been able to give 100 percent. There were so many people invested in the Oilers' fortunes: my teammates, the organization, the fans, the community. How could I have come back unless I was totally committed? Don't get me wrong, it wouldn't have been willful withholding, but I was aware deep down that if I was harboring resentment toward the organization, I wouldn't be able to play with everything I had. I know that there are people who say that shouldn't be an issue, that the two factors of money and performance aren't tied together, but I don't believe that's honest. Whether you're a professional athlete or not, as an employee you always need to feel you're being fairly valued.

That didn't make holding out any easier. A lot of emotions were going through me. I wanted to be there in camp because it was fun to be with my friends, especially after we'd just won a championship. Add in that I felt like a little bit of a sellout personally, making so much drama over money. It got even harder after Glenn, whatever his reasons, eventually decided to come to camp, while Paul and I did not. Paul was making the same $300,000 salary as I was.

It was a truly uncomfortable time. One newspaper writer said we were asking for new salaries somewhere between the levels of "rock stars and oil sheiks." But when it comes down to it, that's the way the business was done back then, and I felt it was what I had to do. You have to make decisions based on what's best for you, and then you have to live with the consequences, right or wrong. And our teammates understood completely. There was no animosity whatsoever.

Eventually, Dad hammered out an agreement for a new six-year deal for me with the Oilers, literally on the day the regular season started. The start of the season was more of a hard deadline for me than training camp, and I was glad to have it sorted. And I was back in uniform just in time to see the 1987 Stanley Cup banner raised to the rafters before our season opener against the Red Wings. I had a first-period power-play goal on an assist from Wayne and Jari, but we lost 4–1. Paul hadn't been able to strike a new deal yet, and he was still holding out. We felt his absence right out of the gate. Only once in the previous twenty-six games had we scored just a single goal.

A lot of people will tell you that Bobby Orr was the greatest defenseman of all time. It's hard to argue. He won the Norris Trophy as the league's best defenseman eight times. He did it mostly because of his unprecedented offensive production. In 1974–75, he scored forty-six goals. It was the third time he had broken his own record for scoring by a defenseman. The last time anyone other than Orr had held the record was Red Kelly in 1960 with twenty. As an offensive-minded defenseman, Orr was peerless.

Defense is the hardest position to play because so much of it has to do with positioning. Defensemen need to have an extreme amount of discipline not to overcommit and open up holes that the other team's offensive players can exploit. Defense also takes an incredible amount of awareness on the ice in order to read the play, which typically has to be built up over years of experience. That's why Scott Stevens, the Hall of Fame defenseman who won three Cups with the New Jersey Devils, said you shouldn't even start to assess a defenseman until he's played more than 250 games in the NHL, because that's how long it takes to understand the nuances of the position. That's also why it was no surprise, and was of no concern, that it took Paul a while to get his footing.

But when he did, and adopted the offensive-minded playing style inspired by Bobby Orr, he became an almost unstoppable force. In his fifth full season, 1984–85, he won his first Norris Trophy. The next season, he not only won the Norris again, but did the unthinkable by breaking Orr's single-season goal-scoring record, netting 48 goals and racking up 138 points.

He was breathtaking to watch. He skated out of our end with the power of a 747 taking off, making everyone else around him look like they were going in slow motion. He set things up for our offense. He could skate it down the ice on his own, or he could make a hundred-foot pass and put it flat on Wayne's stick. That dynamic Paul created with Wayne in particular just wasn't fair to opponents. So often, those long passes up to Wayne would create odd-man rushes, with Jari Kurri waiting on the other wing with his lethal slap shot at the ready.

Paul was so particular about his craft. When we first came up, he insisted on having new laces for his skates every game. That was a little extravagant for those days, so our trainer Barrie Stafford would take the laces out of his skates each night, wash them and iron them, and then put them into an empty package as if they were new.

Paul and Barrie grew to be extremely close. Once, Paul accused Barrie of not doing enough to get him sticks the way he preferred them. They had an angry confrontation which ended with Barrie pushing Paul up against the wall before Lee Fogolin broke it up. You teach people how to treat you, and Barrie must have felt that Paul had crossed a line. Like brothers, they reconciled easily and continued on as friends. There was no caste system on our team. The culture was that everybody was important, whether you scored 45 goals a season, or were the support person who worked to allow someone to do so.

Paul was still holding out eleven games into the season, and we had won six and lost five of those: not a good start for the defending champions. We were clearly missing something without him. But both sides were still digging in their heels.

Paul was asking for a nearly half-million-dollar raise from his $300,000 annual salary. Glen Sather told Jim Matheson of the *Edmonton Journal*: "Gus [Paul's agent] has a ridiculous demand in mind and I told him so. He's sticking to it. I guess sooner or later I'll have to make up my mind whether to trade Paul or sit any longer. If there is no compromise, I'll have to trade him. He's under the impression that you can't trade a player as good as Paul—but you can. You're never going to replace him, but you might replace three or four positions and that'll make us stronger."

Ultimately, players in that kind of circumstance have to decide which fork in the road they're going to take. Every player has to make the best decision for themselves.

The impasse between Paul and the Oilers dragged on into November. In the end, the thing seemed to come down to more of a personality issue between Paul and Glen, not a hockey issue, and that was kind of a wake-up call. When Paul made the decision to request a trade because he wasn't getting along with Glen, it was a huge blow to our team. Finally, on November 24, the forty-seventh day of the season, with our record at a middling twelve wins, seven losses, and two ties, Paul was traded to Pittsburgh.

I hated to see another great friend go, like with Dave Semenko the year before. And I worried about what it would do to the team. At the same time, I respected his decision, as did the rest of the guys. We were seasoned enough to recognize that nothing lasts forever. It wasn't realistic that the Oilers could keep all of us core players together and happy until the end of our careers. We all realized that everybody needed to do what was best for themselves.

PAUL HAD BEEN SUCH A huge part of our success, but great and successful organizations aren't only about stars. On a team like ours, there were a lot of bright lights, and so there were a lot of shadows. Sometimes those who live in the shadows throw off more candlepower than you would ever think. Everybody has value and should be made to feel that way. That was one of our fundamental tenets, and we all bought into it completely. We believed that if you've built the right culture—a culture of inclusion—then an important contribution could just as likely come from a guy who says he's keeping his fingers crossed to hang on with the team as from one of the stars.

There was a defenseman on our first two Cup teams named Don Jackson. He'd played college hockey at Notre Dame and then hung on with Minnesota for a few years before he got to us. He liked to say he considered himself the twentieth man on our roster.

Nobody treated him that way. When he got to town, Wayne had him over for dinner, and Paul got him out of the hotel where he was living and invited him to come stay in his apartment. He later told people we made him feel important. He was.

His attitude influenced others. He was just remarkably positive and believed in what we were about. He was funny, fun to be around, and added a lot to the dressing room.

When we got to our second straight finals against the Islanders in 1984, after they'd swept us the year before, we were maybe a little tight. You would have expected the most important locker room talk would have come from Wayne or one of the assistant captains or any one of a handful of other guys who were most familiar to fans.

Instead Jackson, seventeenth on the team in scoring, sixth among defensemen, stood up.

"A bear and a rabbit are taking a shit in the woods," he said, completely straight-faced. "The bear turns to the rabbit and says, excuse me, do you have a problem with shit sticking to your fur? And the rabbit says no. So the bear wipes his ass with the rabbit."

The joke was profane and silly and exactly what we needed: something to remind us that at our core we functioned best when we had a smile on our faces.

Everybody has to lead, whether it's from in front or from behind. That only happens when people feel valued. A good culture is a circle, not a pyramid—it eliminates hierarchy. That's one of the reasons that when I was playing, a rookie always roomed with a veteran in training camp. It was a way to help kids understand what professionalism was all about. It also worked to solidify team unity and hedge against cliques forming. If you're a veteran and you're headed out to dinner with your buddies, you're not going to leave your roommate behind. Instantly, the new guy is part of the circle. And it meant that when a new or young player came on, no matter who they turned to, they'd hear the same gospel.

Our culture of inclusion extended beyond the players. When we talked about the "organization," it was not a word we used casually. When we won our first championship, it was a point of pride for us to see our training staff—Barrie Stafford, Peter Millar, and Sparky Kulchisky—get their rings. Those rings are important because, unlike the Stanley Cup, you get to take them with you. Some people wear them every day to remember what it took to earn them. Some people display them in their homes so loved ones and friends can get a glimpse.

Barrie Stafford had been a hockey player at the University of Alberta, and then became a trainer because he loved the game so much. "You're a kid who grows up playing this game," he said, "and then they give you that little blue box and it's *my* ring. I just can't describe what it meant to me. The stuff of dreams."

Because they had more than just sentimental value, we all had our rings appraised for insurance. They came in at around $18,000 to $20,000 each. The trainers' rings, though, came back at one-tenth of that.

It turned out that instead of a diamond, their rings had cubic zirconia. All three were upset, but not wanting to seem ungrateful, said nothing. Wayne noticed something was wrong with Sparky, though, and when he finally got it out of him, he was irate.

Wayne took the three rings, and without telling anyone about it, paid to have the zirconia replaced with real diamonds. It wasn't about the value of jewelry. It was a statement about the value of team members. A mistake corrected.

I say this all the time: Culture is your beacon, your lighthouse by which to navigate your way home. There's no better example than the New England Patriots in the NFL. They've always had a culture that's all about the team over the individual. You either grab an oar and row, or you get off the boat. If anybody doesn't want to play that way, they just replace them with someone else. That's the kind of culture that can maintain success even while withstanding huge change. They won their first Super Bowl in 2002. Two years later, they won again, but with a roster that contained only 42 percent of the same players, and only half the same starters.

In our league, although talent is important, it's not sufficient on its own. Winning is about how well things work collectively. Everyone matters. Everyone.

WITH ALL OF THE CHANGE going on around us once again, we had to rely on our culture a great deal during the 1987–88 regular season. On top of the training-camp holdouts and the Paul Coffey trade, Wayne missed the entire month of January with a knee injury. For the first time in his NHL career, he didn't at least tie for the scoring title or win the MVP—though he still led the league in assists, with 109.

Glenn Anderson and I were still skating together on the second line, but now Craig Simpson—who had come over to us from Pittsburgh in the trade—replaced Kent Nilsson on the left wing. He was the primary asset we had received in exchange for Paul. He had been the second overall pick in the draft two years earlier, and he was only twenty years old. As talented as Nilsson had been, Simpson made us just as dangerous, or perhaps even more so.

In hockey, it takes *three* to tango because choreography is everything. Glenn, Craig, and I each brought a different step to the dance floor. A traditional centerman needs to be a pretty good skater. You have to play the full 200 feet of ice. You've got to get in on the forecheck and then get back and help your defensemen at the other end. It's a little bit like a midfielder in soccer, where you're playing both sides of the field. For whatever other talents I had, the core thing was that I thought I could move the puck effectively.

Glenn, on the right wing, was a driver with his own style. In most cases, if you're making a move to the net from the wing, the defenseman cuts you off and forces you to the outside. Most players then go behind the net and try and come out the other side and make a pass. I hardly ever remember Glenn doing that. He was taking the puck to the crease every time, a little bit like Rocket Richard. It didn't matter with Glenn if the defenseman had a step on him—he was going to the crease, incredibly strong and fearless, and he created opportunities as a result.

Craig, on the left wing, was a big guy with soft hands. He could shoot, and he used his size and strength to get in front of the net from the other side of Glenn. Of his fifty-six goals that year, I'm guessing forty of them came from within five feet of the net.

For the first time in seven years, we didn't win our division or finish the regular season with at least a hundred points. That was fine. There had been changes and injuries to deal with, and by this point in our careers we understood that winning the Smythe Division or the Presidents' Trophy had value, but not at the expense of losing steam going into the playoffs. Nobody was throwing you a parade for winning your division.

History is your best teacher. We had a great example of a team that won four Stanley Cups in four years in the Islanders.

You think by the third or fourth Cup they were as concerned with the standings? Or if Trottier or Bossy were winning the scoring title? Sure, it would have been great, and finishing on top has advantages, but that wasn't the primary focus of that Islanders team, and it wasn't ours, either, at this point.

So, despite the challenges of the regular season, we entered the playoffs confident, and rolled to the final, dropping fewer games on the way than we ever had before. We beat Winnipeg in a quick series, four games to one, then swept Calgary, and then took down Detroit four games to one. Then we won our first three games in the final against the Boston Bruins, at which point things got strange.

May 24 in Boston was an unusually hot day, and the old Boston Garden was struggling to maintain equilibrium for game four. Temperatures inside the building rose above 80 degrees and the warm air caused loping clouds of fog to settle on the ice. There was nothing to be done but try to play through them.

Glenn scored off the opening face-off ten seconds into the game, for the quickest goal in Stanley Cup playoff history. We added another score on a power play late in the first period to go up 2–0. But the game had to be stopped periodically so that all forty players could get out and skate around the ice to try to clear away the fog.

The Bruins hung in. They scored one goal near the end of the first period, and eventually took the lead midway through the next period on Glen Wesley's two consecutive goals, the second of which was assisted by our old teammate Kenny Linseman. Craig Simpson scored to tie it back up. And then the lights went out.

Literally.

A 4,000-volt switch overloaded on a transformer outside,

which tripped another switch, which in turn shut down the power in the building.

With the score tied 3–3, the game got canceled and it was decided we would just resume the series back in Edmonton two nights later with game *five*. If there was a need for the series to go the distance, game four would be replayed after game seven.

Huh?

Needless to say, none of us had ever been through anything like this before. A canceled game—or a kinda canceled game—in the finals, no less!

There were a lot of rumors going around. Who knows what really happened, if someone *flipped* the transformer. It is absolutely possible, especially back in those days, when security wasn't what it is now. God, anybody could have gone back there and just pulled a lever.

It might seem unbelievable, but for us it just seemed like another adventure. We were rolling with the punches. We were gonna take our stuff off and get back on that plane. The way we looked at it was: *So what? Now we get to go and win it on our home ice.*

And that's exactly what we did. Two nights later, we swept to our fourth Cup in five years.

There were six new players on our team that year. Watching them experience the realization of everything we'd talked about all year made it seem like the first time all over again, for all of us.

A lot of teams don't want to talk about winning the Stanley Cup—maybe they think it'll somehow be a jinx. But if you don't expect to win, if you don't talk about it, what message are you sending your team?

If that's your perspective, you're cultivating the wrong message, and missing out on an opportunity to shape the vision in a positive direction. There needs to be a galvanizing goal to unify the team from the very start of the season. When personal agendas are put aside and everyone works collectively, there's a palpable energy in the locker room and on the bench—a winning attitude.

Superstitions are silly. Part of our Oilers culture was to be open about our ambitions, and tell the new guys what it would be like to win. We would talk about how great it was to skate around the ice with the Cup over your head; to roll through the ticker-tape parade on top of a float. That's the kind of visualization and motivation that builds the fire every day.

When teams don't talk about it, it's because they don't want to put themselves in a position where anything less than a championship is seen as failure. I think they should see it the opposite way. Concentrate on the positive. Have big goals, and let them drive you.

We'd come such a long way from that confident 1983 squad of limitless potential who had gotten swept by the Islanders in our first Stanley Cup final, but as I skated around the ice at Northlands with the Cup over my head for a fourth time, I was thinking about that team specifically. Not about the ways that we were different, but the ways we were the same.

The common thread was the four Cs: commitment, chemistry, culture, and character.

One of our trainers, Sparky Kulchisky, liked to say it was actually the three Ds: desire, dedication, and Drambuie.

We could laugh now and joke about it all we wanted. We'd navigated an injury that took the best player in the universe out for a chunk of the season. We'd survived key roster changes, even giving up a core player who some would tell you was the best defenseman of all time. And yet we'd had our most decisive playoff run ever to the Cup. We were on top of the world. What could possibly change something this good?

CHAPTER TWELVE

THE TRADE

We can probably all look back on an eventful period in our lives and shake our heads in wonder. Maybe it was challenging or turbulent. Maybe it had moments of pure joy or sudden despair. Any of those would make for a memorable time. The process of winning a Stanley Cup is all of that and more. But what followed that Cup win in the spring of 1988 was a relentlessly wild ride.

I won't say our fourth Stanley Cup was better than any of the previous three, but it filled me differently. In a way, it was more satisfying. I had a better understanding of how hard the road is, how many potholes there can be, and how easy it is to drive off the right path. I was struck with a powerful sense of gratitude as a result. In a team sport, you have to rely on so many people, you're at the mercy of so many lucky or unlucky breaks—it's amazing when it all goes right. You can't do it alone.

At the same time, heading into the summer of 1988, we were all looking forward to some much-needed rest. Four Cups in five years. And five finals in six years. That's a lot of intense hockey—something like 550 games. Win or lose, playoffs are totally exhausting, physically and emotionally. And no matter how good you are, no matter how skilled your team is, it's always a fight when you're playing against world-class competition, and a lot can still go wrong. We'd been very fortunate that in this period a lot had gone right.

Many of us on that Oilers team, players and staff, had been together for ten years. At the beginning, it was all about our team and winning a Stanley Cup. The goal never changed, but we all did—that's inevitable. We were growing up. I think that was also true for Wayne.

By this time, Wayne's world had opened up. He wasn't the small-town kid from Brantford anymore. In July he got married to the actress Janet Jones. The wedding was great—in every sense—but the lead-up almost killed us. We were still recovering from the championship, and it was all we could do to rally and make it there. There's no way to describe the magnitude of the wedding other than to say it might have been literally the biggest thing to have ever happened in Edmonton. It was the story of the year.

Both newspapers in town did full-page wedding *previews*. On the day, tens of thousands of people lined the streets outside the church, behind police barricades, hoping to get a look at what had been described as Canada's royal wedding. There were seven hundred guests and the Edmonton Symphony Orchestra played. The ceremony was broadcast live across the country. I was one of eight groomsmen.

With all the dazzle of the wedding, very few were aware that people had been getting in Wayne's ear about potentially leaving the Oilers, saying it might be time to go somewhere else. I heard rumblings about this but no real details, and didn't put much stock in them.

The fact was, they were true, and the wheels had been turning for weeks.

Wayne would later explain to me that the morning after we won the Cup in late May, he got a call from Nelson Skalbania, a mover and shaker in the hockey and business worlds of western Canada. He had been the owner of the WHA's Indianapolis Racers, which signed Wayne to his first-ever professional hockey contract when he was seventeen. It was 6:30 in the morning when Wayne got the call, and he hadn't even gone to bed yet. Over bacon and eggs with his parents and fiancée, Wayne listened as Skalbania explained he was trying to put together a plan to get Wayne traded to the Vancouver Canucks—and give him 25 percent ownership of the team.

As Wayne says, it all just snowballed from there. This meeting was happening at a point when I think the routine in Edmonton was starting to get a little stale for Wayne, and tensions between him and Glen Sather—just the typical kinds of things that can happen between a player and his coach, who was also the general manager—seemed to be coming to a head. For the next six weeks, Wayne was on a roller-coaster ride, with different teams coming into the picture, and him not knowing who he was going to be playing for. On August 9, Wayne's wedding became the *second*-biggest story of the year when it was announced that the Oilers had traded him to the Los Angeles Kings.

When I had first heard the rumors that summer that he might be dealt, I remember I was lying in bed and thinking, *How could this even be possible?* He's twenty-seven, at the peak of his career, and coming off four Stanley Cups. It would have been like the Bulls trading Michael Jordan—it was just unthinkable. I didn't believe it could happen. So it truly was a total shock to me when it did. I was playing golf at Edmonton Country Club with some buddies on that day in early August when the trade was announced. We'd stopped after nine holes and were standing at the halfway house, having a beer. The television was on and in came the special report. It had actually happened, Wayne was gone.

Time has a way of killing deals, and I think in this case everybody involved knew that, so it all happened very fast. The Oilers had proposed a contract extension but Wayne hadn't signed it. The Oilers were a small-market team and both Wayne and the team owner, Peter Pocklington, knew the club couldn't afford to give him the money he could earn elsewhere for a long-term deal. But the team still owned his rights, so in a preemptive move, Pocklington started looking around to see what he could get in exchange for Wayne in a trade. It wasn't just Skalbania trying to lure Wayne away, either. Wayne later said the Rangers and the Red Wings had made offers to the Oilers, but his father convinced him L.A. was the best situation.

Pocklington arranged a deal that sent Wayne to the Kings along with Mike Krushelnyski and Marty McSorley, in exchange for $15 million in cash, three future first-round draft picks, and two top-shelf young players, Martin Gélinas and Jimmy Carson. A year earlier as a rookie, Carson had scored 55 goals. The only other teenager to have ever accounted for more than 50 had been Wayne.

When I got back from the golf course that afternoon, I called Wayne. He said he was disappointed he wasn't going to be part of what the Oilers would do next, but he just had to move on. He could've signed the extension and stayed in

Edmonton another two years. Some people thought that might have been the right thing to do. But that's not really fair.

Wayne wanted to see what was out there. He was the best player in the game and deserved to be paid like it. Ask yourself what you would have done. Chosen a path that was best for you, your family, and your career, or chosen what was best for others? I certainly couldn't blame him for the one he took. Anybody who thought Wayne was selfish just didn't know him. He felt so guilty for leaving, and indebted to the team and the city of Edmonton. He died a thousand deaths because of what he was leaving behind: the fans, the organization, his teammates, the training staff, Joey Moss. It tore him apart.

That emotion was clear the next day at the press conference announcing the deal. Wayne spoke to a bank of microphones, a field of reporters, and a live television audience before he broke down in tears. The last thing he said was, "I promised Mess I wouldn't do this."

Shock enveloped the city, the country, and the world of sports. Three weeks after his wedding, Wayne was back on the front page of the *Edmonton Sun* along with another twenty-one pages covering his departure. Nobody could imagine it would end for him in Edmonton this way. A trade in his absolute prime? Jim Matheson of the *Edmonton Journal* once said, "It was like selling the Mona Lisa."

When Babe Ruth was sold by the Red Sox to the Yankees in 1919, he was a developing talent who'd hit only forty-nine home runs in five seasons. And we've all seen countless examples of superstars who get traded at the end of their career to a big market to chase one more championship or extend their career. This wasn't any of that. The Kings were getting the sport's biggest superstar in his prime. There had never been a trade like it.

Out on the plains of Canada, in the league's third-smallest market, Wayne was doing things for an expansion franchise that nobody anywhere had ever done. How could anyone be more essential than that?

The *Edmonton Sun* columnist Graham Hicks wrote: "He was our best reason for living here."

But I think most people in town supported Wayne. He was revered. Sometimes when a star player leaves a team, he's vilified. When LeBron James left Cleveland, some fans burned his jersey. There was hardly any of that. People were sad more than anything.

As for the players, we were mad: not at Wayne, but at the organization. To put it bluntly, we felt betrayed. How could they do this to a brother, to Wayne of all people? There was a lot of emotion to deal with, but in the end, it's a fact of life for professional athletes. We all had to accept that it's a business, and we were not in control.

The trade was going to have an enormous impact on our professional lives, but mostly we were thinking about our friend, hoping he'd made the right choice. We wanted him to be happy. The reality soon set in, though. Wayne had been traded within our division and that was really going to change the landscape. It would be incredibly hard to play against him not only physically, but emotionally. Instantly, the L.A. Kings became a team we were going to have to go through to keep winning.

ONE MONTH TO THE DAY after the trade was announced, we opened training camp. The numbness we all felt had faded and we started to focus on the future.

We weren't the only ones thinking about this. There'd been

whispers that we were "nothing" without Wayne. We were the defending champions going into the 1988–89 season, but nobody considered us a threat. True, we were clearly not the same team without him, but we were still very good. That speculation became an incentive for the team. As shocked as we were about the trade, and as pissed as we were at the Oilers management, we knew that we had to let it go. We had a responsibility to win, for one another, for the fans, and for the organization.

We still had the bulk of our core intact—Kevin, Glenn, Jari, Grant, and others. These guys understood that the worst thing an athlete can be is comfortable. We certainly wouldn't allow ourselves to slip into the mindset of being satisfied with our past performance, given the circumstances. We would keep finding that perpetual edge that never dulls. We adopted the mentality that we were setting off on a run to another Cup. We still had three of the top thirteen scorers in the league—Jari, myself, and now Jimmy Carson—and to add to that, we had added an enormous chip on our shoulders.

There was another unanswered question for fans: Who would be the new captain? When Lee Fogolin had stepped aside and given the captaincy to Wayne, it was because as a leader he recognized it was Wayne's time, and what the team needed. This was different. I was named the new captain, and the void that I had to try to fill was massive.

I was lucky, though: I wasn't in it alone. Our team culture was well established, and our roster was full of experienced veterans who were not only tremendous hockey players, but knew how to support a captain, and help lead the team. I think that speaks volumes about what we had created. You don't have to have a "C" on your sweater to be a leader.

We didn't have a game on the day the season opened, so

some guys came over to my place to watch opening night. The Red Wings were playing the Kings in L.A., and we were all curious to see Wayne trot out there in a Kings uniform for the first time. It was a little tough to watch. He did his thing and no one was surprised. L.A. won 8–2. Wayne had a goal and three assists.

The Kings had finished fourth in the Smythe the year before, thirty-one points behind us. It was safe to assume we could expect something different this season. L.A. got off to a hot start, but then won just one of their last nine games going into the all-star break in—where else—Edmonton. (The Oilers didn't fare much better over that nine-game stretch, winning only three of our last nine, leaving us with a middling twenty-seven total wins to the Kings' twenty-eight.) Wayne and Janet came into town with their newborn, Paulina—my goddaughter—who was just shy of two months old.

It was like old times. When he'd been traded away six months earlier, people were saying it was a rough summer in Edmonton: It was "minus 99." Now, at the all-star game, they welcomed Wayne back with signs all over the arena. The equipment guys put him in his old locker. He even skated with his longtime line mate Jari Kurri. But, as if to remind people not to get too sentimental, his other winger was his current L.A. line mate Luc Robitaille.

Before puck drop, the fans of Northlands Coliseum held up the player introductions for a full minute, cheering his return. In true Gretzky fashion, he gave them exactly what they were hoping to see: a home victory, with him in a starring role. Although Wayne was skating for the Campbell Conference all-star team, it must have felt to the fans like he was playing again just for them. Wayne had a goal and two assists, and as the game's most valuable player he was awarded a car. He gave it to his old Oilers bodyguard Dave Semenko, who'd retired at the end of the previous season. Wayne never forgot that Dave was a big part of his career.

The rest of our regular season was something of a disappointment. We had a number of injuries, and during the course of the season we dressed eighteen new players. It's a shame that so often winning teams can't stay together longer, but that's just the nature of professional sports. After the all-star break, we won only eleven more games. I felt responsible for every loss. That wasn't new to me, though—I'd always felt that way, even when Wayne was captain. It was simply the mentality I played with.

The Flames ran away with the division and the Presidents' Trophy. And none of us was surprised that the Kings greatly improved their numbers from the year before, finishing second in the division. We were seven points back from them, in third. That meant the opening series of the postseason was going to be Edmonton and Los Angeles.

Who was writing this script?

Instead of winning another Cup with Wayne, we were going to have to get past him. It felt like I was about to go to war against my brother. Even so, we were determined to beat the Kings. Our two teams had been eerily even in the regular season. We'd each won four of the eight games we played against each other, and both teams had scored thirty-six goals.

Despite all the changes and challenges, we were defending champions and started the series in strong and familiar fashion, winning three of the first four games. I was determined to do anything to win. As *Sports Illustrated* noted, I was a man possessed.

"With due respect to Gretzky, Messier was the series' most dominant player through four games. On every shift, it seemed, the muscular center set up a scoring opportunity by making a slick pass or by drilling either a shot or a King. Sometimes he did all three."

We were in control, but there was a fragility to what we'd accomplished up to that point, and I should have seen the approaching disaster.

In my own stupid way, I'd made it all about me and Wayne. It consumed me. At some point during the season, I started feeling like I needed some kind of validation for replacing Wayne as captain, so I tried to do everything. I was thrust into more of an offensive role, trying to fill some of Wayne's huge shoes. I played more minutes than normal on penalty kills and power plays; I tried to do more defensively in our own zone; I took more face-offs—everything. I would have played goal if there'd been enough room for two of us in the crease. If they'd let me sell popcorn and programs, I probably would have. All the extra effort worked at first, but it wasn't sustainable. I had forgotten the lesson: No one wins alone.

Starting in game five, the Kings roared to life. After a stunning run of success, we squandered a three-games-to-one advantage. Game seven was played at the Great Western Forum—a place that held bad memories for us—on the anniversary of the *Titanic*'s sinking. There was an unpleasant parallel. Not long before, we had been thought of as state of the art and unsinkable, and we went down in the first round. We became only the sixth team in NHL history to lose a series after having been up 3–1.

If we had done all the right things and still lost, it would have been easier to swallow. Maybe they would have beaten us anyway, I don't know. But the way we ended up losing was tough. Because I tried to do everything myself, my teammates weren't being relied upon. They weren't invested in their roles because I didn't have enough trust in the process with the entire team. That's the wrong message to send. You've got to give people an opportunity to do their jobs. In that series against Los Angeles, my ego got in the way—that was our iceberg.

The handshake afterward was awful. Wayne was the last guy on the line. I barely remember the details, but he summed it up perfectly in his postgame comments: "For fifteen days, or whatever it was, I saw those guys and no words were spoken. That's not what life is supposed to be about. You're supposed to be able to talk to your best friends."

In a year's time, things had gone from perfect to perfectly awful. One of my best friends was gone. Our team had its worst record in a decade. We'd coughed up a lead in the playoffs and lost—to Wayne—and to rub salt in the wound, our rivals, Calgary, went on to win the Cup.

In the off-season, the city dedicated a statue to Wayne outside Northlands Coliseum. The Oilers didn't send an official representative to the dedication, but—and this should come as no surprise—around thirteen thousand Edmontonians showed up. Now, going to work every day, we would walk past a symbol of the good times. For me, there was no better motivation to recapture them.

CHAPTER THIRTEEN

PLAYING WITH HEART

O ne of the hardest things to do in sports is win when you're expected to. When you're not the favorite, it can be a lot easier to go about your business. It can also light a fire under you.

That's where we were in fall 1989. The prevailing opinion seemed to be that the talent on our team was outweighed by the questions hanging over it. During the summer, Glen Sather had taken on the general manager job full-time and named John Muckler, his former assistant coach, as our head coach. Jimmy Carson had scored 49 goals the year before, the most on our team. But there were culture-fit problems with Jimmy, and he was unhappy. Our goaltending situation was somewhat unsettled, too, because Grant Fuhr had been at odds with the team. In the off-season, he'd retired, worked out his differences with the Oilers management, and then un-retired, only to then undergo an emergency appendectomy. The young Bill Ranford, whom we'd gotten in March 1988 in a goalie-for-goalie trade from Boston in exchange for Andy Moog, had to take on a bigger role.

In the greater context of the league, there were plenty of reasons to look elsewhere for favorites. It was the year the Soviet Union finally allowed its stars to come play in North America. The Canucks had signed two-thirds of the famous K-L-M line, Vladimir Krutov and Igor Larionov. The defending Cup-champion Flames had signed the other, Sergei Makarov.

Pittsburgh had the league's leading scorer in Mario Lemieux, along with our old teammate Paul Coffey. Between them, they had accounted for 115 goals and 207 assists the year before. And Los Angeles was the highest-scoring team in the league.

Nobody really expected very much from us. Most season previews put us at third in the conference again, behind the Flames and Kings. The Minneapolis *Star Tribune* picked us fourth in our five-team division, and the *Los Angeles Times* referred to us as a "spoiler." You can't let other people define your expectations, but it never sits well to be discounted.

It had been a full year and the story of Wayne's departure just wouldn't go away. It still stung, losing. And it felt terrible to listen to the critics who said we were nothing without Wayne.

While I was on the ice, I wanted to crush him. He expected nothing less when we played each other, and I'm sure he felt the same way about me. That's life in hockey. But our friendship trumped everything.

I remember a playoff game one year against the Kings. The atmosphere was intense bordering on hostile. There'd been a bunch of fights. At one point in the game, Wayne got hit in the head with a shot and it opened up a gash on his ear that would later take thirty-six stitches to close. He likes to tell the story that as he was coming off the ice with a trail of blood following him, he skated past our bench and someone threw a towel to him to stop the bleeding.

It was me.

As intense as we both were, we were able to compartmentalize. There are plenty of examples of real brothers who've played on different teams. You think they didn't get together on the holidays because they wore different sweaters during the season?

So the summer after the loss to the Kings, I decided to go to L.A. I stayed with Wayne and Janet for a couple of days, and then bounced around from Beverly Hills to Malibu, staying in hotels, playing golf, relaxing on the beach, and seeing Wayne as much as possible. My brother, Paul, joined for some of the time as well.

Visiting Wayne was a trip, literally and figuratively. In a city of stars, he was as big a deal as there was. It took some getting used to having Sylvester Stallone come over to our table while dining out to say hi, or going to big Hollywood events. At the same time, he wasn't any different than he'd been. Wayne and Janet were living in Mulholland Estates, on the edge of Beverly Hills and overlooking the San Fernando Valley. There were a bunch of people working on their property—a chef and a gardener—and one day while I was sitting around the house Wayne said, "These people seem really nice, but I don't have any idea who some of them are." Despite all the trappings, we were both just simple Canadian kids.

One year, Wayne invited Doug and me to the premiere of *Die Hard 2*, the big-budget action thriller starring Bruce Willis. After the screening, we went to a party at the home of one of the producers. Everybody from the movie was there. Everybody who wanted to be in the next movie was there, too. At one point we ended up in a conversation with Fred Thompson, who played the chief air traffic controller in the film, and of course Doug made sure to tell him that he runs one hell of an airport, which got a big laugh. Here you've got a Canadian schoolteacher and former minor league hockey player chewing the fat with a movie actor who would actually go on to become a United States senator. Hollywood was an alternate reality.

Wayne had joined the brand-new Sherwood Country Club, and when I came to town, I joined as a national member, too. I think Wayne was the tenth member and I was the eleventh. They put our names on placards on these beautiful lockers, next to those of Jack Nicklaus, Sean Connery, and Ronald Reagan, who were some of the other early members. It was surreal how far we'd come. The club had an incredible golf course, and Wayne and I played often that summer, with Paul and whoever else was around.

One time Paul and I got into a money game against Joe Pesci and a friend of his. The course is set in the midst of a rugged, hilly landscape—the opening credits to the TV show *M*A*S*H* were filmed in the area in the 1970s—and I hit a ball up onto this rocky slope. I climbed the hill, choked all the way up on my club, took a wild, awkward swing, and hit the ball. It landed two feet from the hole. Pesci turned to Paul and in this thoroughly exasperated New Jersey accent said, "Does this son of a bitch ever give up?!" Paul ended up birdieing the seventeenth and parring the eighteenth and we won $3,000. I felt like I was in a movie.

The summer did for me what it always had: afforded an opportunity to reset, recharge, and take my mind to another place. This time, though, around all the fun in L.A., there were some dark times of reflection. It was the first time in my NHL career I had been in a formal position to lead, and I had lived with that responsibility every day and night. People were looking up to me, and I got carried away with something unrelated to what was happening on the ice. We'd had all this success because we'd built an understanding that everybody has to do their part. Everybody has to pull on the same oar, I always liked to say. But I had turned my back on what I knew to be the formula for success and tried to row the boat myself. The loss was on me and there was no running from that. It was painful to accept, but the summer helped me own it.

Wayne had a few cars and let us drive them around. I fell in love with one of them, this black Bentley Eight with red pinstriping. I had my Porsche, but this big, elegant land yacht spoke to me.

Wayne was getting ready to trade it in, and I convinced him to sell it to me instead. A few days later, my time in L.A. coming to an end, Paul and I drove it all the way home, 1,700 miles. We were just so excited to get going that we took off without the right paperwork. It was kind of comical when we got to the border. We put that poor border officer in an awful spot. Here was this nice normal Canadian guy. He had a good government job, although a pretty thankless one. Then one day, I pull up in a $120,000 car (that was a lot more money back then) that is registered to Wayne Gretzky.

The guy had to be thinking that this was some kind of hidden-camera prank, but he was very professional. I guess he felt comfortable that it wasn't stolen, and I suppose he knew where to find me, so they let us through.

When I eventually did get back to Edmonton in August, it was time to get to work.

WE STARTED THE SEASON WITH a pair of wins—one of them at home against Los Angeles. It was nice to get off to a good start, but nothing special: Beating the Kings early in the season wasn't the measuring stick for us. We had gathered again in training camp with the same shared goal to win another Stanley Cup.

Shortly after, we welcomed the Kings to Northlands for another matchup. It had been 432 days since "the trade," but Wayne was still the center of attention. This night there was an added reason.

A big circus was following Wayne around because he was closing in on his childhood idol Gordie Howe's all-time points record of 1,850. And you could never really predict when Wayne might break the record. If he was five points away, you had to be there, you couldn't just wait until the next game, because he regularly scored in bunches. He once had seven assists in a game, and by the time he retired had the most hat tricks of anyone to ever play—fifty!

This night, he was only one point shy of tying the record and it was no surprise when he did. Just four and a half minutes into the first period, Wayne and Tom Laidlaw assisted on a Bernie Nicholls goal and the place went nuts.

The rest of the game was pretty tight and Wayne was uncharacteristically quiet on the ice. He later told reporters he almost didn't play the third period because he had gotten his bell rung a few times. I remember one hit by Jeff Beukeboom, our powerful defenseman, that was particularly bone-jarring.

Still, he was always lurking. Take your eye off him for a split second and he would carve you up. And he did. Late in the game, during a time-out, the crowd started chanting his name. It was as if they knew he wasn't done for the night. We were up 4–3 with about a minute left and there was a face-off in our end. Off the draw, Wayne went back behind the net, to his "office," and when the pass came his way, he snuck out to put in a rebound to tie the game.

Despite all the recent history, the crowd wasn't only rooting for us, they were rooting for him. I got it. You might think we felt a sense of disloyalty, but no way. It was only fitting that he break the record in front of the Edmonton fans.

As much as they were there for Wayne, they were there for history. For fans then, Wayne breaking Gordie Howe's record was a "where were you?" moment. They stopped the game and had a ceremony. Howe was there and said some nice things about Wayne. Wayne was humble, gracious, and sincere—as he always was. He thanked both teams for being such a big part of what he'd been able to accomplish. He thanked the fans of Edmonton and his family, who were all there. He even gave a shout-out to Joey Moss. It was a special night for Edmonton, and hockey fans everywhere.

I remember thinking at the time how important it is to set an example as a leader. Behave with class and humility, not anger or self-absorption. We were still in a game and angry we'd given up the goal. Sometimes, though, you have to take a step back and think about the bigger picture.

I actually thought it was pretty cool to be on the ice for this moment, although it didn't do much for my plus/minus statistics. I cared passionately about winning every game I played in, but this was part of history. And it wasn't like the game was over. The record setter had only *tied* it. Of course, Wayne being Wayne, he scored again in overtime to win it. In a perfect world, Wayne would have broken the record *and* we would have won. Losing the game really stung.

It was a momentous night of history for a favorite son, so it was understandable that another story was overshadowed. Jimmy Carson wasn't on our roster that night. I think playing against his old team, which he'd never wanted to leave, was the breaking point. He'd made no secret about his unhappiness in Edmonton.

He'd been an absolute supernova in junior hockey. In his second season in Verdun (Montreal), he had 153 points in 69 games, and then ended up the number two pick in the NHL draft. He thought he was going to be in L.A. for a long time. He'd bought a house there just before the trade happened.

A few years after he left, he would crystallize his feelings in an interview with *Sports Illustrated*.

"Coming to Edmonton," he told the magazine, "was reverse culture shock. Most of the Oilers come from small farming towns. They think Edmonton is Paris. Their idea of having fun is going to a bar and getting hammered all night. That's not me. How do you give up your values just to be accepted by the team?"

From the start in Edmonton there was a bigger problem, though, than missing L.A. or feeling out of place in our town. How would you like to be the guy who replaces, or tries to replace, not only the greatest player of all time, but a man who is genuinely loved? And in case the thought ever did escape him, Jimmy had to come to work every day and pass a statue the city had built to celebrate its affection for Wayne. Looking back, I wish I'd had more empathy for him.

We needed him to be all in, but it just seemed like his heart wasn't in it. We all had so much invested, so for a guy to say that he didn't want to be there chafed more than a few of us.

There's no middle ground at the NHL level, you have to be

completely committed. Anything less than everything just isn't enough. There's just no way you can have a winning environment, with people going above and beyond, unless everyone's heart is in it. That's just as true outside of hockey.

I think most players who haven't played in a winning environment don't even know what they don't know—how far they can push themselves, their own limits. How could they? Creating that environment, in sports or anything else, boils down to one very simple thing: commitment, which is another way of saying heart or passion. You just can't have excellence with a casual or indifferent approach.

Looking back on our success in Edmonton, I can say we were all committed. It was the same for the New York Islanders, or the Patriots, or the Yankees, or the Celtics, or any great organization that has sustained success. Talented teams, committed to what they are doing, and executing their jobs with passion. That is the winning recipe in sports, as it is anywhere.

How important is heart? You can have heart and commitment without supreme talent and still make a run at it. If you have talent without heart? No chance.

Jimmy wanted out of Edmonton, but he felt trapped. If he played out his contract, the Oilers could just match what anybody else offered to keep him in Edmonton—that was the way it worked in a time before free agency. So, instead, he quit the team the day before our game with the Kings to force a trade.

In retrospect, I have to give him credit. It took guts to stand up and tell us things weren't working out for him. Years later it's easier to see it his way, but at the time when things were raw, it was maddening.

Eight games after Wayne broke Howe's record, Jimmy got

his trade. I remember telling the press, "Who cares? All we're losing is a guy who didn't want to be here." I feel horrible now when I see those words. It was so narrow-minded, but that's the intensity of being neck-deep in something you're passionate about. Now, anytime I'm in a negotiation, I always put myself on the other side and try to understand the reality the other person is living.

The good news was we got a haul of super talent out of that trade. Jimmy was sent to his hometown Red Wings along with Kevin McClelland and a draft pick in exchange for Adam Graves, Jeff Sharples, Petr Klíma, and Joe Murphy (the only player selected before Jimmy in his draft year).

Petr Klíma was a talented winger who came to us as a twenty-year-old with all sorts of potential. He'd been a steady scoring presence on the Wings for a few years after having come over from Czechoslovakia. He had a big personality and loved being an NHL player. He had some money in his pocket and a reputation for enjoying the nightlife maybe a bit too much at times. I could relate to him. None of that mattered to us, though, and we didn't put stock in what other people said: When you came to the Oilers, you were given a clean slate. All that mattered to us was that you came to play, and fit into the culture.

I picked him up when he first got to town. Whether it was myself, or Kevin, or Glen, we all pitched in to make anybody new feel welcome; make sure they had a ride to the rink, or were set up with an apartment, or introduce them to someone who could help with that.

But it wasn't only about making sure they felt welcome, it was about making sure they understood what we were about. What he'd achieved in Detroit didn't seem to match what he was capable of. I thought it was about his level of engagement. It wasn't enough to just have talent.

Petr and I spoke often about team philosophy and what we wanted him to do: work harder in practice, be more focused. It wasn't a coincidence his locker ended up next to mine. At some point, though, we had to hope he was paying attention to the sacrifices that people like Kevin Lowe were making, taping himself together because of all the injuries, falling down with his face in front of slap shots late in regular-season games—not even the playoffs. You hope that when someone new sees that kind of commitment happening around them, words are no longer necessary. Petr got it.

The team had been stuck in neutral up until the trade, but after that we went 33-19-10 to finish the season second in our conference, to the reigning Cup champions, the Flames. Without the high-profile scoring punch of players like Gretzky, Coffey, and Carson, I was called upon to keep playing an even more offensive role and had the biggest numbers of my career. Jari Kurri, Craig Simpson, Esa Tikkanen, and Glenn Anderson all came through the season with north of 60 points, too. Everyone rowing in the same direction.

Not all the contributions show up on a scoresheet, though, and the year wouldn't have been so solid without some key guys on that team whose numbers didn't jump off the page. Kelly Buchberger was a dedicated player from Saskatchewan who'd essentially willed his way into the league. He had tons of heart and was all in for the team. Dave Brown was a six-foot-five, 220-pound enforcer who looked out for everyone. These kinds of guys, willing to do whatever it took to win, and do it with pride, were absolutely essential. Without them, there was no way to win, whether Wayne was on the team or not.

And then there was Mark Lamb, who joined us after a long stint in the minors. For a while we had dubbed the line with Tikkanen and Kurri "The Doughnut Line" because it didn't have a dedicated center. Then Mark stepped in and filled the gap. He was an extraordinary example of what happens when someone completely gives himself to a task.

Mark grew up on a grain-and-cattle farm in Cadillac, Saskatchewan, population ninety-two (that's not a typo). He was skilled with horses and planned to be a professional rodeo cowboy. But all those hours on a tractor working his family's 4,800 acres, he dreamed of hockey. When he was fourteen, his parents moved fifty miles away to Swift Current, a town of sixteen thousand, so the three Lamb boys could be closer to organized hockey.

Mark started as a defenseman, and in 1982, at the age of eighteen, was drafted by Calgary in the fourth round with the seventy-second overall pick. At five feet nine, though, he figured he might be too small for the position, so he told his coaches what every coach loves to hear: "I'll play wherever you need me."

For the next four years, he traveled the minors, eventually playing one game for the Flames. At the end of the season, Calgary didn't renew his contract, so he caught on with the Red Wings, where again he spent most of the season with the farm team. Throughout, he was driven by the burning desire to prove he belonged. "You can give up," he says, "or you can shut up and do what you need to do."

When the Red Wings put him on waivers, Glen Sather claimed him. He liked what he saw. Mark spent the 1988–89 season in the minors on our farm team in Nova Scotia, and after the season got called up for the playoffs.

It just so happened the day our call-ups got to town, the

league was doing a photo shoot with the Cup in our dressing room. It was the spring of 1989 and we were the defending champions. So this kid, who had spent six years refusing to give up on his dream, or himself, walks into our dressing room for the very first time, and there it is—the symbol of everything he had been working for.

Mark never dressed for any of those playoff games, but he never forgot the first thing he saw as an Oiler. He had been the type of player who woke up every day not knowing if he'd have a job in the league. He lived that razor's-edge existence worried that any mistake might send him back to the minors. He was driven and hungry. His heart was completely into it. He was a perfect fit.

LIKE THE PREVIOUS SEASON, THE 1990 playoffs in the Smythe Division were a steel-cage death match. The Flames won the division again, we were second, the Winnipeg Jets were third, five points behind us, and the Kings got the last playoff spot, another ten points back.

That meant our first round would be against Winnipeg. Dale Hawerchuk, their captain, was a tremendous talent and leader. We were not going to just roll over them. They had six 20-goal scorers and they believed in themselves.

Our record at Northlands in the playoffs had always been strong; since 1983 we'd won 83 percent of our home postseason games. But stats never tell the whole story. Sure enough, they came right at us in game one, scoring seven goals to beat us. Six different players on the Jets scored. Hawerchuk had a pair.

We won the second game on a Mark Lamb goal in overtime. We had home advantage and were lucky to get out of there splitting the two games.

Our trip to Winnipeg was a wake-up call. We lost both games and the next thing we knew, we were down three games to one, which was alarming after what had happened the year before against the Kings.

It was all we could do to climb out of that hole, but we did, and Lamb was a big reason for that. He had a goal and two assists as we evened the series, before coming home to win it in seven. Lamb was our third-leading scorer in the series, behind Kurri and Tikkanen.

It's funny, here's this guy who for so long had been hanging on to a job by his fingernails. On any other team, he might not have made it. He had talent, but not at the level you would have thought would bring him here. Nothing stood out about his game other than sheer heart. But we could see that he was someone who looked at his job from a completely selfless angle—the epitome of what's needed to win in the playoffs.

If you look back at the highlights of Oilers history, not much attention is paid to a first-round playoff win against a third-place team. That win over the Jets, though, may have been one of our most significant ever.

It took every last ounce of what we'd learned over the years to survive. The comeback wasn't about the stars, it was about the scars we'd sustained over the years that had taught us the only way out was to keep our heads and play with our hearts.

In the other conference semifinal match, the Kings took out the first-place Flames. Wayne was his usual brilliant self, but they had balanced scoring, too. We'd have to play a better game against them this time around. For fans, this was a much-anticipated rematch, and not just because of the previous playoffs.

A regular-season game in February between our two clubs

had turned vicious. There were a number of brawls, one of which was kicked off when Marty McSorley and I got into a fight behind the Kings' net. We'd been teammates in Edmonton for years, of course, and I have nothing but respect for him. We were down 3–0 at this point, and in games like this, when guys are competing hard, you find any edge you can for your team. Marty knew that as well as anybody, and so we dropped our gloves.

When all the dust had settled, 356 penalty minutes had been awarded—an NHL record that still stands. Not that I'm proud of the fact. But what did make me proud was the way everyone on our team got involved to protect one another, showing real passion. Kelly Buchberger was right in the middle of things, making sure no one on that L.A. team took advantage of our guys. Steve Smith got involved, Jeff Beukeboom and Craig Simpson, too—even Bill Ranford, who'd become our new starting goaltender, left his crease to sort someone out.

I was reminded of one of Doug's early lessons, that a guy who won't stand up for a teammate had lost the privilege of being considered part of the team. We were a team, in every sense, united in our common cause. We weren't allowing ourselves to get wrapped up in some sort of redemption story against L.A., but that didn't mean we weren't driven to win, not by a long shot. It's just that looking forward provided so much more motivation for us than looking back.

The Kings won that regular-season game 4–2, with Wayne scoring a goal and two assists. The playoffs were a totally different story. We outscored the Kings 24–10 and swept them in four games. Twelve different players scored for us.

A year after our first-round playoff exit, we were now one series away from going back to the Stanley Cup finals. We were on a roll, and went into our conference final series against the Blackhawks with confidence, winning the first game. Then things went south. Again.

We lost two straight and found ourselves at the raucous Chicago Stadium for game four. The fourth game in a series can mean the difference between facing elimination or mounting a comeback. I knew that we couldn't afford to go down 3–1 again, like we had against the Jets. It would have been too steep a hill to climb. Game four might as well have been an elimination game.

We were reeling, and there was chatter in the press. Again, people were saying it was Wayne who'd made us a championship team. Some writers were critical of me in particular. It's true that I wasn't playing as well as I expected of myself, but the reasons they were coming up with were pure fiction—for example, they reported rumors that my dad had cancer.

This kind of noise happens when a team isn't winning, and the atmosphere was tight, as could be expected. What mattered was figuring out how to get back on the right track. Then, just before game four, a good friend of mine from Edmonton named Mark Hall casually mentioned something about "light" and "energy," and "the image you portray to others." It hit me like a sledgehammer. I'd never had a true epiphany before, but I was having one now.

I was always an intense player, which was usually a strength, but in this series against Chicago it might have been working against me. I realized my own energy wasn't good. My shoulders were slumped. I was dark, withdrawn. Sullen. My energy was part of the problem, and completely the opposite of what it needed to be. The thought drew me all the way back to my uncle Vic's deck in Hawaii in the summer of 1985.

The slides Vic had shown me that day of Alex Grey's visual conception of the body's energy had stayed with me but not been actively on my mind. I don't know why this happened as I sat in the bowels of Chicago Stadium, but the tumblers all seemed to fall into place. It was a lightning-bolt moment, a complete transformation in attitude. I needed to get myself into a better place emotionally. If I was the leader, I had to think about what people saw when they looked at me and how that might influence them. It may seem obvious now, but I suddenly understood what is truly meant by "follow the leader." The pack only runs as fast as the lead horse.

"It's not an accident that people do amazing things at trying times," says Allyson Grey, Alex Grey's wife and partner in their artistic and spiritual endeavors. I didn't need everybody to buy into the idea exactly the way I did; the important thing was that I had to find a way to identify and extract the right energy from my team. And what was that energy?

If you ever listen to the great basketball player Bill Walton discuss playing for coach John Wooden, you'll learn they talked about life as much as they talked about basketball. It's something that I adapted for my own leadership style. The search for a bigger meaning—why we're all here—can be galvanizing. An effective leader has to be open-minded, and so my epiphany about a "collective energy" was as much practical as it was spiritual. But that energy had to start with me. I project it, everyone else absorbs it.

That night in Chicago, it was like I stepped into a phone booth and came out a different man. I not only exuded calm, I shared it. A weight had been lifted.

We won 4–2. I had two goals and assisted on the other two. After the game, the *New York Times* reported that I "ran roughshod over the Blackhawks, the most terrifying one-man wrecking crew in hockey history." That's some high praise, but it doesn't tell the story of why we succeeded. The team shared that energy, with everyone laying it all down for the greater good. It wasn't something that people in the stands might have been able to sense, but I can tell you that I felt it. It made it possible for me to the play the way I did.

We controlled the next two games and won easily. A year after flaming out in the first round as defending champions, we were headed to the finals for the sixth time in eight seasons. A familiar place, and I felt like myself again.

We were facing the Bruins again, who had the league's best record and were coming into the finals off a dominating sweep of the Capitals. The run-up to a final series in any sport usually offers a variety of compelling story lines, but this matchup featured one that was particularly odd and rich. Two years earlier, in March, we'd traded Andy Moog to Boston for a package of players including the goaltender Bill Ranford. In the Stanley Cup final that year between Boston and Edmonton, Grant Fuhr had played all five games for us and Andy had played two games for the Bruins. This time around, each team would face their former goaltender for the entirety of the series: Ranford, the former Bruin, played every game for us, and Moog, the former Oiler, did the same for Boston.

Both of them had meant a lot to our franchise. Andy helped us win three Stanley Cups in Edmonton and was part of the original core. I don't think any of us will ever forget how he stood up in the dressing room in 1981, when we were first learning to win, and gave an impassioned speech. We'd just swept the Canadiens, who'd made no secret of regarding us lightly. As we were battling the defending Stanley Cup champion Islanders, he implored us to take a healthy dose of how we felt about Montreal, and use it in this Islanders series.

We rode Moog and Fuhr pretty hard for a lot of years, and people in Edmonton got used to having great goaltending, so when Bill Ranford showed up, expectations were high. He didn't blink. Bill had been nothing short of remarkable for us, and under extraordinary circumstances.

He was good enough to keep us in games when we were trying to find our footing, and good enough to win games on his own. Most important, though, he was consistent: We didn't have to think about what kind of performance we'd get from our goaltender each night, which is exactly what you want.

We were confident in our goaltending, but knew the Bruins had every good reason to not worry about theirs. It was all the more important to set the tone early in game one, which we did, jumping out to a two-goal lead. But Ray Bourque, who that season won the first of two consecutive Norris Trophies, scored a pair in the third—the second with just a minute and a half left in the game   to even the score. We then played another fifty-five minutes of overtime without either team able to score. That's almost an entire extra game.

Petr Klíma had sat out most of the game. Maybe the coaches saw something they didn't like in a few early shifts, I don't know. He was on the end of the bench with his laces untied, his helmet next to him, and his gloves on top of it. At close to completing our second hour of hockey, we were at that point where anybody with fresh legs is going in.

Sure enough, with five minutes left in that third overtime period, Klíma got the tap and had to scramble to tie his skates and get his stuff on. He jumped onto the ice and within thirty seconds ended up in a three-on-two with Craig MacTavish and Jari Kurri. Jari dropped him a nice pass and Petr beat our old teammate Andy Moog to end the game.

After a first game like that, we thought we might be in for a long series, but we lost only one game and won the Cup in five.

I had the most productive year of my career and won the Hart Trophy as league MVP. The numbers, I think, were simply the by-product of the system. Everyone bought in.

I've heard some people say that this Cup, our fifth in seven years, was our best because we did it without Wayne. I don't look at it that way. There was a part of me that was a little sad because he wasn't there to share it with us. He was a brother and that would never change. I think more than anything, this Cup was an affirmation of the incredible grit and determination of the players who had surrounded Wayne all those years.

CHAPTER FOURTEEN

MOVING ON

Sometimes I laugh when I hear reporters ask the front-runner of a golf tournament if he'd rather be at the top of the leaderboard, or in a position of close pursuit. I suppose the presumption is that if you're leading, you have to deal with the pressure of someone breathing down your neck. If you're chasing, you get to do the breathing. It's kind of a silly premise. If you're the leader, you've got an advantage.

It is true, though, that once you're on top, there's only one place to go. If you're the Edmonton Oilers of 1984, or the Islanders of 1980, or any great organization in the heart of a run, staying in the lead is a welcome challenge.

That's not where we were in the fall of 1991. Nothing lasts forever.

Jari Kurri was gone. His contract had expired over the summer, and he had decided to go to Milan to play in the Italian league. His confidence as a player was so high that he typically signed a new one-year contract each season—he was totally unconcerned with the security of a long-term deal. He had been with us from the very beginning, for a decade at this point, and I think that after that wild and exhausting ride, he was ready just to change things up and do something different. I was sorry to see him go. (After a year in Milan, he ended up coming back to the NHL and joining back up with Wayne on the Kings.) On top of the incredible scoring numbers he put up—474 goals, 1,043 points—he'd always been an emotional anchor for the team. He never seemed to be affected by the ups and downs: He would just come to work every day, consistent in his demeanor and behavior. Solid as a rock.

Randy Gregg, our "doctor defenseman," who'd been with us since 1982 through all five Cups, lived our team-first culture through and through, and brought a unique perspective to our locker room, was waived over the summer. He had four young kids, and it was another hard moment for me and the team to see him go.

Our outstanding young goalie, Bill Ranford, was back, but our veteran, Grant Fuhr, was not.

In an article published in the *Edmonton Journal* in August, Grant had spoken openly about his struggles with cocaine use, and revealed he'd voluntarily sought treatment in 1989. Although he'd been clean for a year, the NHL commissioner, John Ziegler, responded to the news by suspending Grant for a full year, with the possibility of early reinstatement in February. Ziegler called Grant's conduct "dishonorable and against the welfare of the league." Virtually nobody thought it was fair. It certainly wasn't compassionate.

At the time our teammate Craig MacTavish said: "I mean really, what was Grant guilty of? He was guilty of having a problem, and he was trying to remedy that problem. If that's a cause for suspension, what kind of message does that send to the rest of the league? If you've got a problem, don't seek help, just continue to do it quietly and you'll be able to play hockey."

I agreed with Craig, and I spoke out in interviews at the time, too. It felt like our society's treatment of people with drug issues was Neanderthal. Grant's issues didn't make him a bad or dishonorable person, he just needed help. He was a brother to me. I'm glad we've evolved in North America since then, and the league's substance-abuse policy has followed suit—there are now protocols and supportive policies in place to assist NHL players suffering from these sorts of problems.

On top of Jari and Randy leaving, and Grant's suspension, Glenn Anderson was holding out for contract renegotiations the entire training camp and preseason. The eight-year deal that he'd agreed to in 1985 had been too long, he now acknowledged, and resulted in him being underpaid at this point, five years later. He had a strong case. He'd averaged 80 points a season over that five-year span. In the 1989–90 season, he'd been thirtieth on the top goal scorers list. Yet he was only the league's ninety-eighth-highest-paid player. Even though a new contract hadn't yet been signed, Glenn finally came back five games into the season while his agent continued to negotiate for a raise. It was a strange situation, but we were glad to have him on the ice for our game against St. Louis on October 16.

That game, as it happened, changed our fortunes that season, though it had nothing to do with Glenn's return. About fifteen minutes into the first period, I got wrapped up with one of the Blues' wingers, Dave Lowry, going for a loose puck, and I twisted my left knee. I had to leave the game, which we lost 5–2.

The injury turned out to be a bad sprain to my medial

collateral ligament (MCL). I'd injured my knees before this way and knew it was a four-to-six-week recovery period. In hockey, your foundation on a slippery surface—your legs—is also your motor, so you need to be well grounded. You are moving at speeds up to 25 mph on a pair of three-millimeter-wide pieces of steel. All your stabilizing muscles are taxed to the limit.

Trying to play with a knee that isn't fully functional is a losing proposition. And in order to play a physical game—which was certainly my style—stability was key to receiving hits and hanging on to the puck. You need the agility to be able to pivot and turn, which you can't do on a compromised knee.

The team notched a good win without me in the next game, but then the bottom dropped out. We went on a nine-game losing streak, the longest in franchise history. We also got shut out in consecutive games, another thing that had never happened before.

We were the defending champions, and a month into the season, we were in last place. I hadn't been on a last-place team since I was fourteen years old.

I worked every day with the University of Alberta physical therapist Dr. David Magee. Wayne had given him the nickname "Fibber" after the title character in one of the most popular mid-century radio shows *Fibber McGee and Molly*. I have no clue why Wayne was a fan of an American radio show that ran from 1936 to 1959, but I liked the nickname and used it for Magee as well.

Fibber was way ahead of his time, doing electrical stimulation to the muscles around the knee so they could be strengthened without the joint having to work. That's commonplace now, but back then, it was pretty cutting edge.

After three weeks of working with Fibber, my knee still felt gimpy, but our season was slipping away and I had to make a determination. At less than my best, could I still make a difference? Some people aren't comfortable playing when they're 50 to 70 percent healthy, because they don't want to hear the criticism that will inevitably come if they aren't performing at a high level. No one likes people taking shots at them. But I decided to suit up. I wasn't the first person to try to play hurt. I wouldn't be the last. I wasn't trying to be heroic. I was acting in desperation.

I came back on November 14 at home against Vancouver and had a good game. I had a goal and two assists and we won 5–3. We took fifteen of our next twenty-one and climbed back out of the hole. After I returned to playing, though, all the travel and game-related activities made it impossible to devote as much time as I needed to rehab, and so my knee never got back to 100 percent.

My personal high point of the season came against Philadelphia in mid-January, when I got my thousandth career point. That it came on an assist of Glenn's four hundredth career goal was sweet. That it put us ahead and was the game winner made it even better.

My current contract had two more years to run, and throughout the season, Doug had been trying to negotiate a new deal for me with the team. Every time he'd talk to Glen Sather, Glen would send him to the owner, Peter Pocklington. Dad would go in with a list of things we wanted in the deal, and Pocklington would cross a few of them out. Money was tight on the team, and Pocklington wasn't willing to give anything away for free. But Dad understood what the market was for players, and he was willing to scratch and claw if that's what it took to get me a fair deal. To him, it was just business. So Dad would go back home, make a new list—including the things that Pocklington had crossed out—and go back to meet him again. Pocklington would cross out a few different things, and around and around they'd go. This continued on through-out the season.

In mid-February, we came home from a brutal east coast road slog where we'd lost three in a row to play the danger-ous Pittsburgh Penguins, who were playing great with "Badger Bob" Johnson now coaching. The good news was that we beat them that night. The bad news was that I sustained another injury.

Early in the game, I crashed into the boards with my right hand in front of me and my thumb got bent horribly back all the way to my wrist. To this day, thirty years later, I still wince at the sound my hand made as the tendons in my thumb tore away from the bone. It was one of the most painful injuries I ever had.

Once again, I had to make the same decision I'd made a few months earlier when I'd hurt my knee: I couldn't be the best version of myself, but could I make a worthwhile contribution? This time I was basically playing with a cast on my wrist.

We limped to the end of the season and finished third in our division with the eleventh-best record in the league. Grant Fuhr had been reinstated from suspension on February 18, which provided a big morale boost, but given all we'd been through, I don't think many people expected us to be too much of a factor in the postseason. We surprised the doubters by beating the Flames and then the Kings and making it to the league's final four.

Then we ran face-first into the Minnesota North Stars.

They beat us four games to one. With players like Brian Bellows, Dave Gagner, and Mike Modano, they were younger and stronger than we were. On May 10, they closed out the series to advance to the finals (where they would be beaten by Pittsburgh).

I didn't articulate it to anybody at the time, but as I took off my equipment in the dressing room at Northlands Coliscum that afternoon I had a profound feeling of sadness. It was impossible to ignore and hung over me like a shroud. We'd made it all the way to the semifinals on sheer guts and determination. It reminded me of the Islanders' final run the year we'd beaten them, when they were trying to win five straight. It was unmistakably one last kick at the can.

This was my home. I'd grown up here. I'd been here since the beginning. I'd been part of building something that was maybe the single greatest element of my town's civic identity and pride. I'd made mistakes and learned here. I'd celebrated on the streets with people I'd never met. I'd poured my heart and soul into creating and maintaining something great for twelve years.

The way we had been beaten, it just seemed there was no way to come out of this without the team having to make some major changes. I needed a change as well.

I took my Oilers sweater off at my locker that day for what I was certain would be the last time.

Doing something on the spur of the moment, especially when emotions are high, is rarely a good idea, so I waited a few weeks to let my feelings settle. I would never want to be thought of as a quitter. I'd be leaving my friends and my hometown. That was a heavy thought, full of guilt. But it was obvious that change was coming.

I called Sather and asked to be traded.

I told him I felt like the Oilers needed to turn over and get younger, and I needed a new challenge, professionally and personally. There were a few places I had in mind, but I told him I'd like to be with the Rangers in New York, playing for an original-six team with a passionate fan base.

"I understand," he said. "I'll see what I can do."

Starting someplace new at age thirty would be a little scary, but I think part of pursuing success with abandon means two things: You have to be honest with yourself and you have to be fearless.

WITH SO MUCH ON MY mind, I headed off to South Carolina, which had become my off-season home.

A few summers earlier, my globe-spinning trips with Paul having tailed off, I'd been looking for a warm, accessible place to play golf, and Hilton Head, South Carolina, had been recommended to me. Through a friend of a friend, I found a house to rent near Palmetto Dunes. I'd never really spent any time in the American Southeast, but when I went to Hilton Head, I was astounded by the familiar, tropical feeling of humidity. I liked the size of the island, and the slow, easygoing pace, too. The golf was great, and you could get out on the warm water and fish. I started going there with my family for parts of each summer, renting that same house. By the summer of 1991, my parents and siblings and I were basically spending the entire summer there.

The Canada Cup was on the calendar again that September. Wayne and the coach, Mike Keenan, were calling me often in Hilton Head to try to convince me to play. As much as I loved the event, I just couldn't do it. I hadn't skated since the last game we'd played against Minnesota in May. I wasn't in any kind of hockey shape. And I felt like my knee was only at about 60 percent. I needed time to heal. And with no definitive news about a trade, I also needed time to think about where my life might be headed.

None of this dissuaded Wayne and Mike Keenan. It didn't matter, they said. They were relentless.

I started doing some roller-blading around the island, just to ease in and see how my knee was really feeling and to get a little conditioning—Hilton Head was perfect for that with its long, flat roadways.

When Mike called again, I told him I didn't see any way this could work—the roller-blading hadn't felt too good—but he said: "Why don't you just come up and skate and see how it feels in practice?"

I guess I couldn't resist. The lure of playing for country had gotten me. I flew up to Toronto in late August and had time for one single practice before the start of the tournament. I was super stiff from not having skated, but my knee felt okay, so the next day, I jumped straight into our first game. It was a hectic twenty-four hours. We tied Finland in that game, and afterward, I felt like I'd been run over with a dump truck. All those little muscles you don't even know you have, but are essential for balance and stability—all of them were sore. The knee, though, to my surprise and excitement, still felt all right.

The tournament was a whirlwind, as always—eight games over two and a half weeks. We swept the United States in the best-of-three final, which many remember because the American defenseman Gary Suter took Wayne out with a questionable check. Wayne not only missed the last game, but also the first month of the NHL season. Still, we'd accomplished something amazing: With six wins and two ties, we finished the tournament unbeaten.

On September 17, I flew back to Hilton Head. The NHL season was sixteen days away and I still had no idea where I would be playing.

Two days later, the Oilers traded Glenn Anderson and Grant Fuhr to Toronto. Sather had strapped on his tool belt and was hard at work constructing a new team.

Down in South Carolina, I was in a holding pattern, but I wasn't too worried. Given the success I'd had, I knew I was going to end up *somewhere*, and the best thing was simply to have patience. I was working out a bit more, and my knee was feeling a lot better. Otherwise, I just spent the days with my family, relaxing and having fun, as we always had.

Opening day arrived without any news from the Oilers. It was a Thursday and I was playing golf with my dad and my brother at Palmetto Dunes. It was me and Paul against Doug and the course pro Bobby Downs. I had come to take my golf pretty seriously, especially when my dad was trying to fleece me for a few bucks. I arrived at the sixteenth tee playing perhaps as well as I ever had, and Paul and I were beating Doug and Bobby.

Then the phone rang. It was the New York Rangers' GM, Neil Smith, calling to tell me he'd arranged a deal with the Oilers and I was—pending a physical—now a Ranger.

I'd just birdied three straight holes, something I'd never done. I promptly triple-bogeyed the sixteenth and then just gave up and walked in. So much for focus. My head was spinning.

The next day, the Rangers sent a plane, and Dad, Paul, and

I flew to New York. A limo picked us up and took us over to Lenox Hill Hospital, where Dr. Bart Nisonson, the Rangers' orthopedist, examined my knee.

After he gave the thumbs-up, it was back to the plane and we headed to Montreal, where the Rangers were going to play the Canadiens the next night. At this point, word had started to leak out, and when we got to the Hôtel Bonaventure in Montreal, I figured—for the sake of having as peaceful a stay as possible—it would be a good idea to *not* check in under my own name.

We got to the front desk and I told the clerk I was with the Rangers and needed to check in. "Your name, sir?" he deadpanned.

"Mark Douglas," I said, using my middle name.

The process took only a few minutes, but through it all we kept up the charade that I was Mark Douglas, and the very nice clerk seemed none the wiser, until he handed me my key, smiled, and said very matter-of-factly: "Here you go, Mr. Messier. Enjoy your stay."

Who was I kidding? This was already a big story.

In the morning, I was introduced to the media in a press conference at the most famous place in hockey, the Montreal Forum.

"This is the biggest day in the sixty-six-year history of the New York Rangers," Neil Smith had said in announcing the trade.

Not much pressure, huh?

But that was fine. I'd long ago proven to myself that I could play at a high level and in a winning organization. I'd proven I could help win a Stanley Cup. Now I just needed to figure out a way to take all the lessons I'd learned and implement them in a brand-new environment. Was it daunting, scary? Yes. Was it a bag full of unknowns? Absolutely. At the same time, it was invigorating and I understood the only way to do this was to dig in, one shovel at a time.

The Rangers were the only original-six team that hadn't won a Stanley Cup since World War II. It had actually been fifty-one years. Opponents—most prominently the local rival Islanders, who'd enjoyed an embarrassment of recent Stanley Cup riches—used to chant, "Nineteen forty! Nineteen forty!" when playing the Rangers to derisively remind them exactly how long it had been.

There was no mistaking why I'd been brought in. To stop the chants, to make them obsolete.

I was welcomed by some, but certainly not all. One writer noted that my age, at thirty, was really more like sixty in hockey years because of all the extra games I'd played in the postseason.

In a brief, odd moment at the morning skate, the whole thing, which seemed to have happened in the flash of an eye, became instantly real. For twelve years, I'd been walking into dressing rooms all over North America and, night after night, been seeing the same familiar thing: white or blue sweaters hung neatly above blue pants. I'd played in the Forum and been in this dressing room dozens of times. This time, the door swung open, I walked in, and for a nanosecond my brain tried to convince me I'd taken a wrong turn.

All the pants were red.

It was the tiniest detail, but one that made me immediately aware that things were now different and there was no going back.

That night, we beat the Canadiens 2–1 in overtime. With five minutes left in the third period, I assisted on a goal to

Doug Weight, who tied the game before Sergei Nemchinov won it for us 1:40 into the extra session. It was the first time the Rangers had won in Montreal in six years. Halfway across the continent two days earlier, the Oilers had played their first game in franchise history in which I wasn't a part of the team. Edmonton got crushed in Calgary, 9–2. But I couldn't worry about that.

I was a New York Ranger now.

CHAPTER FIFTEEN
THE DROUGHT

New York is a tough place for a losing sports team. New Yorkers are used to things of consequence happening in their city, in sports and beyond. In fact, they expect it.

The Yankees are one of the winningest, most successful and iconic organizations in sports history. There's great theater all over North America, but shows usually open elsewhere and work out the kinks because they aspire to end up on Broadway. New Year's Eve is celebrated all over, but the country collectively looks to Times Square to definitively mark the occasion. And while there is industry everywhere, the financial center of the nation, and by most accounts the world, is Wall Street.

That was the backdrop against which the Rangers had failed to win a Stanley Cup in half a century. As Sinatra sang: If you can make it here, you can make it anywhere. Left unsaid is the opposite: If you can't make it here . . .

Nobody likes losing, but there are some places where failure is worn with an almost lovable inevitability, though it's never easy to accept. Chicago Cubs fans waited a long time for a World Series.

For Rangers Nation, their team's struggle was more one of perpetual outrage. Struggling, or even being mediocre, was both unacceptable, and the way things had been for a very long time. The club had come close, making it to the Stanley Cup finals three times since their win in 1940, but even those appearances had only brought misery.

In 1950, the Rangers had led the Red Wings three games to two before losing in double overtime in game seven. In 1972, they fell to the Bruins four games to two, losing the last game of the series in a shutout in which Bobby Orr scored the series-winning goal. In 1979, the last time the Rangers had made it to the finals, they teased their fan base by blowing out the Canadiens in the opener, only to have the Habs come back and sweep the next four.

The Rangers had a long black cloud over their heads, and I had been brought in to help blow it away.

I've always felt that success starts with the way you look at things. If your mindset is: "We can do this," you start with a real chance. Otherwise, you really have no chance at all, unless fate intervenes, and as much as I believe in karma, which every now and then allows a little magic to happen, fate is kind of a fairy tale. You'll never stumble into a championship. I believe in what you can control: hard work and commitment.

I arrived in New York pretty confident. I'd just come off five Cups in seven years, six finals in eight. At thirty, I was still playing at a very high level and I thought I could help instill a winning culture, so to come in and try to do something that hadn't been done in half a century was more appealing to me than it was daunting. I looked at it as an opportunity. And it wasn't like the Rangers team I was joining was a mess. Although they had finished the previous season with a disappointing first-round playoff loss to the Capitals, it had been a decent year. The club finished just three points behind the Stanley Cup champion Penguins in the Patrick Division, and so there was good reason for optimism. My trade was thought of as a potential accelerant on a positive trend.

I was excited, but having been in only one place for twelve years, it took some adjustment right from the start. Think about a kid moving towns and showing up midway through first period in a class full of students who've all been together for a while. When I first got to the Rangers, I walked into that dressing room and felt every eye on me. There were kids in the room who maybe looked up to me, but whatever status I may have had, I just wanted to jump into the trenches with them. I was the outsider, the new guy, so I walked around to every stall and stuck my hand out and introduced myself. I don't enjoy being the center of attention—moments like this are actually a bit awkward for me—but it was important to try to make a good first impression.

Except for two players, I didn't yet know any of the guys personally that first day. The twenty-three-year-old left-winger Adam Graves had played the previous two seasons with me in Edmonton and had been signed to the Rangers in September. Mike Gartner, a friend and former teammate dating all the way back to my first year of professional hockey on the WHA's Cincinnati Stingers, had been the Rangers' top goal scorer the previous season by a big margin, with 49. We'd also soon add my former Oilers teammate Jeff Beukeboom, who'd been with us in Edmonton for three of our championships.

It would take some time to get to know the rest of the guys. The top overall points scorer the previous season had been the now twenty-three-year-old defenseman Brian Leetch, who was a local in relative terms, having grown up in Connecticut. He'd notched 72 assists. Doug Weight was a young center from Michigan who was coming off a solid rookie year. The team had good goaltending with two Americans: the former Vezina Trophy winner John Vanbiesbrouck, who had played his whole career with the Rangers since being drafted in 1981, and a young up-and-comer named Mike Richter.

New to the team along with myself and Adam Graves was the twenty-one-year-old right-winger Tony Amonte, an American whom the Rangers had drafted out of Boston University, and the twenty-eight-year-old Russian Sergei Nemchinov, coming to us from the Russian professional leagues, and whom I'd played against in the 1987 Canada Cup when he was on the USSR national team.

I wanted to connect with everybody. But what I quickly realized was that as valuable as all my experience was, the last thing I could do was actually talk about it.

It was early in the season—I don't remember exactly when—and I was in the dressing room talking to the team. I was about to say something like: "I've never done it that way," or, "In Edmonton, Wayne never did it that way."

And just as the words were on the tip of my tongue, I looked around the room and caught myself. I realized that what I was about to say didn't matter.

Successful enterprises are about the here and now. In hockey, it's about the twenty or so guys in the room. Those are the only people who can make a difference. Talking about the strategies that had proved successful in Edmonton was not going to be a productive tool for team building. Rightly, the Rangers weren't too interested in what had happened there—they were focused on what we could do together in New York.

The concepts I had learned were certainly still useful. The words weren't. The only way to make use of my experience was by example, to walk the walk and hope that my new teammates would fall into stride with me. I'm so thankful I was able to catch myself at that moment, because to start talking about the past would have been a massive mistake. I needed to put all my focus into this team.

The New York Rangers had something only five other teams had: They were there from the formation of the league. They were originals. They would always be like the big brothers in a fraternity: looked up to regardless of what their record was from year to year. That was a point of pride, and I thought it could be an identity to rally around.

I had played all my hockey with an expansion team—a very successful one—but I was now part of something unique. I was skating for a franchise where tradition was long and meaningful. I still get chills when I think about putting on that classic Rangers sweater for the first time.

At the end of the 1990–91 season, Kelly Kisio, the Rangers captain, who'd worn number 11, had been claimed in the expansion draft by Minnesota. When Adam Graves joined the team about a month before I did, he'd picked up that number. But when I came to the Rangers, he graciously passed it along to me.

However, when we took the ice for the first game of the season against the Canadiens, in Montreal, the Rangers had yet to name a captain. The next day, GM Neil Smith told me it would be me, and that there would be a "small ceremony" before our home opener the following day against the Bruins.

It's entirely possible he filled me in more completely on the details, but I suppose I was preoccupied with other things as I got ready to play my first home game at Madison Square Garden: finding my way around, getting acclimated to the building, checking my equipment, making a game plan for the night.

The "small ceremony" Neil mentioned was hardly what I was expecting. All the players were introduced in front of the fans, on the ice, and then my name was called. I skated out and there to greet me were former Rangers captains dating all the way back to Don "Bones" Raleigh, who'd worn the "C" in 1953. But it wasn't only captains. The great Rod Gilbert, one of the most popular Rangers of all time, a Hall of Famer and the club's career leading scorer, was there. And the icing on the cake was Murray Murdoch. A member of the 1926 Rangers—the club's first season—he was also a distant cousin of mine.

As I stood there at center ice looking around, I was caught totally off guard. The building was shaking—literally. The riotous crowd was engulfed in a tribal intensity like nothing I'd ever felt. I remember thinking: *What are these people going to be like if they ever get the chance to watch a Stanley Cup final?* The hair on the back of my neck was standing up.

In that moment, I knew I had landed in the right place. It was everything I wanted: the anticipation of starting over, the unknown, a little bit of fear. I was completely invigorated.

The people at the Garden that night didn't leave disappointed. We won 2–1 in overtime. I assisted on both goals, the winner coming off the stick of my old WHA teammate Mike Gartner.

I'VE OFTEN SAID MOVING TO New York felt like stepping into a movie. That first year I lived in a building on Fifty-Seventh

Street right next to Carnegie Hall called the Metropolitan Tower. My apartment was on the seventy-third floor, with floor-to-ceiling windows and a 270-degree view. I could watch planes take off and land across the Hudson River to the west at Newark Airport and to the east across the borough of Queens at LaGuardia. To the north, Central Park's 840 green acres sprawled out before me like my front lawn. It was magnificent.

It was so high up that sometimes all I could see was white because I was in the clouds. Other times it was so windy, the water in the toilets would swish around from the building swaying. I was up there. The elevator was one of those vacuum mechanisms that can whip you up to your floor in what felt like seconds. Of course, there was a doorman. The rent was ten grand a month—a place like this is worth a lot more now but that was pretty hefty back then. The whole thing was just a surreal experience for me, coming from Edmonton.

New York was as thrilling on the ground as it was beautiful to look down over.

I went to the zoo and the Museum of Modern Art. Whenever friends came to town, we'd go to the American Museum of Natural History, where they had the 10-ton, 95-foot-long model of the largest mammal—the blue whale—hanging in the great hall. I got out of the city and traveled north to the countryside, too. There was nothing I didn't do.

It felt like I was invited to every social event in the city. If I wanted to, I could have filled up my dance card every night.

But rule one was that I never went out the night before a game. Never. I might go and have a meal, but never out on the town. I didn't want that to be an issue. I understood that in a media environment like the one in New York City, just the appearance of being seen out at an event, or a bar, could lead to a bad story—let alone how it might have affected my performance. Nothing good could come from it, so I just took it off the table.

You can't talk out of both sides of your mouth, and I knew the failures some athletes faced coming to New York City. It's a great place, but a dangerous one unless you pay attention to what you came for. I knew I could never do anything to jeopardize my performance. That said, there were still plenty of opportunities to have a good time. I didn't get shortchanged on any of that.

Brian Leetch was the only other player on the team who lived in the city—the rest of the guys were out in the surrounding suburbs—and we became fast friends. He showed me around, gave me rides to practice, and we would go out and have a good time together. With him and other friends, I went to plays and concerts, all sorts of restaurants and clubs. It was the China Club one night, Au Bar another. Out to dinner, you'd run into everybody—it was a small world, so when I say that, I mean everybody. The circles of acting and music and sports all seemed to find common points of intersection. It didn't seem at all unusual to be out and run into Robert De Niro or Howard Cosell. Bruce Springsteen and his wife, Patti, used to come up to our greenroom at MSG after games. Tim Robbins and Susan Sarandon were there a lot, too. Eddie Vedder from Pearl Jam was a friend of Brian Leetch's, so sometimes he would come out with us.

Being from where I am, to be exposed to those kinds of stars was unusual and fun, but I was never really affected by it. We were all just having a good time, and I think people who are celebrities, outside of their own core group of friends, seem to feel comfortable around other people in the public eye, because they figure there's an understanding of the life they lead, and maybe also a deeper appreciation for what they do.

It wasn't that we had developed the kind of friendships where we'd see one another a couple of times a week or anything. People just kinda ended up in the same places—you'd see them around, seemingly by total chance. New York's funny like that.

It reminded me of going to visit my brother when he was playing in Mannheim. We'd just go out to the local place and "run into" everybody there, and the evening would take shape from that point.

You think of New York as such a huge city, but it always felt so much more intimate to me than that. It felt like I inhabited a small community that just moved around from place to place. And everybody was kind of going through their own grind, whether it was the hockey player or the banker, the famous actor or the struggling musician. You'd cross paths in places where everybody was just trying to decompress or celebrate or forget someone, or remember better days. Those late hours in New York brought people together as New Yorkers, not fans and performers. Sharing a drink with someone you didn't know was part of the New York experience.

Invariably, things would end up in the newspaper. The *New York Post* had a famous spread called "Page Six." It's still an active and popular gossip site, but in the days before social media, it was an even louder megaphone. I did my best to keep my name out of it, but occasionally it was no use.

The previous summer during the Canada Cup, Wayne's wife, Janet, had been working on the movie *A League of Their Own*. Madonna was in the film and they became friendly, and Janet was trying to get the two of us together.

When I got to New York, we finally went out and had dinner. I met her at a place on the Upper West Side. It was meant to be kind of under the radar, but of course it showed up in "Page Six."

It was a crazy time. The Rangers literally played on the city's biggest "stage," so life seemed a bit surreal. I was single, and I was having a good time. But I was also thirty when I came to New York, and had the maturity to keep things in perspective. I didn't let distractions get the better of me. And I never forgot an important lesson that Wayne had taught me: Hockey is always the priority.

I'd come here with the intention of winning. There was too much at stake to ruin that.

WE GOT OFF TO A good start that first season, winning three of our first four games, including one at the Garden against the Islanders, which was particularly satisfying. No team was more hated by Rangers fans than the Islanders, probably because the Islanders had been able to do what the Rangers couldn't: win the Cup.

In early November we were in Philadelphia for an afternoon game. I hadn't signed my new contract yet—the lawyers were still dotting the *i*'s and crossing the *t*'s—and Neil Smith, the GM, invited me up to his room to talk about how well things were going. So I told him: "Neil, I'm gonna be honest with you. Don't get too excited, we're not there yet. We're not even close to where we're gonna need to be if we want to win."

He looked at me like I had three eyes, and said, "Whadya talking about? We're in first place, we just won four in a row."

"We're playing okay, but are we in a position to win a Stanley Cup? Based on my experience, no," I told him.

We won that day in Philly, too, and two days later we shut out the Flames. It was true, we had talent. We also had issues. There's a huge delta between championship teams, or teams that are on the cusp of a championship, and those that are a work in progress.

Championship teams need to have the obvious components—talented players, depth, a great coach, a dynamic offense, a solid defense, and superb goaltending. These are easy to recognize. But championship teams also need to have the intangibles—chemistry, character, determination, leadership, experience. Recognizing the intangibles that you're missing, and finding a way to implement them, is the hardest part of building a winning team. They're the glue that brings all the pieces together. Maybe to be successful you need a little more grit and a little less finesse (or vice versa). More than anything, though, you've got to have the right attitude.

Another one of the intangibles is having the right attitude toward winning. When I first got to New York, winning was kind of a touchy subject. Be positive privately but don't talk about it too much—that was the feeling—because if you do, you might jinx it. I think they didn't want to set expectations too high and risk disappointing the fan base. The holding company that owned the Rangers organization, Paramount Communications, was also publicly traded, and didn't want to create expectations that might not be met.

There were no pictures of the Stanley Cup in the offices or the dressing room. Nothing in the environment seemed aspirational. The idea was just to come to practice every day and play the games. Everybody wanted to play well, but nobody wanted to rock the boat or take a risk even *talking* about it, because if you do and don't accomplish your goal, what does that say about you, or the team, or the organization? That's the message I was getting.

Funny thing is, to me, that's the exact opposite of what you have to do to be successful. Everywhere you turn, there should be a reminder of why you're there: to win the Stanley Cup. That doesn't mean you're a failure if you don't, any more than any other team that falls short of bringing home the Cup, but that should be every team's stated goal. Isn't that the point of putting on your skates? Why would anyone deny that? You should talk about that and use it as fire, every day.

From there, you have to understand that everything you do is either a step toward winning the Stanley Cup or a step away from it. This isn't only about attitude. It's expressed in your habits.

To me, not much can be more important than practice and how you go about it.

The great golfer Ben Hogan used to talk about "practice with a purpose." He would think of every shot he hit on the practice range as being a rehearsal for a specific shot he would face in competition. He didn't just go out there and slap a bunch of balls with a seven iron. You need to practice like you play. Concentrate as if you're playing.

At the NHL level, there's no reason why when you're doing a line rush in practice you can't put the puck flat on a guy's stick, just as you'd need to in a game. The only reason you'd put it in his skates, wobbling instead of crisp, is because your concentration isn't there.

This emphasis on the intensity and concentration level that you bring to practice was one of the things I learned from Wayne. He played and practiced at such a high level that he raised everybody else up, because they wanted to emulate him. So instead of talking about the right way to do things—as I caught myself almost doing early in the season—just go do them instead.

Then the hope is those good habits you're demonstrating spread across the fabric of your team. We often hear about peer pressure as a negative influence, but on a healthy and successful team, the opposite couldn't be more true. In a positive winning environment, peer pressure makes everyone better, because you hold one another accountable. The last thing you want to do is let your teammates down.

Our season was judged to be a big success by most everybody. For the first time in a half century, the Rangers had the best record in the league. We beat the Devils in a tough seven-game first-round playoff series. We then lost in the next round to the Penguins.

The Penguins were the defending champions, the class of the league. It wasn't like you could point a finger at anybody or anything being obviously at fault when we lost. There was no shame in the result of that series. They were better than us. Bigger, stronger, everything. Simple.

Brian had won the Norris Trophy, becoming one of a handful of defensemen to ever score more than 100 points. And I'd won the Hart Trophy as league MVP. But I wasn't happy. I believed that what we'd accomplished with our great regular-season record and first-round playoff victory was misleading. I felt that our loss to the Penguins, and the easy way we could write that off as falling to a better team, camouflaged our imperfections. We weren't ready to win yet, and it wasn't only cultural. After the season we'd had, which to many was a success, and unquestionably an improvement, we were far from a finished product.

The next year told that story. There were injuries and we were really struggling, and then things got messy.

This is where it gets a little uncomfortable for me.

THE 1992–93 SEASON, MY SECOND in New York, started off decently. In early December, we traded for Kevin Lowe, who had been such a great teammate in Edmonton. Then, in mid-December, Brian got injured taking an awkward fall into the boards in St. Louis. Nerve damage in his neck and shoulder caused him to be out of the lineup for thirty-four games. He'd emerged as one of the best players in the league, skating more than thirty minutes a game for us, and it was a huge loss.

In that time, a pall fell over the team. By the end of December, we were in third place in our division, and the alarms were sounding. After losing two straight games, we arrived in Pittsburgh on New Year's Day, and our coach, Roger Neilson, called a meeting that night with Mike Gartner, Adam Graves, and Kevin Lowe.

He told them he felt that, for whatever reason, I hadn't been leading the team, and that he wanted them to take over more of that leadership role. The right way to handle it would have been to come to me if he had a problem.

I was very frustrated. I didn't speak publicly about it, but there was no question that as an organization, the Rangers were aware that Roger and I weren't seeing eye to eye.

We lost the game the next day, and two days later, on January 4, Roger was fired. He was replaced with Ron Smith, a disciple of Roger's who had been the coach of our farm club in Binghamton, New York.

The media came to the swift conclusion that while the

team's "dismal record of late was the direct cause for Neilson's demise . . . the coach's problems with Messier were, just as certainly, the catalyst for yesterday's action," as the *New York Times*'s Filip Bondy put it. It was a difficult stretch. I was booed at the Garden. Other local sportswriters really mauled me.

"Instead of elevating Ron Smith from the minors as interim coach yesterday," Joe Lapointe wrote in the *New York Times*, "the Rangers brass should have given Messier another 'C' [for *coach*] to wear on his jersey."

Bob Raissman was even more pointed. In the *New York Daily News*, he wrote: "You can slice and dice this thing any way you want, but the bottom line is this—Rangers inmate Mark Messier is running the asylum."

I guess I should be grateful there was no such thing as Twitter in 1993.

As uncomfortable as this was, winning meant so much to me that I could stomach it. I hadn't come to New York to play on a good team. I came to New York to play on a championship team.

I remember I heard Howard Cosell say something once. I have no idea where he got it from: "What is right is not always popular. What is popular is not always right."

If winning or excellence is important to you, you have to be willing to be criticized for the choices you make—if you believe they are right. Leadership in its most difficult moments is about conviction. And winning was more important to me than my popularity.

We bobbed and weaved in mediocrity the rest of the year. Brian came back in March, by which time we were in third place. But his return was short-lived.

On March 20, we beat San Jose 8–1 at the Garden. After

dinner later that night, Brian fell while climbing over a snow-drift trying to get to the sidewalk in front of his apartment. The rumor around town was that he and I had been drunkenly wrestling. For the record: not true.

The next day it was discovered his swollen right ankle was actually a broken fibula. He was gone for the rest of the season.

Two days later we fell to fourth place. A week after that we were in fifth. By the second week in April, we were tied with the Flyers for last place, and on April 15, we claimed the cellar all to ourselves.

We became the first team in league history to have the best record in the game one season, and then miss the playoffs the following year.

Coming to New York, I knew it wasn't going to be easy. I knew there were going to be ups and downs and challenges, and it would take a while, but I don't think anybody on our team thought of the 1992–93 season as anything but a colossal failure. Maybe you could chalk it up to injuries, but the issues went so much deeper than that.

It was tough when we didn't make the playoffs, but it would have been tougher for me if I had settled for us having a decent team that never got any better. It would have been the same as not going to help a teammate because you're afraid of getting punched in the nose—the kind of inaction that keeps you up at night.

I knew better, and honestly, I think that's one of the reasons I was brought in: to provide that kind of guidance. The Rangers hadn't won in a half century, and they didn't have anybody who really understood what a championship culture was about. So, if I wasn't willing to take a risk and change things, who would? There's a backlash when you take a stand, but if you're uncomfortable with that, you shouldn't be in a leadership position.

The only bright side was that maybe, in a strange way, by failing we were progressing. It's kind of ironic, but it forced us to realign things.

On the final day of the season, Mike Keenan—who had coached the Flyers, Blackhawks, and my 1987 and 1991 Canada Cup teams—was hired to replace Ron Smith. When we got to training camp that summer, one of the first things he did was assemble the team to show us a videotape.

It had nothing to do with hockey.

The summer after we finished the season as one of the worst teams in the league, our new coach's first order of business was to show us coverage of the New York Mets' ticker-tape parade after they won the World Series in 1986. What he was saying with his first move was: This could be you. This is what we're here for.

My first thought? *Fucking right.*

CHAPTER SIXTEEN

LIGHTING A FIRE

I was standing on Columbus Avenue, desperately trying to hail a cab, in a black wig, platform shoes, and a sequined jumpsuit, when a guy walked past me and, without breaking stride, casually turned his head to say: "Hey, Mess."

He just kept on walking.

Nothing fazes New Yorkers, apparently not even one of their professional athletes looking for a ride while dressed as Elvis Presley. Of course, this wasn't a normal night, and I was on the way to oversee important business.

Most people might never guess it, but the key to leading a successful hockey team is a good Halloween party. The hockey season usually starts in mid-October, so two weeks in is the perfect time to exhale and have a team meeting. Why not do it in costume and with good food?

At the Rangers' party, wives and girlfriends were welcome. Team staff members were there, too. It was about inclusion and making a statement that our team wasn't composed only of those who carried sticks. The idea was to let your guard down and get to know people.

We took it very seriously—at least the preparation. Midway through the evening, the music would stop and we'd have a contest where we'd give away prizes for the best costumes: big-screen televisions and vacation packages. The party would go on all night, but the stories would last all season, and that was the point. It was an experience we could all share.

This was in the days before camera phones, so our team masseur, Bruce Lifrieri, would bring a Polaroid and take dozens of pictures. We'd show up in the dressing room before our next practice or game, and they were all posted on a big board—each image a small piece of good-natured glue that would connect us through a long season, and beyond.

It was a perfect way to create an environment where cliques didn't exist. But team parties were also critical for another reason.

When I was on the Oilers, we traveled to games by commercial airlines, but the Rangers traveled by charter. That meant no more waiting until the next morning after a game to catch a flight out, and so we lost the countless postgame gatherings—for meals or beers—where we simply bonded over things that had nothing to do with work. That kind of interaction knits people together.

And our team needed to come together, after the challenges of the previous season. Standing on Manhattan's Upper West Side, decked out like Elvis that night, I was eager for better times. The 1992–93 season had been a disaster, and a test for me personally. For the first time in my career, I walked away from the rink with a bitter aftertaste. I had to steel myself to remember why I had been brought here.

Things, though, were looking up again. The new 1993–94 season had gotten underway decently, and the day before Halloween, we had started a run that would eventually stretch to eleven wins and a tie. That was both because of, and in spite of, our new coach, Mike Keenan, who had brought a very different energy to the team, though one that was familiar to me from playing on the 1987 Canada Cup team that he coached, and against his Flyers and Blackhawks teams over the years. I knew that he was a hard-driving guy who held his players accountable, so when I heard he'd been hired, I thought he was a good choice for the Rangers.

One of a coach's biggest responsibilities is to make sure everybody is engaged, paying attention, and ready to play. Sounds simple, but in a long season, all teams go through a malaise at some point. It's important to have *fire starters*, guys who are like sandpaper, a little aggravating. Someone who drags the team into the fight. Usually it's a player, but in this case, that was Mike Keenan. There was never a dull moment with him. He sought harmony through chaos.

At one point in March he was unhappy with the way we were playing and suggested to the media that the answer was to bring the former Islanders captain Denis Potvin out of retirement.

The New York tabloids exploded. Denis Potvin was a Hall of Famer and four-time Stanley Cup–winning defenseman, but more significant, he was probably the single most vilified Rangers opponent of all time.

In February 1979, the promising Rangers center Ulf Nilsson had broken his ankle after a collision with Potvin. Nilsson missed the rest of the season, and Rangers fans never forgave Potvin (even though Nilsson did, saying that it was a freak accident).

Ever since, the most enduring and exuberant cheer at

the Garden—regardless of the opponent—has been a brief, spritely melody played on the building's organ punctuated by words every Rangers fan knows: "POTVIN SUCKS!" It's still the case to this day.

Keenan knew exactly what he was doing. Potvin wasn't coming back, of course, but Keenan was changing the narrative—stirring up the media to take the focus off us. Another time that season, he was angry about how one of our lines was playing, so he sent out three defensemen to play forward. His methods were sometimes amusing, but rarely subtle. He kept things bubbling.

It didn't matter who you were, if he had a problem with what you were doing on the ice, he would sit you in a heartbeat—star players, too, myself included. And that spoke volumes. Up and down the bench, the thinking was clear: *If they can sit* him *down, then we'd better get going.*

He moved goalies in and out of games like he was rearranging vegetables in his refrigerator. Mike would pull one out and then maybe put him back in later. Nobody had really done that before. I don't disagree with his thinking here, because if a goalie isn't mentally prepared, why should he stay on the ice while defensemen and forwards regularly get benched for the same type of thing?

Sometimes, though, the way he went about it seemed heartless. We had a game at Nassau Coliseum near the end of the season against the Islanders, and sure enough he pulled Richter and put in Glenn Healy, who had played the previous two years for the Islanders and been a popular part of that team. Just eleven minutes later, Keenan pulled Glenn and put Richter back in.

It was humiliating and Glenn was livid, but we came back

to win the game, the first time we'd beaten the Islanders on their home ice in five years. That was all Mike cared about.

Mike liked keeping people on edge, and that wasn't limited to games.

There was a trash barrel outside our dressing room where guys would put used tape and broken sticks—it had been there for years. One day, Mike came in and got one of our trainers, Joe Murphy, out in the hall and started screaming at him: "Why is that fucking garbage can right outside our dressing room door?" Of course, everybody came out to see what the ruckus was about. Mission accomplished. His message had been delivered to the whole team at once: We run a tight ship around here, and every detail matters.

I liked Keenan's style of practice—short, up-tempo, and fun—which reminded me of the way we did things in Edmonton, but sometimes at practice, he would make a show of his outrage if things weren't being done properly. There were rumors that he would half-saw the shafts of sticks so that when he slammed them across the pipes of the goal, they would shatter, making for effective optics. I don't know about that, but his antics certainly taught people to be careful around him.

It was a regular thing for Mike and our PR guy, Barry Watkins, to get a sandwich together before games in a room that had been set up right across the hall from our dressing room at the Garden.

Once, by the time they'd gotten to the front of the line, the food-and-beverage people had run out of a few things. "No rolls?" Keenan asked. They both just put some cold cuts on their plates and sat down. Not a minute later, an employee came scurrying into the room with a bag full of rolls. Keenan was feared enough that he didn't always *have* to do something dramatic. He *would* do what he felt was necessary, though. And it seemed to be working.

By February 23, 1994, we had the best record in hockey and an eight-point lead in our division.

We were facing the Bruins that day at home. For months, Mike had been preaching the importance of shortening our shifts so we could stay fresh. You never wanted to be on the ice too long and get worn out, especially on defense.

Left unsaid was what we'd all understood since our Pee Wee days. In hockey, there's a rhythm to the game. It's important that when your line mates change, you come off the ice, too. It's just how hockey works.

Alex Kovalev, a twenty-year-old left-winger, who'd been a star for the Russian national team and was in his second season with us, apparently hadn't been tuned in to Mike's decree. Alex was a tremendous talent who had steadily improved. We were trailing the Bruins 5–1 with five and a half minutes left in the second period at Madison Square Garden, with Alex's line on the ice. His two line mates came to the bench, but Kovalev was oblivious and kept on skating.

The guy who was supposed to come in for him was standing there with one leg hanging over the boards, raring to go.

Alex just kept on skating.

Finally, the guy gave up and sat down. We were all watching this thing unfold, knowing Keenan was about to go absolutely nuclear. Keenan was trying to get Kovalev's attention and get him off the ice, but eventually, he shifted his strategy and instead of trying to get Alex *off* the ice, decided to leave him out there—to punish him.

Alex apparently didn't see it that way. He thought this now marathon shift was a reward for playing well. He had a huge gas tank—he was young and superbly conditioned. A normal shift might last forty-five seconds, but that was a yawn for Alex. Keenan kept him out considerably longer than a yawn. I remember thinking that even Alex must have been feeling the pain. Keenan was furious with him, but for the rest of us it was absolutely hilarious.

The punctuation mark to this circus episode was that with thirty-two seconds left in the period, Alex scored on a laser beam of a slap shot. His shift lasted an incomprehensible five and a half minutes. The next day, he turned twenty-one. Happy birthday, Alex.

Mike was hard on a lot of guys. Coming in as a new coach, it's important to understand the players you're working with. Sometimes you've got to put players through a stress test to see how they react, but that evaluation can be perilous.

He was particularly hard on Brian Leetch, which I didn't quite understand. I think part of it was Mike trying to figure out who Brian was, although it was hardly a secret. Just two years earlier, Brian had won the Norris Trophy as the league's best defenseman. Knowing Brian the way I did, the last thing Keenan had to worry about was getting maximum effort and productivity out of him.

Very early in that season, we lost a game at the Garden to the Mighty Ducks of Anaheim—who had come into the league just that year—and Mike was furious. He came into the dressing room, looked right at Brian, and started in on him.

"Brian Leetch," he says. "Brian fucking Leetch. Chris Chelios is *way* better than you. I would trade you right now for him. This organization has you rated way too high!"

It was a gut punch for Brian—and a gut check.

Chelios was a Stanley Cup–winning defenseman who Mike had coached with the Blackhawks. We all knew Chelios was a warrior and had a lot of talent. But Brian Leetch was everything that Chris Chelios was, and maybe more. Mike was a new coach at this point and should have taken more time to look at his hand before deciding that he knew what he was holding, especially since he had gotten Brian so wrong.

But as mad as Brian was at Mike, he still had one of the best years of his career. It's entirely possible that at some point Brian's attitude toward Mike became: *Fuck you—I'm not in this for you. I'm in it for my teammates.*

And a lot of times Mike would *want* the team to galvanize together against him, which is a strategy. I don't think that it's necessarily always the best strategy, but it has worked before. Herb Brooks carried the U.S. Olympic team to a gold medal in 1980 by uniting everybody in their contempt for him.

There's no question he got the most out of his players. He held people accountable. His teams never got run out of an arena because they were intimidated. Some people might tell you that strategy wasn't the strongest part of his game, but I liked his practices and game style, and he also had keen assistants in Dick Todd and Colin Campbell to handle the finer points of the *x*'s and *o*'s.

Ultimately, the coach is the leader. He's the one who sets the pace, culture, and psychology of the team. Everybody then has to follow, whether they like it or not. Coaches make mistakes, too, as Mike certainly did. Thankfully, we had enough experience and leadership on our team to absorb Mike's coaching style, figure it out, and then keep everybody focused on our goal. The results that year speak for themselves.

I'M NOT SURE IF IT was Ben Franklin, John Wooden, or the Reverend H. K. Williams who first said, "Failing to prepare is preparing to fail," but what's indisputable is that although you can accidentally stumble upon a good moment, the only way to be sure to repeat it is by preparing.

The mistake many people make is not understanding that success is a *lifestyle*. Nobody was a better example of this during the 1993–94 season than our goalie Mike Richter. He was a maniac about preparation. He used to say, "Preparation isn't like a jersey you put on. It's more like your skin. You can't take it off." It was the way he trained, the way he ate, even the way he *thought*. Everything. He was constantly in search of exactly the right formula to produce optimal results. He kept a log of his sleeping habits, charting how many hours he slept and when. He kept track of whether his sleep was uninterrupted and then cross-referenced it to his performance the next day. These days, that is hardly uncommon in professional sports, but twenty-five years ago, it bordered on radical.

"Take three days with not only a lack of sleep, but a lack of *good* sleep," he says, "and see how you handle a parking ticket, let alone a hundred-mile-an-hour slap shot."

Mike loves Indian food, but he never ate it on game day. He ate the same thing—chicken and pasta for lunch, maybe some fruit and orange juice, then some scrambled eggs and a sports drink for a late-afternoon snack—*every* game day. Personally, I avoided building routines around anything I couldn't completely control. My thinking was: *If I decide that I'm going to eat Raisin Bran every single day at five o'clock, what happens when the road hotel is out of it?* I remember one time Wayne had hot dogs before playing a great game. He got it in his head that he needed to eat hot dogs between periods to get a certain number of goals! But in Mike's case, the monotony had nothing to do with superstition. He had figured out the perfect fuel mixture for the Richter machine to run at peak efficiency.

And Mike's routine was inviolable. Every game day—home or away—he stayed in a hotel so he could have a controlled environment with few distractions. There might be a great football game on TV, but he would shut it off, because his routine called for sleep in the afternoon.

In addition to working like a madman on every physical aspect of his game—strength, flexibility, nutrition, sleep—he also worked with a psychologist, because as much as the game is played between the pipes, it's also played between the ears.

Collectively, all of this was Mike's way. Some might have found it eccentric—and Mike admits he could get a bit anal about sticking to the plan—but he knew that the biggest battle any athlete fights is with *himself*, and you need to figure out your own blueprint for success.

As for me, I had my own methods for getting the best from myself and from our team. When I got to New York, one of the first things I did was move the furniture.

The old Rangers dressing room had a table right in the middle, which was usually loaded with training supplies and a couple of big coolers of Gatorade. I immediately asked the trainers to have it taken out. We didn't need instant access to sports drinks. We needed to be able to see one another.

Some of the most powerful times I'd ever had in hockey were those last few minutes in the dressing room before a big game as the ice was being cleared and the fans were making the arena shake above us. Those are the raw moments when words aren't needed.

Each of us has an energy that circulates around a room, and I didn't want anything blocking that. If our eyes are indeed the window to the soul, then I wanted to make sure that everybody was connected, spiritually and emotionally, at these crucial moments.

A leader's job is actually very simple: Make those around you better. I never graduated high school, but I love to read, in part because it transports me to beautiful places, but also because I often discover new ideas that I can apply to my life and work.

Every year at Christmas, I would give my teammates a book, something I hoped would help them unlock something in themselves. One year it was Pat Riley's *The Winner Within*, another year it was Phil Jackson's *Sacred Hoops*—a book that really speaks to me in how it lays out the importance of sacrificing the "me" for the "we" in winning cultures.

They weren't always sports books, though. One of my favorites that I gave my teammates was *Endurance* by Alfred Lansing. The book told the story of an expedition that went to the Antarctic in 1914 and got stranded for a year. Ernest Shackleton was the leader and brought everyone home alive (although when he got back, he had one of his crew jailed for insubordination). It was a book not only about leadership, but about how the only hope of survival for a team of people was to work together.

Culture isn't built in a day, but a year after the messy failure and dysfunction of the 1992–93 season, we were working together like we had written the book. On March 21—the trading deadline—we had the best record in hockey, but the New Jersey Devils were nipping at our heels. So, at Keenan's urging, Neil Smith reluctantly started making deals, like a broker trying to beat the market's closing bell, to bolster our depth.

He made five trades in the day's closing hours. Twenty-five

percent of the roster was changed. When the trades were made, we were in Calgary, and Glenn Healy later told John Kreiser, of NHL.com, that going from the hotel to the Saddledome for practice that day was very strange.

"The bus was empty," he said, "because we had traded so many guys."

Among those gone were Mike Gartner and Tony Amonte. Between them, they'd accounted for 90 points thus far that season. We picked up my old teammates Glenn Anderson and Craig MacTavish, along with Brian Noonan and Stéphane Matteau.

There was some outcry from fans who didn't want to see some of our team's stars leave, and didn't understand why they were being traded. The changes mirrored the classic disagreement between the architect and the builder, but when tested, Keenan's construction project came out looking pretty solid. We lost only two of our last twelve games and ended the season thirty-three points better than the year before. For the second time in three years, we won the Presidents' Trophy, this time with the best record in franchise history.

That was fine, but now came the real test. We were ready. It would last at least sixteen games and take two months. That's a long time to play high-intensity hockey, but it's not so long when you consider the city had been waiting fifty-four years for a championship.

CHAPTER SEVENTEEN

"NOW I CAN DIE IN PEACE"

First up in the 1994 playoffs was our rival the New York Islanders. We made quick work of them, sweeping the series, and then we rolled past the Capitals, losing only one game. Sometimes the stats can make it look easy—we outscored those two opponents 42–15—but it's always hard, and it was about to get harder. Eight wins down, eight to go.

In the Eastern Conference finals, we would be facing the New Jersey Devils. We had the best record in the league, but they had the second-best. Buzzing around in the back of our brains all year had been the suspicion that if we were going to have a chance to finally win a Cup, we were going to have to get past the Devils.

Going into that series with the Devils there was already friction—it was a fact of pure geography. Our home arenas were eight miles apart. No two teams in the NHL shared closer proximity and we weren't exactly the friendliest of neighbors, mostly because everything about us seemed to be in conflict.

The Rangers were an original-six team that played in the self-described "World's Most Famous Arena." The Devils were an expansion franchise that moved to New Jersey in 1982 and played in a swamp (literally, the arena was built on wetlands). They had needed permission from the Rangers just to locate there in the first place. We were Broadway, they were the New Jersey Turnpike. They played a stultifying defensive trap. We played a high-energy breakout offense. We got a lot of attention. They felt they never did.

As the New York radio talk show host Joe Benigno told Tim Sullivan for his book *Battle on the Hudson*: "All the Devils really provided at first was a place to see the Rangers a few more times."

And he was from New Jersey!

So with a manhole-sized chip on their shoulders, the Devils were motivated. They were also young and talented, and we knew we would have our hands full. All season, they'd ridden a young goalie named Martin Brodeur to success. They had strong forwards in Bill Guerin, Bobby Holík, and Claude Lemieux. Scott Niedermayer was still pretty new, but his skill was already evident. And leading them was the captain, Scott Stevens, as bruising a defenseman as there ever was.

The puck dropped for game one on May 15 at the Garden. Fans on both sides of the Hudson River got what they might have expected. We scored, they tied it. We scored, they tied it again. I assisted on a Steve Larmer goal about halfway through the third period, and it looked like we were going to hold on, but in a desperate attempt to tie the game in the waning moments, the Devils pulled their goalie. With just forty-three seconds left, Claude Lemieux scored.

It took almost two more full periods of scoreless overtime hockey before Stéphane Richer swooped in on the left side and won it for the Devils.

And that's the way the series continued to go, back and forth, often to the brink and beyond. We won the second game with far less trouble, keeping the Devils scoreless. But the third went to double overtime again. This time it was our new addition Stéphane Matteau who ended it, and we took a two-games-to-one lead.

As the puck dropped in New Jersey for game four, we were in a good place strategically and emotionally, but the Devils scored a couple of goals in the first period. Keenan promptly did what Keenan does. He sat Leetch for long stretches despite the fact that he was leading all players in the postseason in plus/minus, the critical stat that indicates combined offensive and defensive effectiveness. He also pulled me and Richter.

We went into the dressing room at the first intermission down 2–0, many of us thinking: *What the fuck was that all about?* We weren't playing poorly. Anybody can get down 2–0. Clearly, Mike was trying to jolt the team, but these were some questionable moves. We lost the game.

The next day at practice, I went in to have a talk with Mike. I don't remember it being emotional, although others have reported it as such. I just said to him: "Come on, what are we doing here? How is this going to help us, at this time of the year, when there's this much pressure on us, when we're playing a team that arguably is just as good as us?"

Twice before—in Philadelphia and Chicago—Mike had coached teams to the Stanley Cup final, but failed to win. He was a great coach, and I appreciated how he wouldn't accept anything other than maximum effort, but there's a time for the stick and there's a time for the carrot. I think he'd sometimes lost sight of the distinction between the two over the years.

I wanted him to understand that the time for being a

disciplinarian was over. We weren't going to win every shift. We weren't going to win every period. We weren't going to win every game. We just needed to win four games out of the seven. Here we were on the threshold—everyone exhausted, nerves frayed, and we were all in, we were with him. The hierarchy between player and coach dissolves in these moments. He had to jump in the boat with us. I told him: "The time for head games is over; now is the time for you to let the guys know you believe in them."

It was a good talk, and he didn't push back. The next night in the dressing room he apologized. It was an honorable thing to do, and although we were a team with players who knew how to compartmentalize little disagreements and focus on the task at hand, I think it helped us move on. Coaches are human, just like the rest of us, and we all make mistakes. As long as they're acknowledged, they're easily forgiven.

Unfortunately, we promptly went out and lost game five. Sometimes the other team plays better, and the Devils simply outplayed us that night. Which meant we were now one game from elimination. This set the stage for an episode that, for some people, has come to define me.

Although we played our games at Madison Square Garden, we practiced at a rink in an amusement park called Playland in the suburban community of Rye, twenty-five miles north of the city. It's a cool old place that was built in 1928 and featured in the movie *Big* with Tom Hanks.

The next day after our 11:00 a.m. Playland practice, a bunch of writers gathered in front of my dressing stall. There must have been thirty people there, and I told them what I believed.

"We're going to go in there and win game six," I told them.

"We know we're going to win game six, and bring it back for game seven."

It wasn't empty rhetoric. Including this series thus far, we'd played the Devils eleven times that year, and won eight of the games. We'd outscored them 35–18. They were good. We were better. At the time, I was focused on nothing more than sending that message to my teammates. We had to change the way we were thinking.

Consider the context, though. The best team in hockey, after a half century of misery, stands on the brink of underachievement yet again, only to have their captain guarantee a win. There are two ways this could have played out. It could have ratcheted up the pressure on my teammates and worked against us; or it could have told them I was supremely confident in who we were, how we had prepared, and what we were about—and gotten us back on track.

The next morning, "the guarantee" was all anyone was talking about on the radio. The back page of the New York tabloids had my picture and a giant headline that said: "WE'LL WIN." Brian Leetch—who has the most deadpan sense of humor—and I had driven up to the practice facility together, as we usually did. When he got in the car, he opened up the paper and was quiet for a minute or two. Finally, he said: "I guess we're gonna win, huh?"

It's good to have a bit of levity when the air gets thin. If I had any doubt about how this might play out, it was dispelled as soon as I got on the bus at Playland. Everybody was reading the papers, and the atmosphere seemed good.

Was I concerned about providing "bulletin board material"? Not really. And if that kind of media storm was what the Devils needed to get them over the top, it was a good sign for us.

At a time like this, the difference between winning and losing comes down to the smallest things. We had a lot of guys on the team who had won, but we also had a lot who hadn't. This is where experience is crucial. Every team on its way to a championship has to face this moment at some point, where you look around and decide collectively, have we had enough this year, or are we going to push harder? Veteran guys help everyone find more to give, and get them through the moment, because they've done it before.

If some people thought saying what I did was a risk? So be it.

WHEN GAME SIX GOT UNDERWAY it looked like we weren't going to right the ship. I don't think we played very well in the first period. The Devils scored two goals and had all the momentum. They threw everything at us—but Mike Richter completely kept us in it. They couldn't quite bury us thanks to him, and seeing that level of compete and heart from our teammate inspired us.

In the second period, Keenan switched things up and put me on a line with Adam Graves and Alex Kovalev, and sure enough, with about a minute and a half left in the period, Alex scored. The complexion of the game changed dramatically right there.

They'd been battering us for the better part of two periods, but were only up 2–1. Something had changed and we could see the whole momentum shifting. We went into the dressing room with hope, feeling we were one shot away from tying it. And I had to imagine in the Devils dressing room they were thinking they had to hang on.

And that's how it went. We started the third period attacking and the ice tilted for us; they started sitting back. Two and a half minutes into the period, I scored on a backhander that came out of a nice pass from Alex and we never looked back.

I went on to score twice more and we won 4–2. Because of that hat trick, and my promise that we would win, most of the attention was focused on me after the game. But I have always maintained that Richter was the star that night. If he hadn't kept us in it early, it wouldn't have mattered how many goals I scored.

It was a great moment for us, but more a lesson: Belief can take you a long way, as long as you've prepared. I can't recall anybody thinking of Richter as an eccentric after that.

We didn't have a lot of time to bask in the win, though. The minute that game was over, we had to focus on the next. We were coming back home for game seven, but we knew it was going to be the hardest one yet.

And it was.

The game started on a high note for us. Nine and a half minutes in, Leetch scored on this balletic spin move he'd once seen done by the future Hall of Famer Doug Gilmour. Brian had never tried it himself, but executed it flawlessly and slid the puck past Martin Brodeur. For almost the entire game, that was all the scoring. But with eight seconds left, Valeri Zelepukin put one in on a scramble in front of the net and we went to sudden death to see who got to play for the Cup.

A goal that late, when we thought we might have won it, could have been paralyzing, but we had enough experience on the team to absorb that kind of body blow.

"You know, if it wasn't so damn hard," Kevin Lowe said in the dressing room, "it wouldn't feel so good to win. This doesn't come for free. Let's go out and take it from them."

Neither team scored in the first extra session, and twenty-seven years later, I still shake my head. The two best teams in a sport, occupying the same market, with a deep and long-standing antipathy to each other, played a series just to get a chance to *play* for the Cup, and three of the games went to double overtime. Who wrote this script?

There are many great moments in sports history, but only a select few are remembered for the broadcast call that described them. Who will ever think of the U.S. 1980 Olympic victory—the Miracle on Ice—without parroting Al Michaels's legendary call: "Do you believe in miracles? Yes!"

Four and a half minutes into the second overtime, Stéphane Matteau swooped around the left side of the net, and as Scott Niedermayer tried to hook him, slipped the puck in between Martin Brodeur's blocker and the pipe.

In the Madison Square Garden radio broadcast booth, the play-by-play announcer Howie Rose erupted in a call that may well be what Rangers fans remember the most after a half century of heartache.

"MATTEAU! MATTEAU! MATTEAU! The Rangers have one more hill to climb, baby!"

And so we were off to one last series. It had been 969 days since I had first put on the Rangers sweater, and this was why I had come.

I'VE HEARD MORE THAN A few people say that our series against the Devils may have been the greatest in NHL history. Perhaps it was, but we couldn't afford to dwell on it. We had gone from two hyperintense elimination games into, just four days later, game one of the finals. The playoffs are a two-month chess game, and when there are only two pieces left on the board, everything is just different. We had to prepare.

The Vancouver Canucks' trajectory to the Stanley Cup final was the complete opposite of ours. They had started with a tough series against the Flames, which ended with a double-overtime win in game seven. They then dropped just one game in each of the next two rounds. Their captain, Trevor Linden, was a gifted goal scorer, but their team was built around the electrifying Pavel Bure, a speedy Russian winger, dynamic player, and all-around catalyst for their offense. He made the players around him better. Our strategy, in simple terms, was to shut Bure down.

So the Canucks were coming in hot, and we had just barely survived our last battle, though we came out of the series with hope and energy. We carried that energy into the finals, and in game one outshot Vancouver 54–31. But their goalie Kirk McLean was amazing. We lost on a Greg Adams goal with just four seconds left in overtime.

I wasn't happy. We had played well enough to win, except we didn't. But there was no cause for alarm. We'd certainly been on the other side and won games we maybe shouldn't have because of Mike Richter's outstanding play. The message was just to move on and not change anything. Things would even out, and they soon did.

We won game two, again at the Garden, then dominated them in game three in Vancouver, winning 5–1. Brian Leetch scored twice in that game. Then, as we were getting ready for game four on the road, a bombshell: Reports had surfaced that Keenan was poised to take the vacant head-coaching position in Detroit after the season.

Everybody in our dressing room knew there was some level

of dysfunction between Mike and Neil Smith, so was this a shock? Not even a little bit. But it was potentially a distraction.

It could have totally derailed us. But after all the drama we'd gone through with Mike that year, it was just a moment of turbulence—the flight attendants didn't even need to take their seats. We were far down the road on our journey, and had enough levelheaded people on the team to keep this from rattling us. We fell behind by two goals in game four, but came back to win 4–2.

We got on the plane that night, every one of us knowing that when we played our next game at home, the Cup would be in the house. That was invigorating. It was also a challenge.

The reason the Cup was there, as each and every one of us knew and understood, was because this was a potential series-clinching game, and those are the toughest to win.

It's human nature to get ahead of yourself. And it's a hard thing to balance these kinds of high-stakes situations, on every level: organizational, coaching, managing, playing, and even from the standpoint of the fans. Where are you going to celebrate? Who are you going to include? Neil Smith said he was already fielding questions about the champagne setup in the locker room and requests from the city about the parade route. Organizations *have* to think about these details and have plans in place, there's no way around it. The players can't ignore it. But it's crucial to make sure that the energy is going in the right direction. At this point in the season, 100 percent focus is required: Against a team like the Canucks, up against the ropes, desperate and likely to play with abandon, nothing less would do.

The Canucks came out in game five and took a 3–0 lead. We clawed our way back to even it, but they put three more on top of us to win and send the series back to Vancouver. Now things were very different. They had all the momentum, and when we got dropped 4–1 two days later at Pacific Coliseum, Rangers fans, who'd endured so much misery, were fatalistically shaking their heads. You could forgive anyone for believing the curse on this franchise was real.

The series should have never gotten to a game seven. But it didn't matter how it happened, all that mattered was for us to again regroup and get back to doing what we had all year.

When we got back, New York was manic. Between the possibilities of winning or losing, fans were hyperventilating.

There was some suggestion we should perhaps get out of the craziness and spend the day and night before the game in Lake Placid. Mike left that up to the team, and there was almost complete unanimity: Let's just go home and enjoy the experience. Let's be with our families, and sleep in our own beds. And importantly, let's engage in the routine that had been so successful for us all year. We'd played forty-eight games at the Garden since the season started and lost only ten of them. Those were pretty good odds.

I've heard people say that you shouldn't get too high when you win or too low when you lose. I couldn't disagree more. I always wanted my teammates to feel the emotion. You should feel elation when you achieve, and you should feel the pain when you lose something important. You should use those feelings as benchmarks, something to shoot for or avoid. Use your emotions to fuel you.

There may be some athletes out there who play only for their teammates (or even just for themselves), but I can tell you this: We knew what this meant to the franchise and its fans. We felt at a deep level how important this moment was to everybody who cared about the Rangers and the city. That emotion drove us even more to do something special.

For an evening game, I would usually leave my place on the Upper West Side around three o'clock to head to the Garden. When I went downstairs that day, there were all sorts of people gathered on the street waiting to wish me good luck.

From that moment on, there was nothing normal about the day. It was supercharged with emotion. On the ride down Broadway, listening to the radio, it was clear: In this powerful, vibrant city where so many important things happen every day, nothing was more important today than the game we were about to play.

The energy it would take to block out something that powerful would itself be a distraction. It would be pointless. You are better served to embrace that energy, and use it. It was no time for the faint of heart.

It's why sports is the ultimate reality TV. The evening would contain every emotion you could think of—for players *and* fans—all wrapped up in this condensed, combustible moment, inside a contained space, bursting at the seams with anticipation.

Before the game, Mike came in and got ready to speak. It had been a year of frayed nerves, ass-kickings, and hard feelings between coach and players. I don't know what anybody was expecting, but what he said was raw and vulnerable.

"We've come this far," he said. "I know I've been hard on you. I want you to know that I believe in you."

There were still some players who had a rough time with Mike, but I think overall they could respect what he was doing there. His words and the sentiment were appreciated. It was definitely the right thing to do.

With the building shaking above us, with fifty-four years of frustration and angst, I reminded myself and the team that all year long, we had been the best in the league. Anytime there was a challenge, we met it. It didn't matter what happened, when we needed to win a game, we did. Now our singular focus was to do what we had done better than everybody else. We wore our psychological muscle memory like body armor as we took to the ice.

There hadn't been a Stanley Cup game seven in this building—or either of the previous two Madison Square Gardens that had served as the Rangers' home ice—ever. It was mayhem, a religious tent revival complete with over-the-top fervor.

Brian Leetch and Adam Graves opened the scoring for us in the first period. With a two-goal lead going into the second period, we lost a little ground when Trevor Linden scored for Vancouver and cut our lead in half. We scored eight minutes later to put us up by two again. As we went to the dressing room to gather before the final push in the third period, it seemed we were controlling the game—not that it was at all easy.

The third period of game seven in the Stanley Cup final. We were so close. But then Linden scored again about five minutes in, and for the rest of the period we just had to hold on, keep playing our game. There were some close calls, including a face-off in our zone with just seconds left. But we controlled the play and the seconds ticked by—and all of a sudden it was over.

There was a sign in the crowd, made by a fan, that through the years has come to symbolize the meaning of the accomplishment:

"NOW I CAN DIE IN PEACE."

We didn't get out of the Garden until 2:00 a.m. Last call in

New York City is supposed to be 4:00 a.m., but on Manhattan's Upper East Side, the cops looked the other way. I've heard that neighborhood—with bars on every block—described as "the fifth year of college."

My buddy Johnny Barounis's place on Eighty-Ninth Street, the Auction House, generally had a more refined feel, but that night, *refined* would have been the last word to describe the place, or its surroundings. The streets were filled with thousands of fans, some hanging from fire escapes. Imagine the density of the crowd at Times Square on New Year's Eve—but in a much smaller space. Inside, police officers, who'd closed the street to vehicular traffic, were taking pictures with the Cup alongside John McEnroe and the actor Burt Young, who lived in the neighborhood. Everyone wanted to celebrate this historic night.

At some point I went home and went to sleep. When I woke up and knew it was real, two things occurred to me: Number one, it would be *our* parade that others would one day watch for inspiration. And number two—I needed some aspirin.

CHAPTER EIGHTEEN

ALL GOOD THINGS . . .

I t felt like a dream. I was traveling through Europe with "The 99 All Stars." Organized by Wayne Gretzky, we were some of the NHL's most exciting players up against local teams in Sweden, Finland, Norway, and Germany over an eleven-day exhibition schedule, raising money for charities and promoting hockey. Also with me and Wayne were Paul Coffey, Marty McSorley, Jari Kurri, and Grant Fuhr—we had gotten the original Oilers band back together.

But it was mid-December, which meant we *weren't* playing NHL hockey. As much fun as we were having in Europe, the whole situation felt like a kick in the teeth.

Over the summer, after our historic Cup championship, the NHL Players Association (NHLPA) and team owners grappled over a new collective bargaining agreement that would significantly affect player salaries. The disagreement continued into the fall of 1994, and when the two sides still couldn't agree, on October 1 the owners locked the players out.

The timing couldn't have been worse for the Rangers. Our Stanley Cup win had elevated our team's profile to new heights, and we should have been able to carry that momentum into the next season. There's something universally appealing about the never-win team finally succeeding, and it seemed that all kinds of sports fans, even those not typically focused on hockey, were enjoying the ride. Network late-night shows had us on—we did the "Top Ten List" with David Letterman and had a good time. But as the fall dragged on with no resolution in sight, the sport lay in mothballs.

I was eager to see our championship banner raised in MSG, and we all wished we were playing in the NHL, but with that option off the table, this trip with some of my best friends was the best of a bad situation. We shared memories of the little things that made our years together in Edmonton so good—like the salmon sandwiches Glenn Anderson's mom used to pack for charter flights. Our dads were along for the trip, too, with Walter Gretzky and Jack Coffey reminiscing—as Roy MacGregor of the *Ottawa Citizen* observed—about how their boys were once fourteen-year-old Bantam teammates in Toronto. (Can you even imagine how good that team must have been?)

Back on home soil, though, the dialogue between owners and players was pretty contentious. For my part, I believed that any solution had to work for everybody. A scorched-earth policy on either side wouldn't be good for the game, and we were *all* part of the game. But that said, when it came to taking sides, I was fundamentally with the players' union. Early in my career I hadn't paid much attention to the NHLPA. But by this point, I had come to recognize the necessity of being an educated and active union member. I felt strongly that when you sign up to be part of a union, you sail on the wake of those who've gone before you, and are responsible for making gains that will benefit future generations.

As we considered a way through the collective bargaining dispute, I was thinking about people like the Hall of Fame winger Ted Lindsay, who was the first president of the NHLPA, and my dad, who had fought for health insurance as an AHL player for his and his teammates' kids, and an extra fifty cents a day for meal money. Unions are teams, too. You need to be in it for the collective, not the individual. Otherwise, it's not going to work. Don't get me wrong: That's not easy. There's sacrifice involved. In the case of this lockout, some players never played again. Families lost income. That can't be ignored or forgotten. The only thing I could do in response was remember that we were fighting for the players who would come after us.

Late 1994 was a messy and unsettled time within the Rangers organization, too. We all knew there was a lot of turmoil at the management level. I didn't focus on that much right after we won. We'd just done something that hadn't been accomplished in fifty-four years and I was kind of lost in euphoria. And, because it was my nature, I just kept thinking, *How about everybody puts aside their differences and we try to do it again?*

Mike Keenan, though, had made it clear he wanted out. There was no fixing his relationship with Neil Smith. And so, less than a month after our ticker-tape parade in front of an estimated 1.5 million people through New York's Canyon of Heroes, during which he told the crowd, "We're indebted to you," Mike informed the team that it was in breach of his contract. A bonus payment had arrived one day late—and he was quitting.

That was only the first domino to fall.

In my original contract with the Rangers, there was a provision that I had a right to ask for a renegotiation if we won the Stanley Cup, so that June we made the formal request.

My contracts and endorsements had become a more complete family affair at this time—Doug, Paul, my sister Mary-Kay, and her husband, Aldo, created a company called Messier Management International. They handled the negotiation (and were soon representing a couple other players as well). Their initial discussion was with Neil Smith and Bob Gutkowski, the president of the Garden, whom I liked very much. I once heard someone say that he ran the Garden like it was his living room. He was proud of it and made everyone feel comfortable.

But in August, Madison Square Garden Corporation—which included the Rangers and the NBA's New York Knicks—was sold by its parent company, Viacom, to ITT/Cablevision. Gutkowski was out, and Dave Checketts, who had been president of the Knicks, was elevated to run the Garden. From that point forward, the negotiations slowed.

You never want to make contract negotiations personal, but this one felt very much that way. I was asking to be paid like a top player in the league. I didn't see what the problem was, and it seemed simple enough after what we'd just accomplished. In my view, there wasn't even that big a gap between our positions.

Maybe it was the new executives at ITT and Cablevision holding the line, I don't know, but the negotiations dragged on to the eleventh hour. The lockout finally ended on January 11, with a compromise that didn't seem to make anyone happy, and a shortened season was set to begin on January 20, 1995. That day, I was up in the Rangers offices with my dad and my brother, still trying to hammer out an agreement, more than five months after we'd first started talking about it.

In a few hours, the Garden was going to be full and pulsing

as the Stanley Cup banner was raised—fans had been waiting decades, even generations, for this moment. The front-office executives didn't want me to miss the event. And I wouldn't do that to my teammates or the fans. It was an awkward stare-down.

At the last minute—literally—we came to an agreement for a three-year deal. It should have been a joyous affirmation of all the work we'd done; instead, I had a bad aftertaste as I walked out of the office and went down to get dressed for the long-delayed first game of the season. My relationship with the organization was never the same after that.

And then, as if none of it had ever happened, I was skating around the ice with the Cup in my hands again. Watching the Cup banner being hoisted to the Garden ceiling stirred many thoughts: the closeness with my teammates and hard work it had taken to make it happen, the dedicated and raring support of the fans, and perhaps most of all, the journey, not over one season, but three. We had gone from the highs and inflated expectations of that first year to being lower than a snake's belly just a season later, and then to as high as you can get, winning it all. And now, as I held in my arms the thing that made it all worthwhile, I was ready to do it all again.

It was an emotional night, for many reasons. Back in the summer, after we won, our director of PR, Barry Watkins, called to tell me about a thirteen-year-old named Brian Bluver who had been waiting for a heart transplant, but was in really bad shape. Nick Kypreos, one of our tough role players that year, and I were heading up to Yankee Stadium with the Cup in hand to throw out the first pitch. On the way, we made a detour to Brian's hospital room with the Cup.

He was a great kid, so courageous. I told him he'd be right

there on the bench with us on opening night the next season to watch the banner raised.

"To tell you the truth," Brian's dad, Bill Bluver, told the *New York Post*'s Steve Serby, "I think it kept him alive for the next five days," until he finally got his heart transplant.

None of us knew that banner celebration would have to wait until January, but here it was, and here was Brian Bluver. My name would be on the Stanley Cup, but Brian Bluver's soul was in it.

I only wish our opening night, and our season, could have had as inspiring a story. We narrowly lost to Buffalo in that home opener. Keenan had moved on to become the coach and general manager of St. Louis, and had been replaced by Colin "Soupy" Campbell, one of his assistants, who had actually been a teammate of mine my first year in Edmonton. Soupy and I got along just fine. He was a solid *x*'s-and-*o*'s coach who had been a gritty defenseman.

The roster was mostly the same, but new faces inevitably were needed in the long grind of a season, even a shortened forty-eight-game schedule, instead of the regular eighty-two.

On February 16, we were playing .500 hockey when Nick Kypreos went down with an injury. The next day, the team called up a twenty-four-year-old from our Binghamton farm club, who was less hotshot and more long shot. Darren Langdon had bounced around the minors for a few years. The next night in Montreal would be his first-ever NHL game.

The best teams care for and support one another. They have to. Who's going to give his all, or function at his best, if he doesn't feel like he belongs?

The first time I saw Darren was when he showed up the day before our game with the Canadiens. It might seem quaint now, but anytime players traveled back then, or went to and from the arena, we were required to do so in a jacket and tie. But here comes Darren, about to meet his new teammates, big smile on his face, in khaki pants and a sweater.

He was dressed like he was going out to get pizza, while everyone else looked like they were heading out for a board meeting. It wasn't that he was being disrespectful of the rules. This simply might have been the best he had with him. We *did* give him a little bit of a good-natured ribbing—but really, what good was it going to do us to make this guy feel bad about himself?

And imagine how he felt? An undrafted newbie out of Deer Lake, Newfoundland, showing up to become a part of the defending champions, a room filled with all-stars. But he'd earned his spot, and it was up to us to make him feel welcome.

So I called up a guy I knew in Montreal who owned a men's clothing shop, and the next morning, when Darren got to the Forum for our day-of-the-game skate, there was a suit hanging in his locker.

"I'd never even heard of Hugo Boss," he said.

A tailor took his measurements, altered the suit that day, and when he showed up that night for his first NHL game, he looked like a million bucks. We lost 5–2, but Darren scored his first NHL goal.

I think everybody could relate to his journey in their own way. He was another tough kid—like Mark Lamb—who paid his dues in the minors and just refused to give up. There's not only a lesson with people like that, there's value.

When businesses and corporations recruit, they might want to look past glossy résumés to find people who've maybe struggled and failed and built character because of it. You're looking for problem solvers, for character, grit, and determination. I think there has already been a paradigm shift in this direction in recent years.

We welcomed Darren, but I shudder to remember the welcome new players got when I first came into the league. I avoided being hazed, because my first year in Edmonton—having played in the WHA the year before—I wasn't technically a rookie.

But there were definitely "old-school" rituals that happened, on the Oilers and around the league, and they were just about medieval. Veterans would do things like gang up on a new guy and pin him to the training table, tape his arms to some hockey sticks like he was on a cross, and then shave him all over his body. Sometimes they'd take hot muscle balm and put it on the areas where it would hurt the most. It was horrible.

And what was the point? These rookies had worked their asses off to realize a dream. They needed to be welcomed, brought into the fold, and put in a setting where they could give their best on the ice to improve the team. I didn't get the psychology behind it at all, not to mention the dehumanization, and I made a point over my career not to condone it. I think it's become an especially big problem on college teams: It's a terrible thing to do to anyone, and especially foolish when a team should be building a culture of trust.

There are less hostile and more productive ways than old-school hazing to make a rookie earn his spurs. You might ask him to come along to dinner and then hand him the bill. It's a harmless exercise that, at the same time, puts him in a social situation with his new teammates.

Or you'd insist they help the trainers out. During their seventeen-hour days, trainers could use all kinds of help as they did things like load fifty trunks and bags whenever we traveled. On these trips, we'd go to the hotel to sleep while they went to the arena to work, and they were back there again first thing the next morning. The point was to help rookies gain an understanding of all the critical things trainers do, and foster respect for people who are an integral part of our success. The message was simple: This guy's been here twenty years, and if you think he's here to pick up after you, you've got it wrong. It's just as important to be a pro off the ice as on it.

Leadership is teaching someone the right way from the start.

THEY SAY ONE OF THE toughest things to do in golf is follow up a great round with another one, and in fact the rest of the season was disappointing. Our season didn't improve as we struggled to find consistency amid a large number of player and personnel changes. We won seven of our last eleven games to barely sneak into the playoffs. In the opening round we surprised the Quebec Nordiques, coming back to win four straight after losing the first two games. The Nordiques had won our division, and were motivated to go out on a high note because they knew it was likely their final season in Quebec. (In May 1995 they moved to Denver and became the Colorado Avalanche.) But we were then swept by the Flyers in the Eastern Conference semis.

The loss to Philadelphia was a turning point. They were a big, strong, physical team, and I think Neil Smith and the rest of management were convinced that was where the league in general was heading. Later that summer Neil made a trade I presume he thought would help us keep up. I thought it was a critical mistake.

Sergei Zubov, a twenty-five-year-old defenseman, who had 36 points in 38 games the year before, and was just scratching the surface of what would eventually become a Hall of Fame career, was dealt to Pittsburgh, along with Petr Nedvěd, for Ulf Samuelsson and Luc Robitaille.

The way I understood it, the Rangers management thought Philly had physically overrun Sergei in the playoffs and it was time to get tougher on defense. Ulf Samuelsson certainly fit that bill. He was a rugged customer, and it seemed he was always in the middle of a conflict. I hated playing against him, but he would eventually become one of my favorite teammates. So while adding Ulf seemed like a fine idea, giving away a key piece of the nucleus that had won us a Cup seemed incomprehensible. In Zubov and Brian Leetch we had two of the best offensive defensemen anywhere. When you have players that talented, you find other players to support them, you don't trade them.

Whatever the reason we lost to the Flyers, it wasn't because of Sergei Zubov. And maybe the trade wouldn't have happened if Keenan had still been the coach.

The following season, 1995–96, was an improvement. Pat Verbeek, who'd come to the team the previous year, and I each had more than 40 goals, and Brian Leetch had 85 points. As I've said, individual stats like those don't happen unless everyone is doing their jobs. We had definitely become tougher. Ulf Samuelsson lived up to his reputation, and others started to play a more physical game, too.

At the trade deadline, to the surprise of some, Neil Smith traded away the prized rookie defenseman Mattias Norström, along with the veteran forwards Ray Ferraro, Ian Laperrière, and Nathan LaFayette, to the Los Angeles Kings for Jari Kurri, Marty

McSorley, and Shane Churla. This trade had some Rangers fans and radio pundits wondering at Smith's plan.

We were up and down after the trade deadline but were able to finish second in our division, to face the Canadiens in the playoffs. We lost the first two games, but then rallied to beat them, winning the next four. But we lost to the Penguins in the next round.

It was a disappointing end to a pretty good season, with injuries being the number one limiting factor down the stretch— it seemed like every player on our team was banged up, myself included.

What happened next was a true New York story.

Neil called me that summer and said the team had a chance to sign Wayne, who was a free agent. He wanted to know what I thought.

At first, I didn't even understand the question. *What are you talking about?* I thought. *Of course we should get Wayne.* We were talking about the greatest player in the history of our league.

In fairness to Neil, what I think he really wanted to make sure was that bringing in Wayne wouldn't make me feel diminished. I didn't think in those terms. All I cared about was winning. When you win, the stage is always big enough for everybody. I told Neil that the only question he had to ask himself was whether Wayne would make the Rangers better. Of course, he knew the answer.

It had been a long time since Wayne and I were together as NHL teammates—nine seasons—but our relationship had been so cemented during our years in Edmonton that nothing could damage it.

He once almost bought a place a few doors down from me

in South Carolina. He was about to sign the papers when we were out playing golf and he saw an alligator. He went home and told Janet: "We can't live here. We've got two little kids running around. They could get eaten!" He called off the deal.

When he came to New York, it was like slipping on an old pair of shoes for me. We just picked up where we left off, only I wore the "C" this time. We both knew, though, that leadership isn't about letters, it's about actions.

Wayne playing in New York made a splash—the game's best player finally on an original-six team, skating in a "Broadway Blueshirt." We did the Letterman show together. *Sports Illustrated* did a story and put me and Wayne on the cover together. Fox had the NHL network broadcast rights and did a couple of commercials with the two of us. One was a take on the old TV show *The Odd Couple* with Wayne playing Felix to my Oscar. That was really fun.

I still laugh when I think back to him walking into the dressing room that first day. He had a great way of putting the young guys at ease, introducing himself as if he were nothing more than a new teammate—which was the way he looked at it. Meanwhile, once Wayne had moved on a bit, the kid would turn to the guy next to him and silently mouth: "Holy shit!"

That 1996–97 season, Wayne wasn't just taking a victory lap in New York. He was our leading scorer and we were among the highest-scoring teams in the league. I hadn't agreed with all the personnel decisions Rangers management had made over the previous two years, but bringing in Wayne was the right move. The fans loved it, too. We had a mid-season stretch where we lost just three of twenty.

But then things started to go sideways. Alex Kovalev tore up his knee in January and was gone for the season. In February we went winless for an eight-game stretch, and as the season closed we finished fourth in the Atlantic Division.

We were the bottom seed in our division for the playoffs, so I'm not sure people expected much from us, especially after we got shut out in our opening game, against Florida. Somehow, though, we came to life, returning the favor and shutting them out in game two and then winning the next three to end the series. Our veteran team had the experience to battle through and win all three of those consecutive games against the Panthers by a one-goal margin. Two were won in overtime.

Amazingly, the pattern repeated in the next series against New Jersey—a shutout loss in game one, followed by a shutout win and then a winning run to finish in five games. In the Eastern Conference finals, though, the Flyers beat us four games to one. Once again, they knocked us out of the playoffs. Along the way, Wayne had a pair of hat tricks, but as a team we were severely injured and living on borrowed time.

Brian Leetch injured his wrist badly against the Flyers and had been profoundly limited in his play. Pat Flatley, one of our gritty wingers, tore a rib cage muscle in the Philly series, too. Another winger, Niklas Sundstrom, had broken his arm in the previous series against the Devils, and the forward Bill Berg broke his leg in the opening round against Florida. With so many injuries, we were thin. It was all hands on deck just to field a full team.

Dallas Eakins was a journeyman who'd played five years in the league and been with five different teams. Great guy, but he didn't have a lot of experience. Yet there he was—a defenseman forced to play out of position as a forward—in the lineup in the Eastern Conference finals against Philadelphia.

He'd played on our top minor league team, which was

already out of the playoffs. A bunch of their guys were sitting up in the press box where the extra players on our roster who weren't dressing for the game would watch.

There was a face-off and Eakins skated over to Wayne, asking, "Gretz, where do you want me to be on the draw?" Wayne said, "Well, where I'd *really* like you to be is up in the press box."

And then Wayne gave him a smile.

I shake my head about that season sometimes. We made it to the conference finals on half a roster running on fumes, and lost to a Philly team running on all cylinders. Maybe if we'd been healthy, we still wouldn't have won, but that doesn't diminish the fact that everybody gave their hearts. What we were able to accomplish that year can't be looked on as a failure. If you do, you overlook the integrity of what *was* done. If under-achieving is among the worst things in sports, then pushing beyond what you think you're capable of is a badge of honor.

It was inspiring to see how far we were able to get with what we had. I took a lot of positives out of it. Sometimes you have to celebrate and acknowledge the small victories on the way to something bigger. There's growth in loss. It was becoming more apparent, though, in the weeks following the season, that the way I looked at things differed from the way the Rangers' management did.

My contract was up and I wanted to stay and finish my career in New York, but there was too much in the way. There was bad blood left over from my last negotiation and I think my presence put a certain amount of pressure on the franchise—a constant reminder of what we were expected to do.

They made me an offer, but I knew they weren't trying to

keep me. And they knew me well enough to know I wasn't going to stay under those terms. It was an easy way for them to get out from underneath that kind of pressure. We all understood what was happening.

Playing with Wayne again had been fun, but as a player, you know when you're welcome or not. It tore my heart out to leave, but I felt I had no other option.

In an interview with Garden CEO Dave Checketts on New York talk radio, he was asked why he was allowing Mark Messier to slip away.

"How long," he asked, "am I going to have to keep paying for that Stanley Cup?"

CHAPTER NINETEEN

VANCOUVER

I remember the day as mostly beautiful, and entirely complicated. We were drifting in San Francisco Bay on a massive and opulent sailboat with the skyscrapers of the city beside us, the Golden Gate Bridge behind us, nothing but blue sky above, and uncharted territory ahead. At least for me.

It had become clear that the Rangers didn't want me to return, so Doug, Paul, and I explored other options. We went down to visit Washington, as they'd expressed interest in bringing me to the Capitals. Nice people, and they made a serious offer, but playing for the Caps was literally too close to home. There would be five or six games against the Rangers—maybe three trips to Madison Square Garden every season, and possibly more in the playoffs.

I had such a deep emotional connection to the Rangers, those years in New York, and my teammates. Brian Leetch, Mike Richter, and Wayne—playing against them repeatedly wouldn't be a fun thing to do.

We heard from Detroit, too, but I decided it was best to

get even farther away from the Eastern Conference. Better for all concerned—fans, the Rangers organization, and me personally.

Which is how I found myself on John McCaw's 125-foot sailing yacht on a midsummer afternoon. His family had made a fortune in the early days of cellular communications, and he was now the owner of the Vancouver Canucks. A year earlier, the team had lost out on a bidding war to lure Wayne. It was not McCaw's intention to lose out again.

When the discussion got serious, McCaw sent a negotiating team to Hilton Head for a few days. With the deal close to done, he dispatched his plane to bring my entire family west to work out the last few details. This final talk would be on the water.

My head was swimming that day on the boat. The idea of leaving New York was still really painful. But I was thirty-six and wanted to play. The fact that I'd just come off a season where I scored 88 points in 71 games I thought demonstrated I still could do so at a high level. Now somebody was stepping forward to say they agreed.

We shook hands on a new deal and I collapsed in tears right then and there. It was suddenly overwhelming: the sadness of all I'd left behind and the promise of what lay ahead.

CANUCKS FANS NEVER HAD IT easy. Right from the start, when Vancouver came into the league in 1970, and for a decade after, it was a lonely hockey outpost, a thousand miles from the nearest NHL franchise.

And the club had struggled, as expansion teams so often

did in the NHL. After twenty-two seasons, it had ended a year with a winning record just twice. Things had been improving—they'd been to the finals in 1982 and it had been only three years since Vancouver had last made it to the finals, their loss to us in 1994. They'd had a losing record in the three seasons since, but when I came on board, they were trying to recapture the magic from 1993–94. I was viewed as the missing piece of the puzzle that could help get them to ultimate success. I wanted that, too, of course, and when I joined the team, I did so with the hope and belief that it was within reach.

As the season got underway, however, two things became clear. For one, only nine players remained from the thirty-four who had suited up during the 1993–94 season. Three of the top five scorers from that Stanley Cup final run were gone. It had only been three years, but in 1997, *this* team was no longer *that* team.

Also, there was something in the air that was holding the team back. Management briefed me that the Canucks team had polarized into two different camps. I don't know why. A lot of guys had been there awhile and it was just the way it was. Bottom line: There was a bad vibe hanging over everything. It was unhealthy.

I was the captain, so it was on me to address it—and that is the perfect place to talk about one of the biggest mistakes I ever made in professional hockey.

When I arrived in the fall, Vancouver's captain was Trevor Linden. Not only was he a skilled and experienced player, he was deeply woven into the fabric of the organization's culture. In 1988, he'd been selected second overall in the draft behind the eventual Hall of Famer Mike Modano. Straight out of Medicine Hat, Alberta, he never played a day in the minors, scored thirty goals for the Canucks that first year as an eighteen-year-old, and immediately became a fan favorite. By his third year, he'd become one of the youngest ever captains in the league, and by the fall of 1997, he'd held the position for six years.

It was clear the organization expected me to offer leadership. Whether it was because of that, or because our team was a house divided and it made sense for someone outside to come in and try to pull people together, I was offered the captaincy.

In our Vancouver dressing room before the season opener, Trevor got up and gave a heartfelt speech saying he thought it was best for me to be captain. It was a gracious action, and clearly made with what he felt was the team's best interest at heart.

But the division—a team squared off in cliques—was new to me. I knew problems like this existed on some teams, but I had never really seen it before. I thought I could jump in and fix it. Ultimately, though, you can never fix a problem without the participation of the people who are living it.

My misstep was that I didn't have the equity to function in the captain's role. I had no experiences with these players and hadn't earned the right to lead them.

What I should have done was try to bring those sides together from behind or on the side, as a supportive mediator and not a captain. They were the ones that had created the friction and so had to be the ones to choose one way or another to fix it. A solution needed time, but I was eager to get things moving quickly in the right direction.

And there was some other uneasiness right away that I hadn't anticipated.

As an expansion franchise, that first Canucks team of the 1970s didn't have any star players, but there were some determined and lovable guys whom the Vancouver fans embraced. Among the most popular was a hard-boiled left-winger from Sault Ste. Marie, Ontario, named Wayne Maki. He wore number 11. He was not only an original Canuck, but also a bright spot early on when there wasn't much brightness to embrace.

Then, in what would have been his fourth season with the team, he very suddenly and tragically died of a brain tumor. He was just twenty-nine years old. After Maki passed away, the team didn't officially retire his number 11, but they soon took it out of circulation.

I knew all about Wayne Maki and I would have been absolutely okay *not* wearing number 11. I believed the Vancouver organization had spoken with the Maki family and we had their blessing. I was sad to see it later reported that that wasn't the case.

As the season started, we weren't doing a very good job winning games, which is the biggest challenge of all to team unity. After a mediocre start, we lost ten straight.

That lack of unity was hard to overcome. On our flights, guys put on their headphones, watched movies, and went to sleep. It was just dead from an energy and bonding perspective. All the travel made it hard to go out for a drink or team meal together, but teams have to find ways to connect, no matter the circumstances.

By the middle of November, we'd won only four of our first nineteen games, and General Manager Pat Quinn relieved Coach Tom Renney of his job. Tom was a good guy, but in professional sports, if you don't win, that's all there is to it. Pat then coached a few games himself, and I could see why players loved working with him. He was super honest and smart about the game and had success everywhere he'd been. He was a great motivator and speaker. But as with Tom Renney, it all comes down to wins and losses. Ownership soon decided to let Pat go, too.

It was clear by this point that to get to where they wanted to be—to make the Canucks a real contender for the Cup the team wasn't just missing a piece: It required a rebuild. I don't think the fan base was prepared for that.

Mike Keenan came in to take over both the GM and coaching roles. He had been out of hockey since the Blues let him go midway through the previous season.

We won a bit after that, but then sank like a stone.

On November 29, we occupied fourth place in the seven-team Pacific Division. Thirty-five days later, we were in last place, 29 points from the top.

Then, in February, Trevor Linden was dealt to the Islanders. It had nothing to do with Trevor's play. A new coach wasn't going to be enough to turn things around, and part of any rebuild is trading your important assets. The team was hoping to bring in players that would make us younger and more dynamic. But the fact remained, Vancouver had a new captain, and a new GM and coach, and the city had to say goodbye to a favorite Canuck, all while we struggled to win.

Around this time, I had some nagging injuries—I got tendinitis in my biceps and literally couldn't lift a five-pound dumbbell at one point—and my numbers dropped off. With everything else going on, that certainly didn't help the narrative.

We finished in last place. It was my nineteenth season in the league and we had the worst record of any team I'd been a part of.

Over the summer, Brian Burke was hired to replace Keenan as general manager, although Mike remained as coach. It was a homecoming for Burke. He was a lawyer and player agent when Pat Quinn hired him in 1987 to be the director of hockey operations, overseeing every aspect of the Canucks organization.

Most recently, he'd held the same title for the league, which made him, most prominently, the de facto NHL discipline czar. He was definitely a smart guy, with a no-BS attitude, and had his work cut out for him returning to Vancouver.

To start the 1998–99 season, Pavel Bure, our leading scorer the year before, was holding out. The twenty-six-year-old "Russian Rocket" was unhappy with his contract and wanted a trade. On January 17, with the team in third place (out of four teams) in the newly created Northwest Division, Burke dealt Bure to Florida. Two days later Keenan was fired, replaced by Marc Crawford, the former Quebec and Colorado coach who'd won the championship in 1996. Crawford was our fourth coach in three years.

Team dynamics don't change overnight, and I couldn't contribute at the level I wanted to. A concussion and a bad knee injury limited me to fifty-nine games that year. On February 1, we lost 1–0 to Ottawa and dropped into the cellar of the division. We never climbed out.

When a team or an organization is struggling for results, the answer is often in the small details. My uncle Vic used to say those are the times you need to find the "miraculous in the mundane."

The majority of life in professional sports isn't sold-out arenas and adoring crowds. Those moments occupy a tiny fraction of the week and are far outweighed by the sweaty bus rides in full gear after having dressed in a hotel ballroom for an away-game practice, as we used to do from time to time in my Oilers days in places like New York, where ice time is hard to come by. Those moments are no fun, but everyone goes through them together. Winning teams need something—a story, an event—to galvanize them. It can be as simple as an uncomfortable bus trip through the Lincoln Tunnel to New Jersey. Whatever creates bonding.

When hard times come, it's critical to recognize and appreciate the beauty in those small moments—they are what truly brings people together. While you will always remember skating around in front of a wild crowd with the Stanley Cup raised above your head, you will also look back fondly on these seemingly insignificant episodes.

By this point I understood that you can't just jump in and fix everything, moving mountains. Two seasons in a row we missed the playoffs, but you could feel things were changing. The roster had started to turn over, and the team dynamic with it. By the end of the season, there would be only four players left from the day I joined the club. We had early success in the new season, 1999–2000, and winning brings with it an energy that can help bring people together. Two months in, we were in first place in our division, but, starting on December 4, we won just four of our next twenty-six games and plunged all the way to last place.

Burke, to his credit, offered to trade me at the deadline if I wanted to go somewhere and try to win. At that point, I was nearly thirty-nine years old. It was possible I wouldn't play long enough to see a rebuilt Vancouver team really take off. But I knew leaving mid-season wasn't right. And as for going to a different team to chase another Cup, I just didn't see myself as a mercenary. Coming into a new dressing room late in the season would make it all but impossible to connect with a new team. That scenario didn't appeal to me. I told Burke I wanted to see out the year.

As it turned out, we made a late run—we actually had the best record in the league after the all-star break. Can I take any satisfaction from that? I guess at least there was growth in some regard, but it was too late and we missed the playoffs again.

There was a really good feeling on the team by then. And even though we missed the playoffs by a few points, I think the perception internally was that the team had started to take a turn for the better. But it was the last season I played in Vancouver.

I'd like to think we'd planted a seed. The team was taking shape and we had promising new talent in Markus Näslund, Todd Bertuzzi, and Mattias Öhlund and Ed Jovanovski on defense—what you'd expect from a team trying to move up the ladder. The next year Vancouver had a winning record; two years after that, a playoff series win; the following year, a division title.

When I went there, my hope and expectations were to get the team back on a winning track toward a Stanley Cup. I didn't meet my own expectations in Vancouver, let alone anyone else's.

There are a million reasons you could point to for why it didn't happen—in the end, it really doesn't matter. In sports, we're in the results business. If you look back at the standings of any given year, there are no footnotes. Like the Super Bowl–winning NFL coach Bill Parcells said: "You are what your record says you are."

I was the guy who was supposed to get Vancouver over the top. Instead, the record got worse, and the loyal fan base saw so many of their beloved players traded away. Rebuilds are not for the faint of heart. I had all the right intentions, but when we didn't right the ship early on, the narrative changed.

In many ways, I learned more from those few years in Vancouver than I did in all my career before from the things I didn't do, and could've done differently: leading from behind and taking on more of a support role. Leadership comes in different forms. I also learned about myself.

I was almost forty—about a decade beyond the age when a lot of players retire. I didn't feel that I was done. The clock was ticking, though. A year earlier, Wayne had retired in New York, meaning I was now the only NHL player still active who had skated in the WHA.

That night at Madison Square Garden when Wayne hung up his skates for the last time was packed with emotion. The hair on the back of my neck stands up when I think about it.

There's no place like New York.

CHAPTER TWENTY
EVERYTHING CHANGES

It was July 2000, and I was at a Madison Square Garden press conference announcing my unlikely return to New York. Dave Checketts, who was still CEO of the Garden, had arranged for us both to shovel some dirt into a fish tank that contained a small ax. We were burying the hatchet.

"Mark Messier has become synonymous with New York like few other modern-day athletes in any other city," Checketts said. "He arguably has meant more to the Rangers sweater than anyone that has ever worn it. Mark, welcome home."

If you had told me when I left New York in 1997 that I would soon be back playing for the Rangers again, I would have been really surprised. I had tried to move on and not dwell on the parting of the ways, but what my Rangers teammates and I had done was so meaningful to me that leaving—actually, feeling like I'd been forced out—*was* a wound.

The hatchet burying was a PR stunt. If it sounds kind of contrived, that's how it felt, too. But it was important for the fans to see us build some unity.

In fairness to Dave, he came in to run the Garden *after*

we'd won the Stanley Cup. It's one thing to talk about the bull ring, but it's another to be in the ring with the bull. Because he wasn't there, he didn't see the grueling work and long hours it took to put ourselves in a position to not only win the Cup, but get to the conference final three years later on not much more than fumes. In our negotiation in 1997, I imagine for him it was entirely about numbers: wins, losses, goals scored, and my age. If nothing else, the three years since I'd left had helped him understand that the numbers don't tell the whole story. The team had missed the playoffs in all three seasons, not once finishing with a winning record. That might still have happened if I'd been there—there's never one reason why a team struggles—but it was clear something needed to change.

"I think we all make mistakes," he said that day at the Garden, "but the past is the past and today is moving on." Things were certainly changing.

Earlier that summer, the Rangers took what felt like a step in the right direction by bringing in Glen Sather as general manager. He clearly understood all the nuances that made for a successful team. And it wasn't the same team I'd left. There were only three players left on the roster from our '94 Cup: Mike Richter, Adam Graves, and Brian Leetch. They were all at the press conference. Then Brian came up to present me with my Rangers sweater.

I had known that I was going to be the Rangers captain again, taking over the job from Brian, but seeing that blue jersey with the "C" on it overwhelmed me. It's not a coincidence that the letter is positioned over your heart. I couldn't speak for more than a minute, and the tears streamed down my face. I was thrilled to be back, but also thinking about Brian.

I think if you ask anybody who played on those teams Brian captained, they'd tell you he was a great leader. The plain fact is, though, when a team doesn't do well, its captain's leadership doesn't get praised. In this case, I didn't think that was fair. Brian knew as well as anyone, though, that in professional sports, there is no such thing as fair.

It was time to pick up the pieces and try to get back to where we'd been years before, and there was a lot of work to be done.

Midway into December, we were holding our own and playing .500 hockey. It seemed to be a reasonably good first step. In a game against Florida, I played more than twenty minutes and had a goal—my fifteenth of the season—and an assist, my twenty-fourth.

It would take another ten games after that to get our next win, and the season spiraled downward. It was a struggle to find consistency because our lineup was a carousel. That season forty-two different players skated for the team—only fifteen of us stayed in place for fifty games or more. Six different goalies suited up at one point or another.

We won five of our last seven games, but it wasn't close to enough. We'd given up the most goals in the league, and for the fourth straight year, playoff hockey was something I would only watch on TV.

Physically, I felt good. In fact, at forty years old, I'd played a full eighty-two-game schedule for only the second time in my career. I couldn't wait to get back to training camp, and I circled the scheduled start date on my calendar: September 11, 2001.

THOUGHTS ABOUT THAT BEAUTIFUL CLOUDLESS Tuesday come rushing back like a wild current that's overtaken a dam.

For the first time ever, the Rangers were going to hold training camp in Manhattan. Initially the idea was to do it at a vast multipurpose recreational facility on the Hudson River called Chelsea Piers. The logistics, though, didn't work out and it was decided training camp would be at the Garden itself so fans could come and watch.

Had we been at Chelsea Piers, one of the options the team looked at for housing players was the Marriott Hotel at the World Trade Center. A week doesn't go by when that thought doesn't cross my mind.

Training camp opened early that day with all manner of medical tests and physical evaluations taking place in the lobby of the theater at the Garden. New players and rookies reported first, while veterans got the benefit of a few more hours of sleep.

I was still at home on the Upper West Side just before 9:00 a.m. when my dad called. He asked if I was okay.

"Yeah, sure," I asked. "Why?"

"Because," he said, "I'm watching TV and it looks like a small plane just crashed into one of the World Trade towers. It looks pretty bad."

I went into the living room and turned on the TV. Nobody seemed to know what was going on. Maybe the pilot had some kind of medical episode, or the plane had a mechanical failure, but Dad was right. It looked pretty bad.

And then the second plane hit the other tower.

We all learned about it differently. Three weeks earlier, the team had traded for Eric Lindros. He hadn't found a place to live yet, so he was staying with me, but he'd left the apartment earlier to go do an appearance twenty blocks south at the ABC studios on the *Regis and Kelly* morning show. Down at the studios, Eric was just pulling up for his interview and Kelly Ripa came out crying. The planes that hit the towers weren't small, and the discussion had turned ominous with mention of possible terrorism. The show was canceled, and while they stood there in the lobby watching the horrible images, a third plane crashed into the Pentagon.

Meanwhile, at the theater lobby inside Madison Square Garden, many of the players were going through a series of physical evaluations, including one particularly intense test called "the hammer" where a player pushed himself on the stationary bike to give his maximum power for as long as he could. It's usually conducted with the trainers, and other players standing close by, loudly encouraging the man on the bike to go as hard as he can.

The group in the testing room was oblivious to what was happening just three miles south of the Garden until our trainer Jim Ramsay's cell phone rang. It was his friend Ray Barile, the trainer for St. Louis, who was calling from Alaska.

"Are you guys okay?" he asked.

The phone connection cut in and out badly. Barile had no way of knowing that he'd called in the middle of a raucous training session, and so what he (barely) heard on the other end, as America was being attacked, was alarming: He heard screaming. As we all recall, it was just the beginning of a time filled with confusion.

Glen had hired a performance psychologist, Dr. Kimberley Amirault-Ryan, who had worked previously with Canadian Olympians. Her first day of work with our team was September 11. The day also marked her first-ever visit to New York. Can you imagine? On the way to the Garden that morning, she had been knocked down in the street as people rushed madly to get away from the events unfolding downtown. It's a testament to her that she stayed at all.

She got to the Garden that day midmorning, at the height of the confusion. The very first thing she did was instruct all team personnel to record new outgoing voice mail messages explaining they were alive and safe. In the immediate aftermath of the attacks, cell phone service in New York was barely functional. For hours, people across the world trying to check in on their New York–based loved ones could get nothing but voice mail. It was a smart move and she certainly earned her spurs that day. Later on, when we resumed training camp, I made it clear to my teammates—particularly the younger ones who might have been more impressionable—that I intended to embrace whatever counsel she had to offer.

Lindros came back to the apartment along with our VP of hockey operations, Darren Blake, and our VP of communications, John Rosasco. We sat in front of the TV and watched the towers fall. Before they did, I saw people jump to their death.

Those aren't the only images that will haunt me forever.

There were people all day like walking ghosts—trudging aimlessly north from the smoldering cavity, some without shoes, some with torn clothes, all covered in a layer of who knows what. The streets were shut to traffic, and so for hours and miles they walked, an endless parade of the dazed, treading down the middle of avenues and over bridges where cars ordinarily would have been.

All the while the air was filled with smoke, sirens, and dread.

I didn't leave the apartment till that night. The streets were deserted by then. New York is a city where noise is comforting, because it's normal, but the only thing I remember hearing as Eric and I walked up the block to get dinner on Columbus Avenue was the roar of military jets as they ran sorties over Manhattan.

I know so many of us were sharing the same thoughts. We'd lived our lives seeing terrible images on the news of car bombings and carnage overseas, but never did we imagine that we would feel unsafe here, at home.

And nobody knew what was coming. Maybe someplace like Madison Square Garden would be the *next* target? Two days after the attacks, the Rangers moved training camp up to the suburb of Rye. As undone as we all were in those first few days, we knew we had to take the first steps back toward normalcy, but how could we do that? How could anybody do that?

Everyone knew somebody who'd been affected—or worse.

For weeks in Grand Central Terminal there was a bulletin board with pictures of people who had never come home that day, with messages asking, has anyone seen my beloved husband or sister or son? And every day there were funerals. Every day.

Don Maloney, a longtime Rangers great, who was the team's VP of player personnel at this time, had a brother-in-law who died in the towers. One of Brian's best friends from Boston College, John Murray, whom we all knew, was one of the 658 Cantor Fitzgerald employees working in the North Tower who was killed.

Ace Bailey, a player who had taken me under his wing as a temporary teammate in Houston all those years ago when I'd missed an Oilers flight and had been sent down to the minors, was on the second plane to hit the towers.

We were all so numb.

A friend told me about walking into the locker room at his golf club near our practice rink only to find American flags draped over three of the lockers near his.

Five days after the towers fell, a few of us were asked to go down to Ground Zero to try and offer some moral support. It was a humbling day. Eric, Mike Richter, and I, along with Darren Blake and John Rosasco, got in a van that was met at a fenced-off checkpoint. We did a brief stop at police headquarters before continuing on.

Vehicular traffic on the island had resumed, but was still restricted south of Fourteenth Street. I lived in Manhattan, and as close as I thought I was, this was a different world: broken windows, debris from the fallen towers on the street and on top of cars, and a horrible, acrid smell. It was devastated and desolate.

The silence outside was overwhelming. There was no small talk in the van as we rolled through deserted streets. The closer we got to the site, the quieter and heavier the atmosphere became inside our vehicle.

And then there we were, out of the van, on a mountain of rubble that stretched for blocks long and wide. It was still smoking—and everywhere that terrible smell.

I'd had dinner before at the Windows on the World restaurant, which had been on the 106th floor of the North Tower. What a magical place, so perfectly named. Now here I was standing amid the building's ruined infrastructure, the twisted steel beams from the seventieth and eightieth floors looming just ten feet over my head.

We served soup to the rescue workers who were digging through the pile, still looking for signs of life that, at this point, they must have known they were unlikely to find. We shook some hands and told people how grateful we were, how grateful *everybody* was, which is something they might not have known, because this was what they had been doing, day after day, for hours on end. They picked through the rubble looking for the living only to find the dead.

I don't know if our presence or words were at all helpful—maybe they were. They seemed to be. We just wanted to show that people cared about what was going on. I think everyone wanted to help somehow. Even through all this, despite being covered in soot, there were some smiles on their faces. It was a powerful reminder that athletes have a responsibility. Helping people through their daily grind, and giving hope or inspiration, is not a trivial thing.

We stayed for about an hour or so and then went back to police headquarters. There was a holding room in the basement where the loved ones of those who were missing could gather and wait for news.

We spent some time there, shook some hands. We did a lot of hugging. I can still feel the convulsive sobs of more than a few people who leaned into us for support. Grief is better when it's shared. The closer it is, though, the more intense it becomes. You can't say you understand how people are feeling, because you don't. You just try to console the best you can.

I remember one woman who came up to Mike and said, "Thank you for coming down and thinking of us. It means so much and we're going to bring you back when they find them all and we have a parade."

It was heartbreaking. After seeing what we had an hour before, there was no way, at this point, they were going to find anybody alive in that pile. People were clinging to hope.

This was the backdrop against which we started playing games again. We had to. As President Bush said in an emotional address to a joint session of Congress nine days after the attacks: "I ask you to live your life." Somehow, across the country, things had to go on, whether we felt ready or not.

That night, we had a preseason game in Philadelphia, the first two periods of which were marred by a number of fights. President Bush's speech was aired live during the second intermission, on the big screen above the ice. The warm-up stopped. Everything stopped, and everybody—players and fans—watched and listened. "Fear and freedom are at war," President Bush somberly said. When he finished speaking, it just didn't feel like the night to play anything.

Players from both teams glided to the center of the ice, shook hands, and the game was declared a tie.

Two and a half weeks later, we had our home opener at the Garden against the Buffalo Sabres. Neither team wore their traditional jersey, but instead sweaters that simply had "New York" stitched diagonally on the front.

There was a special ceremony before the game, honoring those who had not only rushed in heroically to save lives on 9/11, but were still working on the recovery mission down at Ground Zero. Members of the hockey teams of New York's police and fire departments were on the ice. When they were introduced, the Garden crowd, which had been chanting, "U-S-A," was overcome with admiration and gratitude.

As captain, I was the last player introduced. Without my helmet, I skated out between the officers and firefighters, and took my place on the blue line. I wasn't expecting what happened next. It was one of those New York moments I will never forget, and I know I'm not alone in that.

One of the FDNY guys, Larry McGee, skated over to me. He was wearing his firefighter's helmet, and there was a picture taped to the front, of a man in uniform. Larry explained in that brief moment that the man in the picture was a fire department legend named Ray Downey. He loved hockey and once had been captain of the fire department's team.

A former marine, Chief Downey was one of the most decorated firefighters in the department's history. Over his thirty-nine-year career, he'd been cited fourteen times for bravery. He was a nationally recognized expert on rescue operations and had been the commander of that effort at the World Trade Center on the day of the attacks. As we stood there on the ice that night, Downey was still missing.

Larry said it would mean so much if I would put on the helmet to honor the chief. It was simple and spontaneous, but it had a powerful impact, saying: *We are with you. We are all with you.*

More than four hundred first responders lost their lives on 9/11, including Chief Downey. It would take eight months for his remains to be identified. To this day, I carry around his Mass card in my wallet.

As unimaginable as it was, life went on, and so our season went on. But as it did, the whole metropolitan area remained connected by a sadness and pride in which nobody, regardless of their celebrity, was anything more or less than simply a New Yorker. We were regularly visiting firehouses and police stations, just to say thank you. Walking into these places felt like walking into a cathedral. There was an aura of something bigger. I'd done visits like this over the years where maybe I walked in as the "hero." Now there was no mistaking who the real heroes were.

In our season, we managed to get started on a pretty good run. Late into November, we were in first place. I was playing decently, but my left shoulder was becoming a problem. It was stiff and painful. I didn't know yet what was really wrong.

After a win on December 29 in Los Angeles, we crossed into the New Year still in first place. That's when the bottom fell out. We went nine games without a win, dropping into third.

I was working hard with our trainer Jim Ramsay doing physical therapy to try to get my shoulder right, but it was becoming increasingly painful. At one point my arm felt like a dead weight hanging off my body. It was clear when the league took a mid-February break for the Salt Lake City Olympic Games that I couldn't play anymore, so on March 1, I had surgery. My shoulder was a mess, but I knew I was lucky. How many people could say they'd played twenty-four years of professional hockey and never had any surgery?

The Rangers' team surgeon, Dr. Andrew Feldman, did an arthroscopic procedure to fix a tear in my labrum. He also shaved off a little bit of the clavicle because I had an impingement preventing me from lifting my arm. He cleaned up some arthritis in there, too. There hadn't been any dramatic episode that precipitated the problem. It was just years of wear and tear, years of falling on my elbow and getting into collisions with players and the boards.

The regular season was over for me, although I was told I could be back for the playoffs. It never happened. As a team, we sank further and further, and missed the postseason again.

I'd played forty-one games, the fewest in any season of my career.

After the season, I did what I had been doing for a decade. I went back to Hilton Head to recharge, and to slowly get back into my workout regimen. I worked hard, as usual. The problem was, since I'd never had surgery before, I wasn't rehabbing in the correct way.

Rehab is very different from typical training. You're trying to strengthen, but also break up scar tissue and facilitate range of motion. It's especially critical when dealing with the shoulder, the only joint in the body that rotates 360 degrees.

As a result, when I got back to training camp in the fall for the 2001–02 season, I had something called "frozen shoulder." My strength and flexibility were significantly limited. I could play, but not at full efficiency. It took almost half the season to fully recover. It was yet another reminder for me about the critical role of our training and medical staff. People do what they do for a reason. They're knowledgeable and have experience, and I should have listened more closely to the advice they gave me. In any organization, it's a good idea to let people do their jobs. There's a reason they have them.

Regardless of my injury, by this time the team, and my role on the ice, had changed. I think everybody recognized that at this point in my career I wasn't going to lead the team on the ice like I had in past years. There's no forty-year-old who's going to play the top-line minutes and carry the team.

That wasn't a problem for me. It never meant anything to me to be the number one guy on the team, and I didn't harbor any fantasy about who or what I was. Ego can be a good thing when it fuels your confidence. It can also be a terrible thing if it makes you deluded. Even at the top of my career, I wasn't ever the most gifted, talented player. I started as a fourth-line winger and worked my way up to the top lines. I never had any kind of grandiose ideas of what sort of player I needed to be in order to contribute to a team.

I had always been a player who needed support around me, but even more so now. I knew I could still contribute on the ice, but also push others into those roles that I had formerly played. I didn't have any problem with that, either.

I still loved playing, and I still wanted to try to win. For the 2001–02 season, I had a different role on the team, but I was still trying to create a unified team concept. Altogether, it was a challenge.

I had been so hopeful we could re-create the magic we'd built during my first years in New York, but it didn't work. There were a lot of new faces over the season: Forty-one different players moved in and out of the roster, though we were still a veteran team at our core, and expected to get results. One of the hardest things to do in team sports is build chemistry on a veteran team that isn't winning. Guys seemed to wander in their own directions. We simply weren't connected in any way.

Why is *being connected* so important?

In basketball, your best player can be on the court 90 percent of the time and thus has a greater chance to influence the outcome. In hockey, your best player might be on the ice for only up to half the game, so you have to depend even more on the people around you for success. If you're not an effective, functioning team, in my opinion, the chances for success are zero.

There's a tremendous difference between "a team" and a group of people who are wearing the same shirts. When I played, I never wanted to be part of a *group*, I wanted to be on a *team*, a bunch of brothers who would lay out and put their face in front of a slap shot if they needed to. The saying isn't that he's gonna take one for "the group."

As we approached the 2002–03 season, I felt great physically, and the goal hadn't changed. I played seventy-eight games. But we just weren't good enough. We didn't play well and missed the playoffs again. It was a similar story the next season, my tenth and ultimately final one in New York.

A veteran team with a bad record doesn't offer the hope of success. And without hope, there's no light at the end of the tunnel.

I was tired, not physically, but emotionally.

Professional hockey is a 24/7, eleven-month journey with no letup. And as a leader, every single day you're living dozens of lives, checking in on your teammates, keeping tabs, making sure they feel good.

This wasn't the game I played as a carefree eighteen-year-old. The light was flickering, and after all these years, there was one thing I understood as gospel.

Anything less than everything is not enough.

EPILOGUE

I t had been 652 days since that thoughtful and lonely ride to Madison Square Garden on the night that turned out to be my last home game. I wasn't sure then about retiring, but I was in a different place now, and here I was, back at the Garden, about to take the ice—only this time, in a suit and tie.

As we all feared, the 2004–05 season had been completely lost to a lockout, and in September, before the next season started, I officially announced my retirement. I was humbled by the response from fans and media. Wayne told ESPN that I was the best he had ever played with.

The Rangers held a ceremony to retire my number 11, raising a banner to the rafters of MSG. Their thoughtfulness in making sure every aspect of the evening was perfect was just another reminder of what I felt most of all about my life in hockey: gratitude.

They scheduled it for January 12, 2006, in a home game against the Oilers—the only trip they'd make to New York that season. The ceremony was held on the ice prior to the face-off, in the middle of the two teams with which I had spent the majority of my career. It also allowed some of my closest friends who might not otherwise have been able to make it to be there front and center.

Kevin Lowe, a teammate on all five of the Oilers' championship teams, plus our Cup-winning Rangers team, was there as Edmonton's general manager. Craig MacTavish, with whom I'd played on four Cup teams, was now Edmonton's coach.

The Garden was sold out, but it always was for Rangers games.

I had come to New York all those years earlier from a hockey hotbed, the type of place where there was so much focus on the team that players couldn't step out their front doors without attracting attention. That passionate environment was exciting for me. It pushed all of us to be better, because the fan base desperately cared about the game.

When I arrived, I remember thinking it was a city with so many things to occupy your attention—sports, theater, music—and I was just hoping the Rangers mattered as much in New York as the Oilers had in Edmonton. I was wrong to worry. There was a massive, adoring fan base that had an even longer history with its team than Oilers fans had. There's a symbiotic relationship between the people who play and the people who support them. And what took this to another level was the hunger. It had been three generations since the Rangers and their fans had raised a Cup.

The fan base was rabid, and I was always grateful for their energy, which was our fuel: lifting us up when we were playing well, holding us to an unrelenting higher standard when we weren't.

For the banner-raising, the longtime Rangers favorite John Davidson—he'd been a standout goalie with the team, then later a broadcaster, and eventually the team's president—served

as the master of ceremonies. JD started the evening by introducing a short film narrated by the MSG Network mainstay Al
Trautwig. I watched with PR director John Rosasco on a TV
near our locker room while it played on the big screen inside
the arena. The film talked about leadership, perseverance, and
winning—all over memorable scenes from our 1994 Cup run.
I could hear the crowd in the stands deliriously celebrating the
greatest moment in Rangers history all over again.

The film was stirring, and flattering. It once again reminded
me what can be done when people work together. I sobbed
while watching, completely overwhelmed. This was going to
be a wonderful evening, but it was not going to be easy.

When it was done, I collected myself and then walked past
the entire current Rangers team. I was surprised to see they
had lined the hallway, each of them banging their sticks on the
ground in the age-old hockey salute. Then I emerged out into
the arena. The noise was deafening.

I have never wanted to be the center of attention. Even
when I was a little kid, I was always happier attending events
like birthday parties that celebrate someone else rather than
myself, but on the greatest stage in the greatest city, this was
now my curtain call. As I said to my teammates many times
over the years: "There's no place to hide out here, so let's go."
As I walked out onto the ice, so many of the people who made
the success I'd enjoyed possible were gathered in the building.

The fans who came every night were there, of course, but I
also felt the presence of the thousands more who had lived and
died with us and were watching on TV. There were more than
twenty members of my family gathered on the ice. And then,
one by one, JD introduced my 1994 Rangers teammates. Some
twenty of them had come back to be part of the evening. Esa Tik-

kanen traveled all the way from Finland. GM Neil Smith, and our coaches Colin Campbell and Mike Keenan, were there, too.

As I looked around and saw them all, never was it more clear to me: No one wins alone.

There were warm and lighthearted words, some beautiful gifts, and then a bittersweet moment that crystallized everything for me. My friend the performer Dana Reeve was introduced to come out and sing. I had become friendly with Dana and her husband, Christopher, not long after he had been paralyzed in a horse-riding accident in 1995.

Chris had died in October 2004, and ten months later, in a cruel turn of fate, Dana, who had never smoked, was diagnosed with lung cancer. She was still in treatment, but on the night of my ceremony at the Garden, she had put off a chemotherapy session so she could sing.

That someone would have made the effort to be there while there was that much turmoil in her own life was so meaningful and powerful, it gave me chills.

I stood there on the ice, trying not to let my emotions get the better of me again, but it was never more clear that winning the Cup was about people, and all these relationships. My life was so much richer for them.

The ceremony lasted an hour and fifteen minutes. Then the Rangers went out and beat the Oilers in overtime. When I left the Garden that night, the Empire State Building, a few blocks away, was lit up in the Rangers' colors of red, white, and blue. Less than two months later, Dana passed away.

I THOUGHT RETIREMENT WAS THE end, but I came to see that it was only the start of the next chapter. I had played twenty-six years, was forty-four years old, and had miraculously escaped without any long-term effects from injury. I had a young family, and in reality, my life was just beginning.

While everything changed for me—the routine, the travel, the competition, the people I saw every day—in another sense, nothing changed for me, because the things I have always believed are the bedrock principles of a healthy, successful approach to the team experience are now simply part of the way I do everything else in life.

When I retired, my son Lyon was seventeen and a burgeoning hockey player. He had grown up with his mother in Virginia. I'm sure it wasn't easy for him at times playing hockey with his last name, but he has risen above everything that was thrown at him, and I'm so proud of him. He's made a career out of coaching and mentoring young hockey players, and whether it's hockey or golf or fishing, we've shared so many memorable times through the years. He's a beautiful, caring soul.

My son Douglas was born in 2003. Two years later my daughter, Jacqueline, came along. Since then, with my wonderful wife, Kim, I've been there every step of the way to witness and support their childhoods.

When Douglas was old enough to start playing hockey, I began to coach him, just as Doug had coached me. Standing there on the ice with a whistle around my neck, watching a handful of six-year-olds buried underneath all that oversized hockey gear, I gained a new perspective on an old awareness.

Youth coaching, in any sport, is a tremendous responsibility that should never be taken lightly. You're not only coaching. What you're really doing is teaching and mentoring, you're shaping a life. What you do can have an enormous impact on a child.

How are you going to coach a six-year-old to pass the puck when he might not be at a point developmentally to even share his toys? There are many, many fundamental lessons for a child to learn before they can even think about becoming the next Wayne Gretzky.

For kids, the point of sports is to give them confidence, and every possible opportunity to grow as a person. Youth sports were designed for the physical and emotional well-being of our children, to help them develop, to let them get outside, run around, have some fun. Hopefully at the same time, they'll also absorb the life lessons being taught through sport.

And it's never escaped me that so many of the New York–area parents who have brought their kids out to play were teenagers when the Rangers won the Cup in '94. They were wide-eyed fans with Brian Leetch posters on their walls, and when they eventually had their own kids, the passion they'd developed for the sport made them want to encourage their children to play. That's one of the true, living legacies of that Rangers team. It was about inspiring the next generation of players—these incredible little six-year-olds I was watching fall over one another on the ice.

Unfortunately, in the New York metropolitan area, there's a problem. The passion is there, but the ice isn't.

IN 1985, RUSTY STAUB, THE Major League Baseball player and bon vivant New Yorker known affectionately as "le Grand Orange" for his ample size and red hair, founded the New York Police and Fire Widows' and Children's Benefit Fund. After 9/11, when more than four hundred first responders from the NYPD and FDNY lost their lives, the fund came to be known

as "Answer the Call" and took on a weightier and more profound responsibility.

In 2007, I was asked to serve as the honorary chair of the
organization's annual fund-raising dinner. I eventually joined
the board and came to meet its president, Kevin Parker, who
had two young kids who wanted to start playing hockey, and
so found himself spearheading an ambitious initiative.

In the United States, there is an average of one sheet of ice
for every 100,000 people. But in New York City, it's one sheet
for every 1.2 million people.

In a metropolitan area with three NHL teams, which had
earned the Cup eight times in a twenty-three-year stretch starting in 1980, that's unacceptable. Our kids deserved better.

The potential solution that Kevin and a number of like-
minded people including myself, Stephan Butler, John Neary,
and Kent Correll started working on involved an iconic building in the Bronx that had sat empty for nearly thirty years. It
was, and is, an amazing structure.

The Kingsbridge Armory was originally constructed in
1917 to be the home of the 258th Field Artillery unit of the
New York Army National Guard. It is massive. You could fit
three full football fields on its main drill floor. Over the years,
the building had been used for all kinds of things: concerts,
disaster-relief efforts, car races, film shoots, rodeos. In the
1970s it was designated a New York City landmark. A few
years later, it was included on the National Register of Historic
Places. Through the years, as one project after another for its
use stalled, the building fell into a state of disrepair.

What really got us excited was the opportunity to build the
world's largest indoor ice facility. We figured we could comfortably fit nine sheets of ice on two levels on the Kingsbridge

footprint and create not only a place for hockey, but a full buffet of ice sports. The plan also called for a 5,000-seat arena that could host an AHL team and be a venue for concerts. In short, a real community asset.

Perhaps by the time you read this, we'll have made some more progress toward the project's completion. It's been a complicated enterprise, but I don't look at it as building ice sheets. I look at it as creating access and opportunity for something that just hasn't been available, not to mention the economic impact it would have on the community.

That idea also led to the creation through my foundation of a program called i2i, or "Inline to Ice," that was spearheaded by Kalinda Bogue. We've taught more than five thousand kids from PS 086, the school across from the armory, how to ice-skate by first getting them onto roller blades. The response has been amazing. To see those kids and how much fun they were having with a sport they might have never had a chance to experience is fulfilling.

It's also frustrating. The Kingsbridge project shouldn't have taken a decade to make happen—and we're not done yet. The unvarnished truth is that politics, finance, and commercial real estate have, at times, seemed like an unsolvable Rubik's Cube.

If it wasn't such a great initiative, if it wasn't so meaningful, I would have definitely walked away. But we've spent too much time on it, invested too much sweat and money. Walking away would mean turning our back on tens of thousands of kids right now and who knows how many more in the future. So we are going to keep on fighting to get this done.

And isn't that how it goes? You have to overcome obstacles

to achieve the things worth working for—things that aren't about the individual, but the collective.

EVERY TEAM I PLAYED ON was special to me. The personal relationships, the sense of adventure and the unknown, even the disappointments—together, they added up to something bigger. It was all about the human connection through the game. Professional sport is defined by winning and losing, but you're missing out if you're only concentrating on the end result instead of the journey. And the irony is that if you're paying attention to the quality and depth of the experience, it will lead you right back to the thing you were seeking in the first place: success. I played twenty-six years, but won the Cup only six times. Does that mean that the other twenty seasons should be considered a loss? Absolutely not. I felt I was able to take something positive away from every losing season, that each one could be harnessed, and learned from, to create a winning culture in the future.

My hope is I've been able to convey how powerful it is to be part of something bigger than myself, and how much gratitude I've found in the collective experiences with my family and my teams, which is the most important lesson of all. Maybe you can accomplish good things alone, but if you open your heart, you've got a better chance of accomplishing great things *together*.

My sweater hangs in the rafters in Edmonton and New York. When I look up and see them, I see hundreds of faces. I see an homage to the people I was fortunate enough to sit, work, and skate beside for all that time. It's just a reminder of how lucky I am. And that for twenty-six years, I wasn't in the hockey business, I was in the people business.

Through the ups and downs of my sixty years of life, I've come to recognize that the connections I found in hockey were aimed toward something bigger. I am an ardent believer that what you do shouldn't be who you are. No matter what path you've chosen, if you're open to using your experiences to gain a deeper understanding of yourself, then your life will be richer. That's success. My biggest wish is that everyone will discover this, whether it's through hockey, or something else they love.

Getting there requires an open heart. Perhaps the way I see it all is best summed up through the words of one of Hinduism's core texts, the Chandogya Upanishad.

"There is a light that shines beyond all things on earth, beyond us all, beyond the heavens, beyond the very highest heavens. This is the light that shines in your heart."

"There is a light that shines beyond all things on earth, beyond us all, beyond the heavens, beyond the very highest heavens. This is the light that shines in your heart."

—Chandogya Upanishad

ACKNOWLEDGMENTS

When writing these acknowledgments for *No One Wins Alone*, I was brought back to my retirement night and the last six words I spoke to everyone gathered there: "Thank you, thank you, thank you."

Writing a book was not unlike most things that I have done in life—everything has the common theme of teams and support.

For years I was asked to write a book, but it wasn't until I became friends with Jimmy Roberts that I felt confident enough that what I had to say would be interesting, or at the very least, helpful in some small way. Thank you, Jimmy, for all you did to give shape to my thoughts.

Simon & Schuster emerged as our publisher not because of their vast history but because of the connection we made during our initial meeting. Thank you to editors Max Meltzer and Justin Stoller for your patience and dogged determination to get us over the goal line. Thank you to publishers Jennifer Bergstrom and Kevin Hanson for supporting this book at every turn. And thank you to my literary agent, David Vigliano, who introduced us all.

This book is dedicated to my parents, Doug and Mary-Jean, whose love and support has been my constant through life. And thank you also to my siblings, Paul, Jenny, and Mary-Kay—my original team.

I owe so much to my amazing wife, Kim. And to my children, Lyon, Douglas, and Jacqueline, you inspire me every day.

I want to thank each and every person mentioned in this book who took the time to share their perspectives from the last sixty years. You are too numerous to mention, but I am so grateful. *No One Wins Alone* is itself an example of the amazing people who have supported me throughout my life. It *is* the "Acknowledgments."

With respect and gratitude, I say: thank you, thank you, thank you!

A CONVERSATION
WITH MARK MESSIER ON
LEADERSHIP AND TEAMWORK

No One Wins Alone is as much about leadership and team building as it is about your own professional hockey career. What do you hope people will take away from your story?

As a player, I read *Sacred Hoops* by Phil Jackson and *The Winner Within* by Pat Riley. I was struck by both books, which delve into the team aspect of sport: creating a safe place for players and emphasizing the importance of sacrificing the "me" for the "we." I wanted to write a book about the spirituality of a team, how beautiful team sports can be when you play in a culture that promotes inclusiveness—all important elements of winning. And I was lucky enough to experience this in my professional hockey career. Hockey, like almost everything else, is about people; it's about galvanizing them and maximizing their potential. I think everyone can learn something from those lessons.

What do you think is the single most important lesson of leadership?

I'm asked that a lot and I'm not sure there's one answer. I do know that earning the right to lead people is critical. One of the most important things I did with my teammates was getting to know them on a more personal level: taking the time to understand where they come from, who they are as people, and spending as much time as possible with them away from the rink. You have to establish deeper relationships that go far beyond hockey. This has become more challenging in recent years with the amount of player movement in the game, but you have to establish yourself as someone who is consistent and trustworthy.

So those leadership traits apply off the ice, too?

Yes. The question for a leader is always the same: How do I inspire people? It's a leader's greatest responsibility—inspiring others to motivate themselves. When you create an amazing workplace and a vision that people believe in, they'll find their own motivations. And that has longevity. That's how people can coach and mentor and lead year after year without burning out or being tuned out. There are moments when you have to light a fire, but over the long haul it's better to not hold yourself responsible for motivating others. That's a short shelf-life for any leader. Anytime you're in a leadership position, dealing with people, the same principles apply.

How important is it to foster good leadership traits in others?

When our Edmonton Oilers team was still young, Lee Fogolin, our captain, stood up and announced to us that Wayne Gretzky would be our new captain—I'll never forget it. Lee was nearing the end of his career and he knew Wayne was the future and ready to take over. Wayne was already a leader in so many ways. In my opinion, that was true leadership on Lee's part. It was the best thing for the team, and it also taught us an important lesson.

Later in my career, when I became a captain, I reflected on that selfless action of Lee Fogolin, doing what's best for the team. When you lead by example, those traits permeate the whole team.

Were there any times you think you could have been a better leader?

Absolutely—we all make mistakes and we have to learn from them. One of those times for me was when I became captain of the Oilers after Wayne was traded to L.A. We had a team full of great leaders, but that season, as we went into the playoffs, I felt I had to do everything, that it was all on my shoulders. I compromised my own values as a captain, and my actions showed my teammates that I did not trust them to do their jobs. I wanted to win so badly, but I forgot the most important truth: No one wins alone.

I came to understand that my energy affected the people around me. How I conducted myself, what I brought to the dressing room and the ice, would either help or hurt our team play. This is true for everyone—our energy affects others and we have to be aware of that. When you empower the people around you, and inspire them by setting the right example, then they are free to do their jobs and the whole team prospers.

Leaders don't have all the answers; nobody does. The decisions you make may be the wrong ones. It's necessary to acknowledge when you've made a mistake, step back, take stock, and reassess. Those are important lessons in creating that winning culture and earning that trust.

You mentioned personal energy and how it affects others. In the early eighties, during one off-season, you took a trip to Barbados, where you ended up taking magic mushrooms (psilocybin). It led to some realizations about the body and mind?

I was amazed that something like that could have that big of an effect on me. I had no idea our minds are that powerful. At that point, I was becoming a pro, training my body to be stronger, more resilient. But that experience made me wonder: If the mind is that powerful, how could I train it to do special things at special times under pressure? How can I train my mind as hard as I train my body? That was an awakening for me. We'd done some power-of-positive-thinking seminars early on in Edmonton, about the importance of good self-talk, but that experience in Barbados made me more curious about how else I could become a better player. (Of course, psilocybin is a controlled substance and I'm not an expert on it. It's a good idea to talk to a medical professional if you want to know more.)

So then I became interested in Eastern philosophy, meditation, Buddhism, the spirituality of Indigenous peoples. The power of the mind to create a better aura, or energy, around us. That energy affects people, and learning to use it is a powerful tool for any leader. It made me a better player.

You obviously took leadership lessons from these philosophies. You even end the book with a quote from the Upanishads, a Hindu text.

These philosophies contain so many powerful lessons about the goodness that lives in everybody's heart. When you create an environment that celebrates the diversity of people—not just where they come from but their ideologies too—it allows people to shine in their own ways. In my opinion, it's important to nurture a culture rich with humility and passion and creativity, and all the things that make it fun to come to work. That kind of positive and accepting environment brings the best out of people. The lessons that I took from these philosophies are, I believe, the fundamental building blocks of a championship team.

You played hockey from a young age and have been involved in coaching youth as well. What life lessons can kids learn by playing sports?

I was really interested in the game of hockey because my dad played, but then I fell in love with it when I started to play. There were great benefits beyond learning skills and being active. Sport can be a great teacher, if you allow it. Playing on a team is challenging for a pro, let alone an eight-year-old. Responsibility, accountability, determination, grit, learning to grind and never quit: Is there a scenario in life where those lessons don't apply? I've used them all my life, and they became just as valuable post-retirement.

Sports also teach how to respond to failure. After all, no one wins all the time. What did you learn during those years when you didn't win the Stanley Cup?

If you just look at my own career, having been a part of six Stanley Cup teams over twenty-six years, that means there are twenty years when I lost. But I don't consider those lost seasons. I consider years like that as steps in growth. That's true for any person or organization, as long as you're learning and asking yourself questions. What did we do right? What did we do wrong? What can we do to be better? How can we evolve as players, as people, and as a team? When things don't go right it's important to ask these questions. Finding the answers, individually and as a team, is so important when responding to failure.

In the book you talk about the process of welcoming new players to a team—there's an illustrative story about your Oilers teammate Kenny Linseman. How do you ensure people feel supported in being themselves while also becoming part of the whole?

With Kenny, he had a big personality, and we respected that. It was part of our team culture to celebrate diversity—in people, ideas, styles, everything—and allow people to be themselves. I think Kenny responded well to that dynamic. At the same time, as we'd make room for who he was, we needed him to make room for us and the philosophy that we had as a team. Part of our team identity was to have a strong relationship with our fans, and we treated it as a responsibility. It took Kenny some time to warm to this, but to his credit, he came to understand how important this was to us and he grew to embrace the idea.

I think when you accept people's differences, they become more comfortable and are more likely to feel they're part of the team. This helps them become the best versions of themselves.

The importance of strong connections between teammates is clear throughout the book. What stands out about your relationship with Wayne Gretzky?

It's not often that you can meet someone eight days younger than you and look at them as a role model. Normally the person you look to as an example is older than you, and has much more experience. But for me and the other young guys on the Oilers, our best example was someone the same age as us. We had a core of young players who grew up together, learning from one another, and Wayne was a huge part of that. When we call each other brothers, that's not a term we use lightly.

Leaders want their teams to always succeed, but success and failure are natural parts of life. How important is it to always strive for the top?

I don't think you can be afraid to fail. In my experience, you really need to be forthright in your objective. In professional hockey it's a defined goal. You can have smaller goals along the way and celebrate those, but ultimately you're there for one reason and that's to win a Stanley Cup. It might take some time to put the pieces in place and get the needed experience. But every day you have to ask in the back of your mind: Are we closer to winning a Stanley Cup or are we further away? Is everyone in the organization—players, coaches, managers, trainers, *everybody*—there with the same goal in mind, believing in the philosophy and the vision of the team? Once you have that culture in place, then you just chop wood and carry water toward that goal.

INDEX